DECLINATION IN ASTROLOGY

The Steps of the Sun

by

Paul F. Newman

THE WESSEX ASTROLOGER

Re-published in 2006 by
The Wessex Astrologer Ltd
4A Woodside Road
Bournemouth
BH5 2AZ
England

www.wessexastrologer.com

Copyright © Paul F. Newman

Paul F. Newman asserts the moral right to be recognised
as the author of this work.
All illustrations and diagrams are by the author.

ISBN 1902405226
Original version published under ISBN 1902405188

A catalogue record of this book is available at The British Library

No part of this work may be reproduced or used in any form or by any
means without the express permission of the publisher. Reviewers may
quote short sections.

"Readers familiar with Paul Newman's writing will recognise the quirkiness and diversity of the examples from film, poetry, soap opera and science fiction… an accomplished book which deserves to be widely read"
Anne Whitaker Astrologer and writer

"Astrologers and students looking for a book on declination will be pleased with this one! If you're at all interested in declinations, consider this book an essential addition to your library"
Astrid Fallon The Astrological Journal

"Mr Newman brings to us some new concerns, some very clear thoughts along different lines than the 'old models' handed down from ancient times…I applaud these rare insights"
Edward L. Dearborn *Instigator of the NCGR Special Interest Group on Declination*

"…an entirely new dimension to interpretations"
Chris Lorenz *Dell Horoscope*

"From the earliest festival and ritual to the most current, we have stories that are woven gracefully and usefully into a technical book….
Highly recommended for students and practitioners of astrology"
Erin Sullivan *The Bibliophile, ISAR International Astrologer*

"a fascinating and unique ramble through myth, calendar, folklore and practical application"
Neil Spencer *author True as the Stars Above*

"illuminating"
Michael O'Reilly (Wolfstar) *CirclesofLight.com*

"This very readable book…is written with humor, clarity and is never dull"
Ken Gillman *Considerations*

" This feels like going from viewing with one eye to two eyes…"
"…a mountain of great information that is practical and enjoyable, a wonderful reference…"
Carol Cilliers *Earthwalk Astrology Newsletter*

"*Declination in Astrology: The Steps of the Sun* tells how to watch two movies at the same time…. This book should be in your library."
Alice Kashuba *Sabian Symbol International Newsletter*

"an insightful look at astrology's 'lost' dimension…highly recommended"
Kenneth Irving *Horoscope Guide*

"Newman writes for the thinking reader"
Donna Van Toen *NCGR Magazine*

"I am far, far beyond that island of days where once, it seems, I watched a flower grow, and counted the steps of the sun…"

Elizabeth Smart, *By Grand Central Station I Sat Down And Wept*, Nicholson & Watson, London, 1945.

Also by Paul F. Newman:

You're Not a Person - Just a Birthchart (Wessex Astrologer 1999)

"To deny the validity of either longitude or declination is ludicrous and unacceptable."

Kt Boehrer. 2001.

"Longitude and Declination are the two most important measures from the standpoint of Astrology"

Charles E.O.Carter. 1925

Contents

Introduction

Declination: The Basics	1
The Solar Festivals	33
May Queen and Halloween Jester	33
The Solstice Pause	38
The Twelve Days of Christmas	42
Gawain and the Green Knight	46
The Royal Arch	50
Juliet at Lammas Eve	52
The Sword in the Stone	56
Beyond the Steps: Planets Out of Bounds (OOB)	61
OOB Tales:	
Tarzan of the Apes	62
The Ruby Slippers	66
Two Astrologers:	
1. Ronald C. Davison	71
2. John Addey	77
The Lunar Ranger	81
A Photograph of The Beatles	86
Extreme Venus	91
A Most Unusual Mouse	98
The Two Hemispheres	102
Science Fiction and Soap Opera	104
Omar Khayyám & the Seven-Ringed Cup	111
Cat People	117
Liverpool: Scorpionic City of Dreams	122
The Elephant Man	126
The Invisible Man	129
The Return of the Ancient Mariner	136

Antiscia	144
A Tale of Dark Secrets	145
Stars in Declination	150
First Magnitude Stars close to the Celestial Equator	150
"Death Shall Come on Swift Wings"	157
Declination in Action: The Davison Composite chart	164
Declination at Stonehenge	165
Annual Energy Boosts	168
Three Types of Moon	168
The Path of Ra	171
Appendices:	
1. Ecliptic and Equator: The fundamental astrology of it all	174
2. Named Stars and their Declinations	180
3. Investigating Yods	186
4. Why a Contra-Parallel is not an 'Opposition'	191
Index	193

Introduction

At the time of my last Progressed New Moon in 1996/97 my astrology took a different turn. I had been grappling for some while with the intricacies of Antiscia on the zodiac wheel and, separately, with the eight divisions of the solar year (equinoxes, solstices and cross-quarters) and their correspondence with the zodiac's so-called most powerful degrees. I was soon to realise that these were all based on a common theme - the declination of the Sun - and that there was far more to this idea of declination than I had realised.

A series of coincidences swiftly followed. A short article published in Sylvia Jean Smith's innovative Canadian periodical SHAPE, in which I mused on power points and the solar festivals, was seen by Edward Dearborn in Pennsylvania then founding an official Special Interest Group on declination. He cordially invited me to join this growing band of devotees. Several of the studies in the following pages are based on articles that first appeared in *The Other Dimension*, the Declination Journal, over the past ten years. (The piece about Robert Louis Stevenson "A Tale of Dark Secrets", was first published in slightly different form as "Jekyll or Hyde" in The Mountain Astrologer, November 1994, "The Path of Ra" in a longer form as "The Dec of Cards" in The Mountain Astrologer's Mercury Direct in June 2001, and the tribute to Ronald C.Davison in SHAPE, November 2002).

There are few modern books available on declination and so I have attempted to offer my personal understanding of this ancient concept and the way I use it as straightforwardly as possible. When the Declination Special Interest Group began in 1996, much research had occurred on the horizontal axis (longitude), but only a few had specifically researched any portion of the vertical axis (declination). The results understood today are from the years of researching charts and gathering pieces into a definitive declination premise. While it is impossible to reference every single person and new contribution that added to the whole, special acknowledgement and thanks must be particularly extended towards Ed Dearborn, Nelda Tanner, Leigh Westin, Charles and Lois Hannan, Henrike Mayer, Karen Christino and Astrid Fallon, all of whose work has expanded and enriched my own insights and understanding. For those who would like to delve further *Declination: The Other Dimension* by Kt Boehrer (1994) is the pioneering work and Leigh Westin's *Beyond the Solstice by Declination* (1999-2001) is a highly recommended authoritative study.

Paul F. Newman, Dorset, England
July 2006

1
Declination: The Basics

Declination is a form of *latitude* rather than longitude.[1] It measures how far the Sun and the planets move above and below the celestial equator, rather than around the zodiac circle. It brings a missing dimension back into astrology.

Declination is not intended to supplant the standard zodiac longitude wheel of 360 degrees, rather it is the missing half that completes our study of astrology and explains many of the rules we use.

One of the reasons for its persuasive nature is that the study of declination is as old as astrology itself and close to what we actually see in the sky. In varying levels of application it has bobbed alongside the bulk of recorded astrological practice for at least the last two thousand years.

Simply stated, declination is the measurement of planets north or south of the celestial equator, which is the Earth's equator extended into space. One way of picturing this is to liken declinational measurements to the latitudes of earthly towns and cities in their distances above or below the terrestrial equator. It could be said that a star at the declination of 51 degrees 32 minutes North corresponds to London, or a star at 40 degrees 45 minutes North corresponds to New York City, or at 23 degrees South to Rio de Janeiro, since these are the corresponding terrestrial latitudes.

The tropical zodiac signs of Aries to Virgo are always situated north of the equator while the signs of Libra to Pisces are situated south. As an example a typical western-style birth chart is shown below with the planets and important points given in zodiac longitudes and then with their declination measurements shown separately.

---

1. Declination is only one form of celestial latitude. Declination is latitude measured from the celestial equator. The other form of latitude, most commonly termed simply celestial latitude, is latitude measured from the ecliptic, the plane of the Sun's path. This book is concerned wholly with declination, but for a further explanation of both see Appendix 1: *Ecliptic and Equator*.

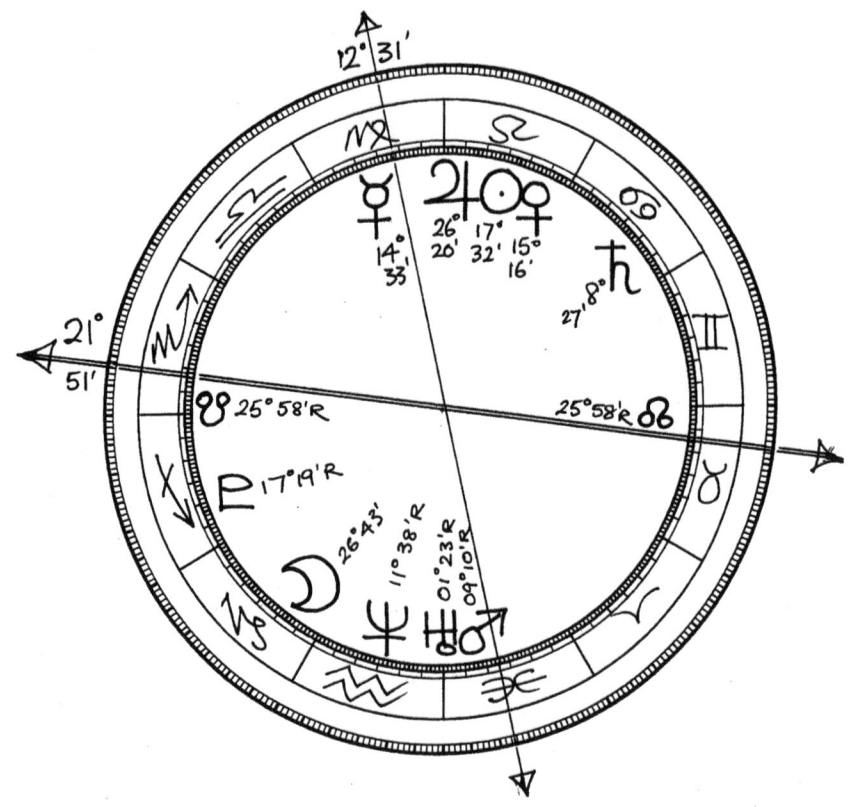

Hottest Recorded Day in Britain
10 August 2003. 2.43pm. Heathrow, England 51N29 00W30
Source: BBC News 10 Aug 2003

This chart has no intended significance other than an illustration. However in keeping with the solar symbolism of this book it is in fact a chart for one of the hottest days ever recorded in the island of Britain since records were kept. The summer temperature topped the 100-degree Fahrenheit mark for the first time ever at 2.43pm on Sunday 10 August 2003. This was recorded at Heathrow Airport, London, and reported on the BBC Television news that same day.

Declinations:

SUN   15N35   (15°35' North of the celestial equator)
MOON   25S07   (25°07' South   "   "   )

Declination: The Basics   3

MERCURY	05N05	(05°05' North	"	"	)
VENUS	17N22	(17°22' North	"	"	)
MARS	14S12	(14°12' South	"	"	)
JUPITER	13N30	(13°30' North	"	"	)
SATURN	22N25	(22°25' North	"	"	)
URANUS	11S43	(11°43' South	"	"	)
NEPTUNE	17S18	(17°18' South	"	"	)
PLUTO	13S36	(13°36' South	"	"	)
NORTH NODE	19N15	(19°15' North	"	"	)
SOUTH NODE	19S15	(19°15' South	"	"	)
ASCENDANT	18S14	(18°14' South	"	"	)
MIDHEAVEN	06N52	(06°52' North	"	"	)

These declination measurements can be obtained from certain ephemerides and all reputable astrology computer programmes. For further clarification the declinations have now been sorted into ascending and descending order above and below the zero line of the celestial equator. (Throughout the book both of these listing options will be shown).

SATURN	22N25
NORTH NODE	19N15
VENUS	17N22
SUN	15N35
JUPITER	13N30
MIDHEAVEN	06N52
MERCURY	05N05

——————————————— (Celestial equator)

URANUS	11S43
PLUTO	13S36
MARS	14S12
NEPTUNE	17S18
ASCENDANT	18S14
SOUTH NODE	19S15
MOON	25S07

It can be seen that none of the planets on the chart above have a declination higher than approximately 25 degrees and this is quite normal as the Sun's highest declination north or south is 23°26' and the remainder of the planets move close to the Sun's path, sometimes tipping over slightly.

The power of the Sun is even more relevant in the study of declination than it is in conventional astrology as its latitudinal movement - as opposed to longitudinal - so obviously marks the growth and decay of the four seasons, the balancing points of the equinoxes, the demarcation of the tropics and the polar circles on the globe and the clear limits beyond which other planetary bodies may or may not tread. These steps of the Sun comprise the fundamental thread of this book.

The Sun's Annual Journey

The diagram on the following page shows the Sun's annual movement as perceived from Planet Earth. The Sun's annual journey begins at the equator (zero degrees of declination) at the spring equinox. The Sun is standing directly overhead at the line around the centre of our Earth providing a moment of equal day and night in both hemispheres. From our Earthly view on this day the Sun will rise due east and set due west - precisely. At this moment the Sun also enters the first sign of the tropical zodiac, Aries, and starts its movement north. The 'tropical' zodiac is so called because it is based on the movement of the Sun turning in this tropical band of up to 23-24 degrees above and below the equator (between the tropics). The other planets also move closely around this solar band.

The Sun's journey through the Northern Hemisphere corresponds exactly with the Sun passing through the signs of Aries to Virgo, the northern signs. It travels upward for three months through Aries, Taurus and Gemini until it reaches zero Cancer, which marks the Sun's highest declination above the equator, approximately 23°26·5' above zero (and is the reason that this boundary line is called the tropic of Cancer). As the Sun moves in this upward journey its height in the sky increases each day and the lengths of day and night alter, the days become longer and the nights shorter for those who live in the Northern Hemisphere; the reverse for those who live in the Southern Hemisphere. At the northern or summer solstice the Sun is at its height in the north, it is Midsummer's Day and the maximum length of daylight occurs. The Sun then travels downwards again towards the equator through the signs of Cancer, Leo and Virgo with both its height in the sky

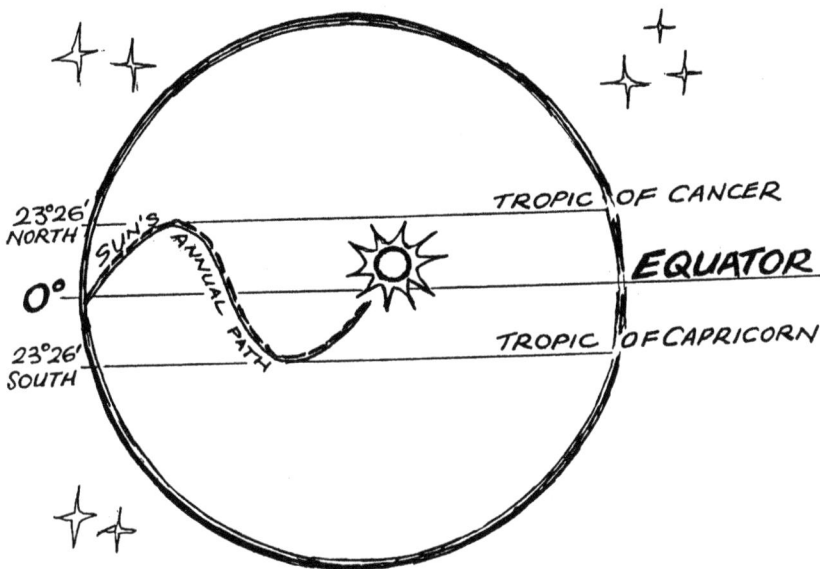

The Sun's movement as seen from Earth

and the amount of its daylight gradually declining until it passes across the zero line again and heads south.

At zero degrees Libra it is the autumn equinox, the Sun is overhead at the equator and day and night are equal. The Sun will now start its six-month journey through the Southern Hemisphere traversing the southern signs of Libra to Pisces. The middle point of this is when the Sun reaches its farthest point below the equator at approximately 23°26·5' South. This corresponds to zero degrees of Capricorn, the southern or winter solstice (and is the reason that this southern boundary line is called the tropic of Capricorn).

Declination Degrees, Parallels, Planetary Eclipses and Occultations

When the positions of planets in astrology are listed in declination they are given in degrees and minutes north or south of the celestial equator (written N or S or sometimes + or -)[2]. The number of degrees will be between 0 and 23, with certain planets occasionally ranging beyond this boundary to a rare maximum of 28/29.

Two planets in the same degree of declination would be parallel to each other in the sky, taking that as equidistant from the zero line of the equator, and their meaning interpreted as a conjunction. These parallels have an equal force to a zodiac conjunction in standard astrology, although on its own terms neither a declination parallel nor a zodiacal conjunction of planets would necessarily appear visually conjunct in the sky. Two planets situated in the same zodiac degree of longitude on a zodiac wheel, for example a 'conjunction' of the Moon and Venus both at - say - 9° Cancer, might appear one above the other in the sky and sometimes be separated by quite an appreciable distance. Similarly two planets in a declination parallel may be separated horizontally by quite a distance, although they would be in parallel.

The strongest possible conjunction in astrology therefore is when two planets are both conjunct by zodiacal longitude and parallel by declination at the same time. They would then come together in the sky. This is what astronomers understand as a conjunction. There are several names used in astrology for this phenomenon including a planetary eclipse, an occultation (usually if the Moon is involved), a cazimi (if the Sun is involved), a parallel conjunction or a zodiacal parallel.[3]

---

2. The abbreviations + and - to imply North or South will be avoided in the remainder of this book so as not to engender confusion when zodiac degrees are written as, for example, 15+ Scorpio (to imply a longitude in Scorpio of 15 degrees and some minutes). Degrees of declination north or south will always be given as N or S or spelt out in full (North, South).

3. There is still confusion over the exact meanings of some of these terms. Strictly speaking a *planetary eclipse* would involve two planets other than Sun or Moon and describe a visual eclipse of one by the other. This is an extremely rare occurrence as these planetary bodies are small from our view on Earth and for one to completely blot out the other involves an incredibly exact alignment. The term *occultation* is taken by some authorities to refer to any planetary eclipse, not necessarily involving the Moon.

Whatever term you use, these are the most powerful conjunctions in astrology. The Jupiter-Saturn conjunction, which occurs in the sky every twenty years, is and has always been regarded as one of astrology's strongest recurring markers. The reason is that both Jupiter and Saturn are planets whose declinations do not vary a great deal from their equivalent zodiacal positions and so they usually form one of these close parallel conjunctions. The result is that the energies of both planetary forces are focused and enhanced.[4]

While the meaning of any such conjunction in astrological terms would depend on the meaning of the two individual planets involved, even an occultation (eclipse of a planet by the Moon) has not been found to occult or reduce the power of the hidden planet, rather it magnifies them both. Jupiter is not automatically more powerful than Saturn in a Jupiter-Saturn conjunction, if it is in front of Saturn from our view. Think of astrology's *cazimi* aspect when a planet is within 17 minutes of the Sun's centre; it is usually regarded as positive and beneficial to both planets. So in an occultation the planet closest to Earth, the occulting planet, is not necessarily the stronger in influence of the two.

A special case must be made however for the solar eclipse, that most awesome of occultations when the Moon dramatically blocks the Sun's light from the Earth. Here the visual revelation of the Sun being eclipsed in its strength must also hold in its astrological interpretation. But in other close joinings of two celestial bodies the concentration of their forces means a fortification of both energies.

Understanding the difference in power between a parallel conjunction and a normal conjunction helps to illustrate the use of integrating declination and longitude together. It can also explain why some transits are more powerful than others - they may only be working one way (making a

---

4.   The conjunctions of the larger, slower-moving planets, like Jupiter and Saturn may not always be narrowed down to one specific day. For example the Jupiter-Saturn conjunction of the year 2000 was exact by longitude on 28 May at 22°Taurus, but the two planets were exact by declination at least a month before this. By 28 May their declinations had moved a degree apart. On 23 April when Jupiter and Saturn were parallel by declination at 15°19' North, Jupiter was still at 14°Taurus while Saturn was at 18°Taurus by longitude. In any case the entire month of May 2000 would have seen a close grouping of their energies.

The Saturn-Jupiter conjunction of 2020 however is closer both ways. The two planets are exactly conjunct by longitude at 0 Aquarius on December 21 when their declinations are only 7 minutes of a degree apart (Jupiter 20°32' South, Saturn 20°25' South). The declinations are at their closest just 5 days later.

conjunction by longitude but not by declination). The study of declination is best understood not as an astrological specialism to be used in isolation but as an additional piece to add to your existing astrology whatever your individual preference or field.

Contra-parallels and Orbs

When two planets have the same degree of declination but are situated in opposite hemispheres, as for example one at 10° North and one at 10° South, the aspect is called a contra-parallel, with an energy loosely similar to a zodiacal opposition. To be more accurate it is a bridging between hemispheres and need not have the negative connotation of an opposite energy. Depending on the planets involved it may be more concerned with linking personal motivations (Southern Hemisphere) with outer agendas (Northern Hemisphere), or as John Willner has put it: negotiating between self and others.[5]

Cynthia Cornell has likened the contra-parallel to two strings on a musical instrument that share a similar vibration when plucked. More a "harmonic resonance" than an opposition.[6] And any two planets in contra-parallel will have as their exact midpoint the powerful zero-degree area of the celestial equator. This would not necessarily apply to two planets in a longitudinal opposition on a zodiac wheel. (For a deeper look at this see Appendix 4: Why a Contra-Parallel is not an 'Opposition').

The orbs used in declination are completely different to those commonly used in zodiacal longitude. While obviously an exact conjunction or parallel remains the strongest meeting of two energies in either system, authorities differ on how far you can stretch the orbs to retain the astrological effect. In declination, orbs for parallels or contra-parallels must go on a sliding scale depending on how far the planets are situated from the zero line, as the degrees are more stretched out near the equator. Charles Jayne suggested an orb of almost 2° around zero declination decreasing to about 1° at 20° North or South declination. Above 20° of declination the orb gets even smaller reducing down to half or a quarter of a degree. As Jayne illustrated in his books *Horoscope Interpretation Outlined* and *Parallels: Their Hidden Meaning*[7] it all depends on how tight an orb you personally prefer to use in zodiac

---

5. John Willner *The Powerful Declinations*, AFA, Tempe, 1998.
6. Cynthia Cornell *Sagittarius Rising*, Newsletter of the Michigan Federation of Astrology, 2003.
7. Both books collected in *The Best of Charles Jayne*, AFA, Tempe, 1995.

equivalents.[8] A rough and ready guide would be to use a 2° orb between declinations 0°-10°, a 1° orb between declinations 10°-20°, and to be allowing only minutes of a degree in orb for declinations approaching the solstices around 23° above or below zero. But the choice is yours.

As mentioned above, the orbs decline in this way because the Sun moves faster through the lower degrees of declination near the equinoxes when it is gaining or losing height rapidly. By the time it is nearing the higher degrees of the solstices the Sun's journey appears to have flattened out and it takes longer to traverse them.

The Solar Festivals

The most powerful degrees of declination north or south are those that mark the Sun's lowest and highest points. These are at zero degrees (the equinoxes) and at 23°26·5' North or South (the solstices). They correspond in the zodiac to the beginning of the Cardinal signs, Aries, Cancer, Libra and Capricorn. On our modern calendar these solar activations take place each year on or very near to the following dates:

The Solar Festivals

---

8. In *Parallels: Their Hidden Meaning* Charles Jayne gives an example of "conservative" orbs, which would be the equivalent of using a 3° orb between planets in longitude. Here the declination orbs range from 1°11'30" at 1°12' of declination to only 0°10'30" at 23°12' declination.

Spring Equinox	21st March (Sun at 0° declination. Sun at 0° Aries)
Summer Solstice	21st June (Sun at 23°26·5' North declination. Sun at 0° Cancer)
Autumn Equinox	23rd September (Sun at 0° declination. Sun at 0° Libra)
Winter Solstice	21st December (Sun at 23°26·5' South declination. Sun at 0° Capricorn)

The terms spring, summer, winter etc. are relative of course. If you live in the Southern Hemisphere summer solstice would be winter solstice, but the dates derived from the Sun's measurements are the same. These four special points and the dates midway between them are the primary solar festivals, honoured in customs and architecture that flow back into antiquity.

The Obliquity of the Ecliptic

The plane of the Sun's path as seen from Earth moves in a band between 23°26·5' North of the equator and 23°26·5' South of the equator. This figure of 23°26·5' is called the obliquity of the ecliptic and is not absolutely fixed. Its precise measurement depends on the current tilt of the Earth's axis and its ebbs and flows or *nutations* are caused by the gravity of other planets and by the Moon's orbit. A standard ephemeris will usually give its monthly position, or if you wish to check its position for any date you can note the closest solstice and its declination.

At the start of the twentieth century this measurement was given as 23°27'06".[9]

At the start of the twenty-first century it was 23°26'18".

Overall the obliquity of the ecliptic had decreased by almost a minute of a degree over the course of a century. The difference is negligible admittedly but it does mark the exact limits of the Sun's highest steps. When the Sun's boundary of 23°26·5' or 23°26' is quoted in this book please be aware that this is a current average figure used for the sake of convenience. (The tilt appears to undergo a vast cycle of approximately 41,000 years with an obliquity difference ranging, as far as is known, from about 21°30' to almost 25°00').

---

9. Neil F.Michelsen, *The American Ephemeris for the 20th Century*, ACS, San Diego.

The Two Hemispheres and the Ingress

The Sun's reliability in its journey through the Northern and Southern hemispheres never wavers. If it is March and the Sun is in Pisces it will be in the Southern Hemisphere, if it is March and the Sun is in Aries it will be in

Zodiac & Declination equivalents. In this example the Sun is shown at approx 20° Taurus, the equivalent of 18° North of the equator.

Zodiac & Declination equivalents.
In this example the Sun is shown at approx. 10° Leo also the equivalent of 18° North of the equator.

The elliptical shape on which these drawings are based were designed by Kt Boehrer in the 1970s. In 1992 Nelda Tanner redesigned Boehrer's graph with permission, and reordered it with north declination at the top and south at the bottom. The full graphic design is copyrighted under RightLeft Graphics.

the Northern Hemisphere. If the Sun is in Leo it will be in the north, if the Sun is in Sagittarius it will be in the south, and so on.

The remainder of the planets however have their own agendas, moving through different signs and degrees of declination to the Sun at any particular time. It is quite possible that on a birth chart the majority of planets may be in north declination while the Sun is in the south, and thus the overall orientation of that horoscope would be towards a northern energy rather than a southern one.

On the Earth's globe there is more landmass above the equator and more water below it. Symbolically this confirms the long-held idea that North = Objectivity, South = Subjectivity. Some of the chapters in this book explore the subtle differences between the two declinational hemispheres including the idea that the Southern Hemisphere may be more karmic in operation. (See more on p.136)

The line of zero declination that divides the northern and southern hemispheres, the equinoctial line, the equator, is one of the most critical positions in declination. It is a change-over point and planets are highly charged when passing here. This equinoctial line of zero degrees Aries/Libra is similar in meaning to that of the "Aries Point" or "Earth Point" of the Uranian school relating directly to the environment and the world [10] and the concept that when it is triggered there is a public projection of the planets or points associated with it.[11]

When a planet crosses the zero line from south to north, as the Sun does when it is born again at the spring equinox each year, a cycle begins that relates to the energy of that planet. This is the golden dawn of the traditional ingress charts and can be studied in terms of the earthly possibilities of that planet's complete zodiacal cycle. It is true whether we are speaking of the Sun and its one-year journey or Jupiter and its twelve-year journey.

---

10. "The cardinal points relate people to the world at large". Charles Jayne in *Parallels: Their Hidden Meaning* credits this observation to Alfred Witte. Charles Harvey in *Mundane Astrology* (Ingresses, Lunations, Eclipses) affirms Witte's viewpoint that the Aries Point "represents the relationship of the individual to the group, to the masses, and to the environment, the nation, and the world in general." Witte-Lefeldt, *Rules for Planetary Pictures*, Ludwig Rudolf / Witte Verlag, Hamburg..
11. C.C.Zain in *Mundane Astrology*, Church of Light, Brea, California, 1999 (originally copyright 1935 Elbert Benjamine, Serial Lesson No.142) said that planets crossing the zero line, or within a degree above or below, "tend to bring a response from the physical environment".

The positions (and declinations) of the other planets on an Ingress chart can become sensitive trigger-points in the life of that planetary cycle.[12]

Beyond the Steps: Planets out of bounds

The Sun marks the boundaries of declination: 23°26·5' North or South of the equator. Other planets will sometimes go outside these boundaries by a few degrees and when they do they are termed "out of bounds" or OOB for short. The term was coined in the 1970s by Kt Boehrer[13] [1923-2004], one of the most important pioneers in the modern resurgence of declination studies.

The Sun can never go out of bounds because it is the Sun that marks the bounds, but the Moon, Mercury, Venus, Mars, Uranus and Pluto do, while Saturn and Neptune do not. Jupiter does occasionally but only by a tiny amount.

Any planet that is very close to the northern or southern boundary line will be powerful by definition, but when a planet is actually beyond that boundary or "out of bounds" it means that the Sun can never reach it by declination. It has stepped outside the borders, beyond the influence of the boss (the Sun). This could be good or bad depending on circumstance, but it provides a natural ability to use the power of that planet without the normal restraints in operation.

Out-of-bounds planets are wild and unrestrained. Their energy is extreme, magnified, uncontrollable, vulnerable, independent, awkward, extraordinary, privileged and creative. We will examine some of their effects in following chapters.

We might note that the "hottest day" illustration chart shown earlier had the Moon out of bounds. (The Moon was at 25°07' South, well over a degree beyond the boundary of 23°26'). The collective public reaction to this event at the time was of emotional surprise. This was something out of the ordinary to the inhabitants of a temperate climate. The knowledge that the summer temperature in Britain had topped the 100° Fahrenheit mark caused feelings of joy to those who liked the heat and fear to those who did not. In other words it was the emotions (the Moon) that were magnified beyond normal. Even the way the information was presented on the News broadcasts was uncharacteristically emotional.

---

12.   For full details of the historical use of Ingress charts see *Mundane Astrology* by Baigent, Campion and Harvey, Aquarian Press, Wellingborough, 1984
13.   Pronounced "Kate Bear".

The unique status of a natal out-of-bounds planet also means that it is rarely touched by another planet in transit - at least not as often as its equivalent zodiac position might suggest. For instance Saturn, a planet that does not go out of bounds, can never reach a natal OOB planet by transit so that its wild natal energy is never tamed or brought into line by the zodiac's harsh teacher.

If you have a chart where none of the natal planets are out of bounds (which is quite usual), they may go out of bounds at some point in your life by progression.[14] If that is the case it represents a time of magnification and further development of the energy of that planet. The force it represents on your birth chart should operate more easily, or at least beyond normal expectations. If you have several natal out-of-bounds planets you are likely to be of a unique character.

At certain times the most regular out-of-bounder is the Moon, meaning that when the Moon is in its OOB cycle it may be out of bounds for a day or so twice every month, usually when it is in certain degrees of Gemini/Cancer or Sagittarius/Capricorn on the tropical zodiac. But this only happens in nine to ten-year chunks. For approximately nine years the Moon can go out of bounds twice a month, then for the following nine to ten years it will remain inbounds all the time and never cross the Sun's boundary lines at all. From approximately 2001-2011 the Moon could travel out of bounds but from 2011-2020 it would stay inbounds. From 1983-1992 it was possible to be out of bounds, from 1992-2001 it was not. And so on. The Moon's maximum declination of around 28°45' North or South, called the Moon's major standstill, will be reached in the middle of the ten-year OOB periods. The Moon's minor standstill of 18°10' North or South (the highest it can reach at that time) will occur in the middle of the inbound periods.[15]

Antiscia

As the Sun takes its annual steps above or below the celestial equator, as it climbs its degrees of declination, it will reflect a series of parallel degrees

---

14. The day-to-a-year Secondary Progressions are the usual method.
15. Astrid Fallon has referred to the major or minor Moon standstill as "a lunistice" and reminds us that they occur when the Moon's North Node reaches zero Aries (major standstill) and zero Libra (minor standstill). Astrid Fallon, "Natural Astrology: Another Door of Perception" *The Astrological Journal*, London, Volume 47, Number 3, May 2005. Astrid produces some very useful annual ephemerides and diaries based on a declination view. (www.fallon.demon.co.uk)

that it meets on the way back down. These *solar parallels* are the days of equal daylight either side of a solstice.

For example in the month of May the Sun is on its way to the northern summer solstice - let us say it is at 18° North and heading upwards - but it will also pass through this same degree of 18 North when it is heading downwards again in August after the solstice. At these parallel times the Sun's energy is similar, the amount of daylight each day is the same, the declination degree is the same and the planetary hours will have corresponding length. This is basic antiscia; a statement of understanding that goes back at least to the time of Ptolemy.[16]

On the tropical zodiac, using the same example, if the Sun were positioned at 20° Taurus in May it would share exactly the same energy and hours of daylight as its position at 10° Leo in early August. So the longitude degrees of 20+° Taurus and 9+° Leo share a likeness, a subtle energy of "vertue" to use William Lilly's description. (V*ertue* meaning effective force)[17]. And every zodiac degree has its antiscion twin situated at either side of zero degrees Cancer or Capricorn, the solstice axis. Anything that affects the one will be felt by the other. A complete table of antiscia-related zodiac degrees is given at the end of this section.

---

16. Interested readers are referred to Deborah Houlding's essay *The Classical Basis of Antiscia and Contra-Antiscia* an article printed in *The Traditonal Astrologer*, Ascella Publications, Mansfield, Spring 1994 ("The Philosophy of Antiscia") and updated on her Skyscript website: www.skyscript.co.uk. An article by Dr Felix Jay in this same edition of *The Traditional Astrologer* makes clear the difference between declination and zodiac antiscia.

17. Lilly's use of the word "vertue" (virtue) is an interesting one. In the early seventeenth century it was something of a fashionable expression, having been used by both Shakespeare and Jonson. From Shakespeare's *The Tempest* comes the quote "the rarer action is, in virtue than in vengeance", and from Jonson's *Oberon the Fairy Prince*: "He is the matter of virtue plac'd high."

Literary scholars have commented on the complicated significance of the word "virtue" in Shakespearean times, suggesting themes of magnanimity and nobility rather than the moral, God-fearing chastity of its later usage. Its original meaning, derived from the Latin *virtus* (manliness), seems to have meant goodness combined with potency and valour.

Antiscia on a zodiac wheel

As long as we are speaking of the Sun these rules are constant. Declination antiscia and longitude antiscia are two ways of looking at the same thing. It is only when we bring the other planets into the equation that the two systems are likely to diverge. One of the more modern researchers into this phenomenon was Charles Jayne [18] who made clear in his book *Parallels: Their Hidden Meaning* the difference between a planet's "bodily declination" and its "ecliptic intercept".[19]

When we look at the movements of other planets the difference between zodiacal parallels and declination parallels comes more noticeably to light, as the planets do not always move in exactly the same plane as the Sun. Pluto is an extreme instance of this, as all modern astrologers including Jayne have noted.[20] For example: Pluto's tropical zodiac position at noon on January 1st 2000 was 11°27' Sagittarius, yet its declinational position was 11°23' South. If the *Sun* had been positioned at 11°27' Sagittarius its corresponding declinational position would be 22°09' South, which is noticeably different to 11°23' South.

---

18. Previous references to the difference between declinational and zodiac or longitude antiscia are referred to in Nichols de Vore's *Encyclopedia of Astrology*, Littlefield, Adams & Co, Totowa, 1976 (originally copyright 1947 by Philosophical Library Inc), and Fred Gettings Arkana Dictionary of Astrology, Arkana,London, 1990 (originally published by Routledge & Kegan Paul Ltd, 1985) which states that Antonio Bonattis (in his *Universa Astrophia Naturalis*, 1687) "was at pains to distinguish the modern sense of the antiscion...from the declination of *antiscium*".
19. Charles Jayne, *Parallels: Their Hidden Meaning*, collected in *The Best of Charles Jayne*, AFA, Tempe, 1995.
20. As above.

Although planets travel in the same band as the Sun against the backdrop of the zodiac, the width of that band is broad. From the point of view of the circular zodiac, Pluto's zodiacal parallel degree in the above example would have been 18°33' Capricorn. We might say that someone with their natal Sun at 18°33' Capricorn at that time would have experienced intense effects similar to Pluto transiting their Sun. But such a prediction is based on rather shaky logic. The true antiscion of Pluto would have had its effect on a planet situated at 11°23' South. Someone with a natal Sun at 29°44' Libra or 0°16' Pisces for example (the exact solar equivalents of 11°23' South) would have been just as likely to feel the Plutonic effects.

Zodiacal parallels therefore are only exact when using the positions of the Sun, the Nodes, the ascendant and the midheaven on a longitudinal chart. Jupiter, Saturn, Uranus and Neptune may not be too far out, but for all other planets (Moon, Mercury, Venus, Mars, Pluto), antiscion use on the round zodiac has to be more symbolic if it is not being related to declination.

Antiscia, when formed by reflecting degrees from the Cancer/Capricorn axis on a longitudinal zodiacal chart, might be more exactly described as a *zodiacal parallel* especially when planets other than the Sun are involved. The true meaning of antiscia is "opposite shadows",[21] from Greek, and was a literal observation of how the Sun threw equal shadows on the ground on opposite sides of a line at certain days of the year. This is determined purely by the declination of the Sun. If the Earth was not tilted on its axis, its annual zodiacal orbit of the Sun would be too uniform to produce these differing opposite shadows; and there would be no seasons either.

Antiscia is a plural word. The singular is *antiscium* or, as is more commonly used, *antiscion*, which has become both a noun and an adjective. For example: "4 Aries is the *antiscion* of 26 Virgo." "The two planets share an *antiscion* relationship."

---

21. *The Traditional Astrologer*, Ascella Publications, Mansfield, Issue 4, Spring, 1994.

Table of antiscia-related zodiac degrees (zodiacal parallels)

Northern declinations

First degree of Cancer (0+) = Thirtieth degree of Gemini (29+)   [Solstice]

Second degree of Cancer (1+) = Twenty-ninth degree of Gemini (28+)

Third degree of Cancer (2+) = Twenty-eighth degree of Gemini (27+)

Fourth degree of Cancer (3+) = Twenty-seventh degree of Gemini (26+)

Fifth degree of Cancer (4+) = Twenty-sixth degree of Gemini (25+)

Sixth degree of Cancer (5+) = Twenty-fifth degree of Gemini (24+)

Seventh degree of Cancer (6+) = Twenty-fourth degree of Gemini (23+)

Eighth degree of Cancer (7+) = Twenty-third degree of Gemini (22+)

Ninth degree of Cancer (8+) = Twenty-second degree of Gemini (21+)

Tenth degree of Cancer (9+) = Twenty-first degree of Gemini (20+)

Eleventh degree of Cancer (10+) = Twentieth degree of Gemini (19+)

Twelfth degree of Cancer (11+) = Nineteenth degree of Gemini (18+)

Thirteenth degree of Cancer (12+) = Eighteenth degree of Gemini (17+)

Fourteenth degree of Cancer (13+) = Seventeenth degree of Gemini (16+)

Fifteenth degree of Cancer (14+) = Sixteenth degree of Gemini (15+)

Sixteenth degree of Cancer (15+) = Fifteenth degree of Gemini (14+)

Seventeenth degree of Cancer (16+) = Fourteenth degree of Gemini (13+)

Eighteenth degree of Cancer (17+) = Thirteenth degree of Gemini (12+)

Nineteenth degree of Cancer (18+) = Twelfth degree of Gemini (11+)

Twentieth degree of Cancer (19+) = Eleventh degree of Gemini (10+)

Twenty-first degree of Cancer (20+) = Tenth degree of Gemini (9+)

Twenty-second degree of Cancer (21+) = Ninth degree of Gemini (8+)

Twenty-third degree of Cancer (22+) = Eighth degree of Gemini (7+)

Twenty-fourth degree of Cancer (23+) = Seventh degree of Gemini (6+)

Twenty-fifth degree of Cancer (24+) = Sixth degree of Gemini (5+)

Twenty-sixth degree of Cancer (25+) = Fifth degree of Gemini (4+)

Twenty-seventh degree of Cancer (26+) = Fourth degree of Gemini (3+)

Twenty-eighth degree of Cancer (27+) = Third degree of Gemini (2+)

Twenty-ninth degree of Cancer (28+) = Second degree of Gemini (1+)

Thirtieth degree of Cancer (29+) = First degree of Gemini (0+)

Declination: The Basics   19

First degree of Leo (0+) = Thirtieth degree of Taurus (29+)
Second degree of Leo (1+) = Twenty-ninth degree of Taurus (28+)
Third degree of Leo (2+) = Twenty-eighth degree of Taurus (27+)
Fourth degree of Leo (3+) = Twenty-seventh degree of Taurus (26+)
Fifth degree of Leo (4+) = Twenty-sixth degree of Taurus (25+)
Sixth degree of Leo (5+) = Twenty-fifth degree of Taurus (24+)
Seventh degree of Leo (6+) = Twenty-fourth degree of Taurus (23+)
Eighth degree of Leo (7+) = Twenty-third degree of Taurus (22+)
Ninth degree of Leo (8+) = Twenty-second degree of Taurus (21+)
Tenth degree of Leo (9+) = Twenty-first degree of Taurus (20+)
Eleventh degree of Leo (10+) = Twentieth degree of Taurus (19+)
Twelfth degree of Leo (11+) = Nineteenth degree of Taurus (18+)
Thirteenth degree of Leo (12+) = Eighteenth degree of Taurus (17+)
Fourteenth degree of Leo (13+) = Seventeenth degree of Taurus (16+)
Fifteenth degree of Leo (14+) = Sixteenth degree of Taurus (15+)
Sixteenth degree of Leo (15+) = Fifteenth degree of Taurus (14+)
Seventeenth degree of Leo (16+) = Fourteenth degree of Taurus (13+)
Eighteenth degree of Leo (17+) = Thirteenth degree of Taurus (12+)
Nineteenth degree of Leo (18+) = Twelfth degree of Taurus (11+)
Twentieth degree of Leo (19+) = Eleventh degree of Taurus (10+)
Twenty-first degree of Leo (20+) = Tenth degree of Taurus (9+)
Twenty-second degree of Leo (21+) = Ninth degree of Taurus (8+)
Twenty-third degree of Leo (22+) = Eighth degree of Taurus (7+)
Twenty-fourth degree of Leo (23+) = Seventh degree of Taurus (6+)
Twenty-fifth degree of Leo (24+) = Sixth degree of Taurus (5+)
Twenty-sixth degree of Leo (25+) = Fifth degree of Taurus (4+)
Twenty-seventh degree of Leo (26+) = Fourth degree of Taurus (3+)
Twenty-eighth degree of Leo (27+) = Third degree of Taurus (2+)
Twenty-ninth degree of Leo (28+) = Second degree of Taurus (1+)
Thirtieth degree of Leo (29+) = First degree of Taurus (0+)

First degree of Virgo (0+) = Thirtieth degree of Aries (29+)
Second degree of Virgo (1+) = Twenty-ninth degree of Aries (28+)
Third degree of Virgo (2+) = Twenty-eighth degree of Aries (27+)
Fourth degree of Virgo (3+) = Twenty-seventh degree of Aries (26+)
Fifth degree of Virgo (4+) = Twenty-sixth degree of Aries (25+)
Sixth degree of Virgo (5+) = Twenty-fifth degree of Aries (24+)
Seventh degree of Virgo (6+) = Twenty-fourth degree of Aries (23+)
Eighth degree of Virgo (7+) = Twenty-third degree of Aries (22+)
Ninth degree of Virgo (8+) = Twenty-second degree of Aries (21+)
Tenth degree of Virgo (9+) = Twenty-first degree of Aries (20+)
Eleventh degree of Virgo (10+) = Twentieth degree of Aries (19+)
Twelfth degree of Virgo (11+) = Nineteenth degree of Aries (18+)
Thirteenth degree of Virgo (12+) = Eighteenth degree of Aries (17+)
Fourteenth degree of Virgo (13+) = Seventeenth degree of Aries (16+)
Fifteenth degree of Virgo (14+) = Sixteenth degree of Aries (15+)
Sixteenth degree of Virgo (15+) = Fifteenth degree of Aries (14+)
Seventeenth degree of Virgo (16+) = Fourteenth degree of Aries (13+)
Eighteenth degree of Virgo (17+) = Thirteenth degree of Aries (12+)
Nineteenth degree of Virgo (18+) = Twelfth degree of Aries (11+)
Twentieth degree of Virgo (19+) = Eleventh degree of Aries (10+)
Twenty-first degree of Virgo (20+) = Tenth degree of Aries (9+)
Twenty-second degree of Virgo (21+) = Ninth degree of Aries (8+)
Twenty-third degree of Virgo (22+) = Eighth degree of Aries (7+)
Twenty-fourth degree of Virgo (23+) = Seventh degree of Aries (6+)
Twenty-fifth degree of Virgo (24+) = Sixth degree of Aries (5+)
Twenty-sixth degree of Virgo (25+) = Fifth degree of Aries (4+)
Twenty-seventh degree of Virgo (26+) = Fourth degree of Aries (3+)
Twenty-eighth degree of Virgo (27+) = Third degree of Aries (2+)
Twenty-ninth degree of Virgo (28+) = Second degree of Aries (1+)
Thirtieth degree of Virgo (29+) = First degree of Aries (0+)   [Equinox]

Declination: The Basics 21

Southern declinations
First degree of Libra (0+) = Thirtieth degree of Pisces (29+) [Equinox]

Second degree of Libra (1+) = Twenty-ninth degree of Pisces (28+)

Third degree of Libra (2+) = Twenty-eighth degree of Pisces (27+)

Fourth degree of Libra (3+) = Twenty-seventh degree of Pisces (26+)

Fifth degree of Libra (4+) = Twenty-sixth degree of Pisces (25+)

Sixth degree of Libra (5+) = Twenty-fifth degree of Pisces (24+)

Seventh degree of Libra (6+) = Twenty-fourth degree of Pisces (23+)

Eighth degree of Libra (7+) = Twenty-third degree of Pisces (22+)

Ninth degree of Libra (8+) = Twenty-second degree of Pisces (21+)

Tenth degree of Libra (9+) = Twenty-first degree of Pisces (20+)

Eleventh degree of Libra (10+) = Twentieth degree of Pisces (19+)

Twelfth degree of Libra (11+) = Nineteenth degree of Pisces (18+)

Thirteenth degree of Libra (12+) = Eighteenth degree of Pisces (17+)

Fourteenth degree of Libra (13+) = Seventeenth degree of Pisces (16+)

Fifteenth degree of Libra (14+) = Sixteenth degree of Pisces (15+)

Sixteenth degree of Libra (15+) = Fifteenth degree of Pisces (14+)

Seventeenth degree of Libra (16+) = Fourteenth degree of Pisces (13+)

Eighteenth degree of Libra (17+) = Thirteenth degree of Pisces (12+)

Nineteenth degree of Libra (18+) = Twelfth degree of Pisces (11+)

Twentieth degree of Libra (19+) = Eleventh degree of Pisces (10+)

Twenty-first degree of Libra (20+) = Tenth degree of Pisces (9+)

Twenty-second degree of Libra (21+) = Ninth degree of Pisces (8+)

Twenty-third degree of Libra (22+) = Eighth degree of Pisces (7+)

Twenty-fourth degree of Libra (23+) = Seventh degree of Pisces (6+)

Twenty-fifth degree of Libra (24+) = Sixth degree of Pisces (5+)

Twenty-sixth degree of Libra (25+) = Fifth degree of Pisces (4+)

Twenty-seventh degree of Libra (26+) = Fourth degree of Pisces (3+)

Twenty-eighth degree of Libra (27+) = Third degree of Pisces (2+)

Twenty-ninth degree of Libra (28+) = Second degree of Pisces (1+)

Thirtieth degree of Libra (29+) = First degree of Pisces (0+)

First degree of Scorpio (0+) = Thirtieth degree of Aquarius (29+)
Second degree of Scorpio (1+) = Twenty-ninth degree of Aquarius (28+)
Third degree of Scorpio (2+) = Twenty-eighth degree of Aquarius (27+)
Fourth degree of Scorpio (3+) = Twenty-seventh degree of Aquarius (26+)
Fifth degree of Scorpio (4+) = Twenty-sixth degree of Aquarius (25+)
Sixth degree of Scorpio (5+) = Twenty-fifth degree of Aquarius (24+)
Seventh degree of Scorpio (6+) = Twenty-fourth degree of Aquarius (23+)
Eighth degree of Scorpio (7+) = Twenty-third degree of Aquarius (22+)
Ninth degree of Scorpio (8+) = Twenty-second degree of Aquarius (21+)
Tenth degree of Scorpio (9+) = Twenty-first degree of Aquarius (20+)
Eleventh degree of Scorpio (10+) = Twentieth degree of Aquarius (19+)
Twelfth degree of Scorpio (11+) = Nineteenth degree of Aquarius (18+)
Thirteenth degree of Scorpio (12+) = Eighteenth degree of Aquarius (17+)
Fourteenth degree of Scorpio (13+) = Seventeenth degree of Aquarius (16+)
Fifteenth degree of Scorpio (14+) = Sixteenth degree of Aquarius (15+)
Sixteenth degree of Scorpio (15+) = Fifteenth degree of Aquarius (14+)
Seventeenth degree of Scorpio (16+) = Fourteenth degree of Aquarius (13+)
Eighteenth degree of Scorpio (17+) = Thirteenth degree of Aquarius (12+)
Nineteenth degree of Scorpio (18+) = Twelfth degree of Aquarius (11+)
Twentieth degree of Scorpio (19+) = Eleventh degree of Aquarius (10+)
Twenty-first degree of Scorpio (20+) = Tenth degree of Aquarius (9+)
Twenty-second degree of Scorpio (21+) = Ninth degree of Aquarius (8+)
Twenty-third degree of Scorpio (22+) = Eighth degree of Aquarius (7+)
Twenty-fourth degree of Scorpio (23+) = Seventh degree of Aquarius (6+)
Twenty-fifth degree of Scorpio (24+) = Sixth degree of Aquarius (5+)
Twenty-sixth degree of Scorpio (25+) = Fifth degree of Aquarius (4+)
Twenty-seventh degree of Scorpio (26+) = Fourth degree of Aquarius (3+)
Twenty-eighth degree of Scorpio (27+) = Third degree of Aquarius (2+)
Twenty-ninth degree of Scorpio (28+) = Second degree of Aquarius (1+)
Thirtieth degree of Scorpio (29+) = First degree of Aquarius (0+)

Declination: The Basics   23

First degree of Sagittarius (0+) = Thirtieth degree of Capricorn (29+)

Second degree of Sagittarius (1+) = Twenty-ninth degree of Capricorn (28+)

Third degree of Sagittarius (2+) = Twenty-eighth degree of Capricorn (27+)

Fourth degree of Sagittarius (3+) = Twenty-seventh degree of Capricorn (26+)

Fifth degree of Sagittarius (4+) = Twenty-sixth degree of Capricorn (25+)

Sixth degree of Sagittarius (5+) = Twenty-fifth degree of Capricorn (24+)

Seventh degree of Sagittarius (6+) = Twenty-fourth degree of Capricorn (23+)

Eighth degree of Sagittarius (7+) = Twenty-third degree of Capricorn (22+)

Ninth degree of Sagittarius (8+) = Twenty-second degree of Capricorn (21+)

Tenth degree of Sagittarius (9+) = Twenty-first degree of Capricorn (20+)

Eleventh degree of Sagittarius (10+) = Twentieth degree of Capricorn (19+)

Twelfth degree of Sagittarius (11+) = Nineteenth degree of Capricorn (18+)

Thirteenth degree of Sagittarius (12+) = Eighteenth degree of Capricorn (17+)

Fourteenth degree of Sagittarius (13+) = Seventeenth degree of Capricorn (16+)

Fifteenth degree of Sagittarius (14+) = Sixteenth degree of Capricorn (15+)

Sixteenth degree of Sagittarius (15+) = Fifteenth degree of Capricorn (14+)

Seventeenth degree of Sagittarius (16+) = Fourteenth degree of Capricorn (13+)

Eighteenth degree of Sagittarius (17+) = Thirteenth degree of Capricorn (12+)

Nineteenth degree of Sagittarius (18+) = Twelfth degree of Capricorn (11+)

Twentieth degree of Sagittarius (19+) = Eleventh degree of Capricorn (10+)

Twenty-first degree of Sagittarius (20+) = Tenth degree of Capricorn (9+)

Twenty-second degree of Sagittarius (21+) = Ninth degree of Capricorn (8+)

Twenty-third degree of Sagittarius (22+) = Eighth degree of Capricorn (7+)

Twenty-fourth degree of Sagittarius (23+) = Seventh degree of Capricorn (6+)

Twenty-fifth degree of Sagittarius (24+) = Sixth degree of Capricorn (5+)

Twenty-sixth degree of Sagittarius (25+) = Fifth degree of Capricorn (4+)

Twenty-seventh degree of Sagittarius (26+) = Fourth degree of Capricorn (3+)

Twenty-eighth degree of Sagittarius (27+) = Third degree of Capricorn (2+)

Twenty-ninth degree of Sagittarius (28+) = Second degree of Capricorn (1+)

Thirtieth degree of Sagittarius (29+) = First degree of Capricorn (0+) [Solstice]

Longitude Equivalents

An illuminating exercise is to translate back the declination positions of natal planets into their solar longitudinal or zodiac equivalents and display them as a round conventional zodiac chart. These longitude equivalents are also sometimes referred to as co-longitudes. The subtle differences of these positions compared to the normal natal ones on the wheel can provide much food for thought.

Table of approximate declination/longitude equivalents[16]

Degrees of declination	Degrees of longitude	
0°00' - 0°23' North=	0° - 1° Aries and	29° - 30° Virgo
0°24' - 0°47'	1° - 2°	28° - 29°
0°48' - 1°11'	2° - 3°	27° - 28°
1°12' - 1°35'	3° - 4°	26° - 27°
1°36' - 1°59'	4° - 5°	25° - 26°
2°00' - 2°22'	5° - 6°	24° - 25°
2°23' - 2°46'	6° - 7°	23° - 24°
2°47' - 3°10'	7° - 8°	22° - 23°
3°11' - 3°33'	8° - 9°	21° - 22°
3°34' - 3°57'	9° - 10°	20° - 21°
3°58' - 4°21'	10° - 11°	19° - 20°
4°22' - 4°44'	11° - 12°	18° - 19°
4°45' - 5°07'	12° - 13°	17° - 18°
5°08' - 5°31'	13° - 14°	16° - 17°
5°32' - 5°54'	14° - 15°	15° - 16°
5°55' - 6°17'	15° - 16°	14° - 15°
6°18' - 6°40'	16° - 17°	13° - 14°
6°41' - 7°03'	17° - 18°	12° - 13°
7°04' - 7°26'	18° - 19°	11° - 12°
7°27' - 7°49'	19° - 20°	10° - 11°
7°50' - 8°11'	20° - 21°	9° - 10°
8°12' - 8°34'	21° - 22°	8° - 9°
8°35' - 8°56'	22° - 23°	7° - 8°
8°57' - 9°18'	23° - 24°	6° - 7°

---

16. Approximate in that the minutes of a degree could vary slightly with the changing obliquity of the ecliptic, but for general purposes this difference is negligible.

9°19' - 9°40'	24° - 25°	5° - 6°
9°41' - 10°02'	25° - 26°	4° - 5°
10°03' - 10°24'	26° - 27°	3° - 4°
10°25' - 10°45'	27° - 28°	2° - 3°
10°46' - 11°07'	28° - 29°	1° - 2°
11°08' - 11°28'	29° - 30°	0° - 1°
11°29' - 11°49' North	0° - 1° Taurus	29° - 30° Leo
11°50' - 12°10'	1° - 2°	28° - 29°
12°11' - 12°30'	2° - 3°	27° - 28°
12°31' - 12°51'	3° - 4°	26° - 27°
12°52' - 13°11'	4° - 5°	25° - 26°
13°12' - 13°31'	5° - 6°	24° - 25°
13°32' - 13°51'	6° - 7°	23° - 24°
13°52' - 14°10'	7° - 8°	22° - 23°
14°11' - 14°30'	8° - 9°	21° - 22°
14°31' - 14°49'	9° - 10°	20° - 21°
14°50' - 15°07'	10° - 11°	19° - 20°
15°08' - 15°26'	11° - 12°	18° - 19°
15°27' - 15°44'	12° - 13°	17° - 18°
15°45' - 16°02'	13° - 14°	16° - 17°
16°03' - 16°20'	14° - 15°	15° - 16°
16°21' - 16°37'	15° - 16°	14° - 15°
16°38' - 16°55'	16° - 17°	13° - 14°
16°56' - 17°11'	17° - 18°	12° - 13°
17°12' - 17°28'	18° - 19°	11° - 12°
17°29' - 17°44'	19° - 20°	10° - 11°
17°45' - 18°00'	20° - 21°	9° - 10°
18°01' - 18°16'	21° - 22°	8° - 9°
18°17' - 18°31'	22° - 23°	7° - 8°
18°32' - 18°46'	23° - 24°	6° - 7°
18°47' - 19°01'	24° - 25°	5° - 6°
19°02' - 19°15'	25° - 26°	4° - 5°
19°16' - 19°29'	26° - 27°	3° - 4°
19°30' - 19°43'	27° - 28°	2° - 3°
19°44' - 19°56'	28° - 29°	1° - 2°
19°57' - 20°09'	29° - 30°	0° - 1°
20°10' - 20°21' North	0° - 1° Gemini	29° - 30° Cancer
20°22' - 20°34'	1° - 2°	28° - 29°
20°35' - 20°45'	2° - 3°	27° - 28°

20°46' - 20°57'	3° - 4°	26° - 27°
20°58' - 21°08'	4° - 5°	25° - 26°
21°09' - 21°18'	5° - 6°	24° - 25°
21°19' - 21°29'	6° - 7°	23° - 24°
21°30' - 21°39'	7° - 8°	22° - 23°
21°40' - 21°48'	8° - 9°	21° - 22°
21°49' - 21°57'	9° - 10°	20° - 21°
21°58' - 22°06'	10° - 11°	19° - 20°
22°07' - 22°14'	11° - 12°	18° - 19°
22°15' - 22°22'	12° - 13°	17° - 18°
22°23' - 22°29'	13° - 14°	16° - 17°
22°30' - 22°36'	14° - 15°	15° - 16°
22°37' - 22°42'	15° - 16°	14° - 15°
22°43' - 22°48'	16° - 17°	13° - 14°
22°49' - 22°54'	17° - 18°	12° - 13°
22°55' - 23°04'	18° - 19°	11° - 12°
23°05' - 23°08'	19° - 20°	10° - 11°
23°09' - 23°12'	20° - 21°	9° - 10°
23°13' - 23°18'	21° - 22°	8° - 9°
23°19' - 23°21'	22° - 23°	7° - 8°
23°22' - 23°23'	23° - 24°	6° - 7°
23°24' - 23°24'	24° - 25°	5° - 6°
23°25' - 23°25'	25° - 26°	4° - 5°
23°26' - 23°26'	26° - 27°	3° - 4°
23°26 - 23°26'	27° - 28°	2° - 3°
23°27 - 23°27'	28° - 29°	1° - 2°
23°27' - 23°27'	29° - 30°	0° - 1°
0°00' - 0°23' South	0° - 1° Libra	29° - 30° Pisces
0°24' - 0°47'	1° - 2°	28° - 29°
0°48' - 1°11'	2° - 3°	27° - 28°
1°12' - 1°35'	3° - 4°	26° - 27°
1°36' - 1°59'	4° - 5°	25° - 26°
2°00' - 2°22'	5° - 6°	24° - 25°
2°23' - 2°46'	6° - 7°	23° - 24°
2°47' - 3°10'	7° - 8°	22° - 23°
3°11' - 3°33'	8° - 9°	21° - 22°
3°34' - 3°57'	9° - 10°	20° - 21°
3°58' - 4°21'	10° - 11°	19° - 20°
4°22' - 4°44'	11° - 12°	18° - 19°

Declination: The Basics 27

4°45' - 5°07'	12° - 13°	17° - 18°
5°08' - 5°31'	13° - 14°	16° - 17°
5°32' - 5°54'	14° - 15°	15° - 16°
5°55' - 6°17'	15° - 16°	14° - 15°
6°18' - 6°40'	16° - 17°	13° - 14°
6°41' - 7°03'	17° - 18°	12° - 13°
7°04' - 7°26'	18° - 19°	11° - 12°
7°27' - 7°49'	19° - 20°	10° - 11°
7°50' - 8°11'	20° - 21°	9° - 10°
8°12' - 8°34'	21° - 22°	8° - 9°
8°35' - 8°56'	22° - 23°	7° - 8°
8°57' - 9°18'	23° - 24°	6° - 7°
9°19' - 9°40'	24° - 25°	5° - 6°
9°41' - 10°02'	25° - 26°	4° - 5°
10°03' - 10°24'	26° - 27°	3° - 4°
10°25' - 10°45'	27° - 28°	2° - 3°
10°46' - 11°07'	28° - 29°	1° - 2°
11°08' - 11°28'	29° - 30°	0° - 1°
11°29' - 11°49' South	0° - 1° Scorpio	29° - 30° Aquarius
11°50' - 12°10'	1° - 2°	28° - 29°
12°11' - 12°30'	2° - 3°	27° - 28°
12°31' - 12°51'	3° - 4°	26° - 27°
12°52' - 13°11'	4° - 5°	25° - 26°
13°12' - 13°31'	5° - 6°	24° - 25°
13°32' - 13°51'	6° - 7°	23° - 24°
13°52' - 14°10'	7° - 8°	22° - 23°
14°11' - 14°30'	8° - 9°	21° - 22°
14°31' - 14°49'	9° - 10°	20° - 21°
14°50' - 15°07'	10° - 11°	19° - 20°
15°08' - 15°26'	11° - 12°	18° - 19°
15°27' - 15°44'	12° - 13°	17° - 18°
15°45' - 16°02'	13° - 14°	16° - 17°
16°03' - 16°20'	14° - 15°	15° - 16°
16°21' - 16°37'	15° - 16°	14° - 15°
16°38' - 16°55'	16° - 17°	13° - 14°
16°56' - 17°11'	17° - 18°	12° - 13°
17°12' - 17°28'	18° - 19°	11° - 12°
17°29' - 17°44'	19° - 20°	10° - 11°
17°45' - 18°00'	20° - 21°	9° - 10°

18°01' - 18°16'	21° - 22°	8° - 9°
18°17' - 18°31'	22° - 23°	7° - 8°
18°32' - 18°46'	23° - 24°	6° - 7°
18°47' - 19°01'	24° - 25°	5° - 6°
19°02' - 19°15'	25° - 26°	4° - 5°
19°16' - 19°29'	26° - 27°	3° - 4°
19°30' - 19°43'	27° - 28°	2° - 3°
19°44' - 19°56'	28° - 29°	1° - 2°
19°57' - 20°09'	29° - 30°	0° - 1°
20°10' - 20°21' South	0° - 1° Sagittarius	29° - 30° Capricorn
20°22' - 20°34'	1° - 2°	28° - 29°
20°35' - 20°45'	2° - 3°	27° - 28°
20°46' - 20°57'	3° - 4°	26° - 27°
20°58' - 21°08'	4° - 5°	25° - 26°
21°09' - 21°18'	5° - 6°	24° - 25°
21°19' - 21°29'	6° - 7°	23° - 24°
21°30' - 21°39'	7° - 8°	22° - 23°
21°40' - 21°48'	8° - 9°	21° - 22°
21°49' - 21°57'	9° - 10°	20° - 21°
21°58' - 22°06'	10° - 11°	19° - 20°
22°07' - 22°14'	11° - 12°	18° - 19°
22°15' - 22°22'	12° - 13°	17° - 18°
22°23' - 22°29'	13° - 14°	16° - 17°
22°30' - 22°36'	14° - 15°	15° - 16°
22°37' - 22°42'	15° - 16°	14° - 15°
22°43' - 22°48'	16° - 17°	13° - 14°
22°49' - 22°54'	17° - 18°	12° - 13°
22°55' - 23°04'	18° - 19°	11° - 12°
23°05' - 23°08'	19° - 20°	10° - 11°
23°09' - 23°12'	20° - 21°	9° - 10°
23°13' - 23°18'	21° - 22°	8° - 9°
23°19' - 23°21'	22° - 23°	7° - 8°
23°22' - 23°23'	23° - 24°	6° - 7°
23°24' - 23°24'	24° - 25°	5° - 6°
23°25' - 23°25'	25° - 26°	4° - 5°
23°26' - 23°26'	26° - 27°	3° - 4°
23°26' - 23°26'	27° - 28°	2° - 3°
23°27' - 23°27'	28° - 29°	1° - 2°
23°27' - 23°27'	29° - 30°	0° - 1°

Time Equivalents

Degrees of declination are irregular in time as compared to the one-degree-a-day approximation of zodiac longitude degrees. Declination degrees near the equinoxes, the lower numbers north and south, are the equivalent of a lesser number of longitudinal degrees than those declination degrees nearer the solstices. A closer study of the table just given on Longitude Equivalents will bear this out, but the same information is presented in a different form below where the Sun's degrees of declination are shown in relation to the calendar days of a year.

As can be seen the Sun takes two to three days to travel through one degree of declination at the first part of its solar year from the March equinox to early May. By mid-May it is averaging four days in one degree, rising to six days by late May, nine days in early June and twelve days as it nears the solstice.

Journey of the Sun from Equinox to Equinox

Calendar day	=	Sun's declination	=	Calendar day
March 21		0 - 1° North. Equinox		September 23
22		"		22
23		"		21
24		1 - 2°		20
25		"		19
26		"		18
27		2 - 3°		17
28		"		16
29		3 - 4°		15
30		"		14
31		"		13
April 01		4 - 5°		12
02		"		11
03		"		10
04		5 - 6°		09
05		"		08
06		6 - 7°		07
07		"		06
08		"		05

30 *Declination in Astrology*

	09	7 - 8°		04
	10	"		03
	11	8 - 9°		02
	12	"		01
	13	"	August	31
	14	9 - 10°		30
	15	"		29
	16	"		28
	17	10 - 11°		27
	18	"		26
	19	"		25
	20	11 - 12°		24
	21	"		23
	22	"		22
	23	12 - 13°		21
	24	"		20
	25	"		19
	26	13 - 14°		18
	27	"		17
	28	"		16
	29	14 - 15°		15
	30	"		14
May	01	"		13
	02	15 - 16°		12
	03	"		11
	04	"		10
	05	16 - 17°		09
	06	"		08
	07	"		07
	08	"		06
	09	17 - 18°		05
	10	"		04
	11	"		03
	12	"		02
	13	18 - 19°		01
	14	"	July	31
	15	"		30
	16	"		29
	17	19 - 20°		28

Declination: The Basics 31

	18	"	27
	19	"	26
	20	"	25
	21	20 - 21°	24
	22	"	23
	23	"	22
	24	"	21
	25	"	20
	26	"	19
	27	21 - 22°	18
	28	"	17
	29	"	16
	30	"	15
	31	"	14
June	01	"	13
	02	22 - 23°	12
	03	"	11
	04	"	10
	05	"	09
	06	"	08
	07	"	07
	08	"	06
	09	"	05
	10	"	04
	11	23 - 24°	03
	12	"	02
	13	"	01
	14	"	June 30
	15	"	29
	16	"	28
	17	"	27
	18	"	26
	19	"	25
	20	"	24
	21	"	23
	22	" Solstice	22

The tables on the previous pages show the approximate link between declination degrees and calendar days in any year from the March to September equinoxes.

As can be seen, the Sun's highest degree of declination (23-24° North) covers a total of 23 days in the northern midsummer. In terms of days the Sun remains longer in this one degree of declination than any other.

> 22-23° covers 18 days in total (two separate periods of nine days).
> 21-22° and 20-21° cover 12 days each.
> 16-17°, 17-18°, 18-19° and 19-20° each cover eight days.
> And the first 15 degrees cover five to six days each on average.

A similar kind of pattern takes place when the Sun travels the Southern Hemisphere from the September to March equinoxes.

2
The Solar Festivals

"I am the maker of the hours and the creator of the days. I inaugurate festivals."

So spoke the Sun god Ra in *The Egyptian Book of the Dead*.[17] The choice of the word "inaugurate", in "I inaugurate festivals", is meaningful as it stems from the same root as "augury". To inaugurate something suggests more than making an official beginning of it, it implies that the starting moment is divined and therefore divine. As Geoffrey Cornelius discusses in *The Moment of Astrology*, inaugurate means the "ritual inception of a major matter".[18]

The Sun god has decreed by his movement that certain times are divine and that these charged moments should be celebrated by festival. In fact he relies on our participation for his power to be realised.

In the same vein as that old advice that it is better to participate in one's personal astrological transits rather than be passive or hide from them, ("if you want to walk with the gods you should put yourself in their path"), we need to make things happen collectively by honouring the Sun at its festivals.

May Queen and Halloween Jester

The energy of the Cross Quarters

The great festivals of the solar year are the equinoxes and the solstices, the four Cardinal zodiac points marking the Sun at its highest and lowest declination. Dividing these four annual points or quarter-days equally again gives us the so-called cross quarter-days, astrologically the mid-degrees of the Fixed signs. This is the eight-part year corresponding to eight annual festivals that celebrate the Sun's relationship to the land.

---

17. E.A.Wallis Budge, *The Book of the Dead*, Gramercy Books, New York, 1999. (Originally published in 1895). Ra is stating his many attributes in the story where Isis is attempting to heal him by learning his secret name.
18. Geoffrey Cornelius, *The Moment of Astrology*, The Wessex Astrologer, Bournemouth, 2003. Particularly Chapter Seven on Katarche.

However, the Sun does not move precisely one zodiacal degree of longitude every day. It moves faster through zodiacal degrees around winter solstices (southern solstices) and slower at summer solstices (northern solstices). Because of the Earth's elliptical orbit and axial tilt there are about eight more days in the half-year running between the March and September equinoxes than there are between the September and March equinoxes, yet the number of designated zodiac longitudinal degrees remain the same. While there are 180 zodiac degrees between zero Aries and zero Libra, there are approximately 186 calendar or solar days. Similarly while there are 180 zodiac degrees between zero Libra and zero Aries there are only approximately 178 solar days.

In turn this gives rise to other anomalies: The cross-quarter festival of Beltane or May Day (May 1st) is neither halfway between the spring equinox and the summer solstice on a count of days, nor is it halfway between zero Aries and zero Cancer on a count of longitudinal degrees. In other words, the Sun is not positioned on May 1st at 15° of the Fixed signs. On May 1st the Sun is positioned at approximately 10° Taurus, rather than 15° Taurus, just as its annual opposite point at Samhain or Halloween is closer to 9° Scorpio, rather than 15° Scorpio. And this is true of the other cross-quarter festivals too.

When we look at declination, we find that on the eve of May 1st the Sun usually reaches 15°00' North, with its exact solar parallel around the eve of August 12th. There is an equal amount of daylight therefore on both May 1st and August 12th as they are both an equal number of days from the summer solstice (approximately 52 days). When we check on Halloween, the night of October 31st, we find that the Sun is around 14°30' South or 9° Scorpio with its solar parallel point at 21° Aquarius around February 9th. These are both an equal number of days from the winter solstice (again approximately 52 days). Correctly therefore, if we allow the calendar dates of May 1st and November 1st to remain for Beltane and Halloween, the annual solar festivals should take place on, or very close to, the dates shown below.

Vernal Equinox   March 20th/21st   (Sun at 0° declination)

Beltane   May 1st   (Sun at 15° North, solar parallel of Lammas)

Summer Solstice June 21st   (Sun at 23°26' North)

Lammas	August 12th	(Sun at 15° North, solar parallel of Beltane)
Autumnal Equinox	September 22nd/23rd	(Sun at 0° declination)
Samhain	November 1st	(Sun at 14°30' South, solar parallel of Imbolc)
Winter Solstice	December 21st	(Sun at 23°26' South)
Imbolc	February 10th	(Sun at 14°30' South, solar parallel of Samhain)

It is important to note that some of these dates do not coincide with the days of the year that such celebrations now take place. Lammas for instance, tends to be celebrated - if it is celebrated at all - on August 1st, rather than August 12th, and Imbolc or Candlemas or Groundhog Day on February 1st or 2nd, rather than February 10th. Of all the solar festivals these last two mentioned: Lammas and Imbolc, are not great public holidays today. Their celebration dates became meshed into the solar calendar somewhere in the past so as to take place on a convenient first of the month. In Scotland Candlemas and Lammas formed one axis which is bisected again by Whitsunday on May 15th and Martinmas on November 11th for the legal purposes of quarterly rents and tenancies.

The Christian Church played an early hand by incorporating pagan festivals into its own calendar and grafting specific new saints on to older amorphous figures. Beltane Eve leading to May Day became St Walpurgis Night, but was encouraged to be shunned by good Christian souls because the Devil was said to be riding about. The Horned One was similarly abroad at the Eve of Samhain six months later, which was the Eve of All Hallows to the Church. So powerfully must this celebration have been entrenched in the public mind that November 1st was officially declared All Saints Day, presumably to rally every saintly force against the perceived fairies, hob-goblins and ancestral spirits at this Halloween time. In England in the seventeenth century the Protestant authorities were glad to be able to defuse Halloween and get it off their doorstep by heaping it all on to the Catholic "Gunpowder Plot" and the person of Guy Fawkes, who was thereafter decreed to be celebratedly burnt on fires every November 5th. The February cross quarter became the Christian Candlemas with an older goddess of light taking shape as Saint Brigid or Saint Bride and the rural importance of looking for light and shadows in the shape of Groundhog Day, while the Lammas festival was a first harvest celebration.

What seems to be beyond question is that the Sun running from equinox to solstice, Aries to Cancer and Libra to Capricorn, was regarded as more important at its mid-point festivals of Beltane and Samhain than the reflective points, the antiscia, at Lammas and Imbolc respectively. Before the solar years were universally dated to begin on January 1st, some old customs had the year beginning and ending at Samhain (Halloween). As 14-16° North and South relate now to the festivals of Beltane and Samhain, some additional meaning to these declination degrees may be gained by investigating the old customs and beliefs of May Day and Halloween.

Fifteen degrees North, May Day, is a fertility celebration above all. In the Northern Hemisphere it is abundantly spring in full bloom; and to ensure and celebrate the continuing fertility a kind of try-out marriage between lovers was once permissible. Thus Greenwood Marriages were contracted for a year and a day, and everyone danced around the phallic May Pole. The Sun god married the Earth-goddess, the Oak King partnered the May Queen and childless couples wishing for children would sleep together at a sacred spot with any offspring conceived regarded as special to the gods.

The Lammas festival in August was a fainter echo of the fertility theme, concerned with the first harvest of summer and the life-giving spirit of the corn. It honoured the growing family as well as the lovers and we might suggest therefore that the declination degrees of 14-16° North have the keyword "Fertility", the figure of the May Queen, and abundant growth attached to any planet or body situated there. Note how Juliet of Romeo and Juliet, one half of the famous pair of lovers, was said to be born at Lammas.

Fifteen degrees South (Halloween) is the great celebration of death and regeneration. The year once began and ended here. Family ancestors and the dead in general were close in spirit and were honoured and remembered with candles and fires. Both Beltane and Samhain are still regarded as potent times for divination.

The echo of Halloween at Candlemas or Imbolc or St Bride's, in February, also concerned new life in the dead of winter. It coincided with lambs being born and the first signs of approaching spring breaking through the earth. The legend of the Groundhog emerging from the dark to look for his shadow has a similar folk status.

Groundhog Day

The essence of the American groundhog superstition is the belief that making a tricky choice through observing the current state of nature determines the future. By old tradition the state of the weather in early February in the

Northern Hemisphere gave farmers a clue as to an early or late spring. This belief found echoes in many agricultural societies. In Britain there is an old rhyme "If Candlemas Day be bright and clear, there'll be two winters in the year". In the United States, Pennsylvanian folklore centred on the groundhog, a little animal believed to emerge from its winter sleep on this day to see if it could find its shadow on the ground. If it saw no shadow the groundhog decided the climate was mild enough for it to remain above ground, and human observers predicted an early spring. However if it did see its shadow the groundhog knew it was still too cold and returned underground for another six weeks of hibernation. At this time in early February the Sun in Aquarius helps towards an offbeat nature which is on a par with Halloween in the sense that both are solar parallels or antiscion points. Its 'tricky' nature reflects the similarly tricky spirits abroad on the night of All Hallows.

So we might suggest the keywords of "Death and Regeneration" for the declination area of 14-16° South, and the grinning mask of the Halloween Jester for any planet or body situated there.

The solstices and equinoxes, the highest and lowest degrees of declination, are critical points. But so also are 14-16° North or South. It seems clear that these were once celebrated in relation to the Sun in customs that continued long after their original meaning was lost. Perhaps the most strongly surviving cross-quarter custom today is the revelry at Halloween. This could be an indictment that of all the eight solar festivals, it is the energy of death and regeneration that most sweeps the world today. At the modern Halloween we manufacture our own ghosts and spirits or dress ourselves in their costumes to be reminded of the unseen energies that were once believed to abound as the Sun reached midway South. And it is not just Halloween that has this monopoly on spirits. When Shakespeare depicted the games the fairy folk play in *A Midsummer Night's Dream*, his sixteenth century audience accepted it readily knowing that this whole cast of otherworldly characters were not only confined to Midsummer Night, but were recognisable in all the eight solar festivals. (Santa Claus's "Ho, ho, ho!" comes from Puck's traditional cry.[19])

There is strong evidence here that the Sun does activate the Earth in a way that is more than visually obvious and the early Christian church and civic authorities, wishing to discourage the direct worship of the Sun, concentrated on these power-points to turn the acceptance of the spirits of

---

19. William Shakespeare, *A Midsummer Night's Dream*, Act III, Scene II.

nature into a fear of evil demons. There was nothing necessarily evil about Halloween originally; the energy was there to be used for good or ill. Surviving through the centuries as quaint customs to appease the world of Faerie on the eve of solar festivals was the knowledge that the Sun's power had an animating effect across the Earth at these special times.

The Solstice Pause

The word *solstice* literally means the Sun making a stand or the Sun standing still, and although there is a precise moment for this solar peak it has invariably been celebrated on Earth as a pause that lasted for several days.

For those observing the daily movement of the sun from the Earth, visually noting not only its changing rising and setting points on the horizon but also its declinational height in the sky, it would be obvious that as it started to reach a solstice its arc broadened out. It was no longer climbing so rapidly. It had reached a high pause. In this sense the 'standstills' of the Sun appear to stretch longer.

Saint John and The Christ

Saint John and Jesus Christ, the two most important male figures in the earlier history of Christianity, stand at opposite ends of the year associated with summer and winter solstices. (Saint John's Day - June 24th, Christmas Day - December 25th). Yet, as far as records show, their anniversaries have always been celebrated several days after the divine moment of solar peaks. This surely could not have happened by chance.

Medieval customs suggest that the period of standstill was expected to continue for several days. An extended festivity took place which culminated at the last day of the period rather than on the solstice itself. Written records of royal observances in England make it clear[20] that the most important celebratory feast of the midsummer turnaround took place annually on June 24th, St John's Day[21], three or four days after the actual solstice. Until very

---

20.　For a detailed overview on this and other historical customs of the solar year see *The Stations of the Sun* by Ronald Hutton, Oxford University Press, Oxford, 1996, and *The Oxford Book of Days* by Bonnie Blackburn and Leofranc Holford-Strevens, Oxford University Press, 2000.

21.　Originally there were two feasts of Saint John in the year, one in midsummer for St John the Baptist and the other in midwinter for St John the Evangelist. Legend has it that John the Baptist lost his head on midsummer day and he was thus associated with the beheading game of the solstices, explored further in *Gawain and the Green Knight*.

recent times this was still officially (and somewhat confusingly) called Midsummer's Day in diaries and calendars.

A similar case can be seen in the adoption of Christmas Day as taking place on December 25th, usually four days after the solstice. (See more on this in *The Twelve Days of Christmas*). All surviving records of folkloric customs connected with the solstices show that the communal lighting of candles or burning of fires or rolling of blazing fire-wheels through a town, took place three or four days after a solstice. This was obviously not an oversight on the part of the participants but a deliberate attempt to celebrate the climax at the end of this special time of 'standstill' as the Sun started to move again.

Lady Day, Easter and Michaelmas

Neither was this delay peculiar to the solstices only. The custom can also be observed at the equinoxes, although there could be no similar solar observance in the sky to back this up as around the equinox the Sun is climbing rapidly, not standing still in the same manner as it does at a solstice.

Lady Day, the Christian festival of the Annunciation, which commemorated the Angel Gabriel's announcement to the Virgin Mary that she would have a child, was once an extremely important date in the calendar and took place on March 25th, four days after the equinox. From the twelfth to the eighteenth centuries it marked the formal beginning of the year and was a favourite date for the payment of quarterly rents and dues. Whether this was an echo of an earlier pre-Christian celebration is difficult to ascertain but from the Church's point of view March 25 was exactly nine months before Christ's birth on December 25 and as all these things were taken literally it obviously marked the Annunciation. It seems however that there was still a necessity to make a holy day coincide with a time of solar importance.

Easter, the great spring equinox celebration that honours the Moon as well as the Sun, is always observed *after* the equinox, never before. (See more on this in *The Sword and the Stone*).

At the time of the Libra equinox, the official recognition became Michaelmas, the feast of Saint Michael the Archangel, now fixed on September 29th, usually five or six days after the solar balance. This coincided with end-of-summer fairs, harvest festivals and general revels, although the date as a civic or legal marker did not have quite the same force as Lady Day.

Moons and standstills

In the same general vein, old cultures celebrated New Moons a couple of days after the actual moment of lunation. This was and is still the case with the Muslim calendar for instance whose months begin one or two days after each exact lunar-solar coupling. The reason here is visual. Only when the thin crescent of the New Moon is observable in the sky does the New Moon begin.

Contrary to the way that our current commercialism forces us to celebrate seasonal markers in advance of their time and drop them as soon as the day is over (Halloween masks on sale before the equinox, Christmas goods on display before Halloween etc.), there appears to be something in human nature that deeply needs to absorb and climax a celestial energy retrospectively.

Midsummer's Day and Midwinter's Day, two appellations of the solstice, are confusing titles as they mark the beginning of summer or winter rather than the middle of it - at least in terms of seasonal climate. The hottest summer temperatures and the coldest winter ones tend to be experienced about a month or so after the solstice, the Sun's standstill. And a similar retroactive case can be made for the effects of the Moon's standstills, which take place every nine to ten years. The feeling of collective security, the "nest and invest" impulse to use Bruce Scofield's words,[22] is conjectured to follow the Moon's minor standstill by about two years, but has peaked and begun to slide about two years after the major lunar standstill.

All this may lend weight to the idea that, in terms of concrete results, a separating astrological aspect is more powerful than an applying one, or that the greatest effect to the human or to the Earth comes after the moment of cosmic exactitude.

How to celebrate the solstice

In the west, society has largely forgotten the periods of fast that always preceded collective celebrations. It is more than likely that the actual days of equinox and solstice, especially the solstice with its built-in 'pause', were fasting days. This was a ritual time to be pure, a time to pray, a time to divine and make contact with the spiritual worlds. The gorging of food and wine and the general excess and revels, all just as important at the Sun's special times, would follow a day or so later.

---

22. Bruce Scofield, The Moon and the Megaliths, *The Mountain Astrologer*, Cedar Ridge, California, June 1996.

As the relationship between the Sun and the land is at its peak at the turning point of the solstices it follows that the forces of Yang and Yin are also at their highest point of interchange. With such macrocosmic shifting and balancing taking place human activity should step back and wait. In ancient China no official business was conducted at the solstices and no personal activities took place that might have over-stimulated the universal Yang energy and upset the balance. Solstice days are therefore times to try and withdraw from the hustle of daily life and be deliberately inactive, to be in tune with the turning celestial/terrestrial tides but to honour them quietly. It is wise to be relaxed and tiptoe through the day. To light a candle but not a fire.

Although not strictly connected to the Sun, the beginning of our current century, the night of the Millennium, was an interesting case in point. Because of the particular order of the meshing of solar and lunar days at the end of December 1999, Vedic astrologers would have recommended January 1st to be a day of fasting with celebrations to come later.[23] It was not the best celestial energy to support partying and the drinking of alcohol in excess. However January 1st is not a solar festival and other than being somewhere in the middle of the Twelve Days of Christmas it has no particular astrological significance. In general New Year's Eve, or New Year's Day, is an echo of how we naturally have the need to celebrate the change of tides from old to new, how we wipe the slate clean and make new resolutions for the immediate future. This would have greater effect if it was in tune with solar tides.

Most certain is the collective benefit to those on Earth to live in accord with the annual steps of the Sun; to honour it first in quiet meditation and then follow on with sustained and noisy joy. And we should be in no rush either to curtail the process of thanksgiving as soon as each solar moment has passed.

---

23. Information from a talk by Komilla Sutton on *Remedial Measures in Vedic Astrology*, London, 2000.

The Twelve Days of Christmas

> "Ev'n the poor Pagan's homage to the Sun
> I would not harshly scorn, lest even there
> I spurn'd some elements of Christian pray'r"
>
> Thomas Hood (1799-1845)

It has long been debated that the seasonal song **The Twelve Days of Christmas** has origins in the twelve zodiac signs. Historically the "Twelve Days" may be more a concept than an actual count, a bunch of intercalary days at the end of the year representing each of the solar months that have passed or were yet to come. Some sources even suggest they were once lunar, the twelve days supposedly left over when a year is divided into twelve moons.

At the Council of Tours in AD 560 these special days were officially accommodated into the Christian festival and became the Twelve Days of Christmas. By late medieval times the celebration is recorded as ranging loosely from its beginning at the winter solstice, with peaks at December 25th (Christmas Day), January 1st (New Year's Day) and January 6th (Epiphany - the adoration of the Magi). This could stretch the Twelve Days to a period of several weeks and for many centuries Christmas was regarded as a six-week season not ending until Candlemas. (Candlemas Eve was once the time to take down the holiday greenery). The usual official version however was that the twelve days ran from Christmas Day to Epiphany.

The popularity of the idea of the Twelve Days or Twelve Holy Nights of Christmas suggests that the winter solstice season can easily be seen as the year in miniature, and in one form or another the birth of the new sun (son) is required to be celebrated. The solar power stored in the Yule Log's rings is released and renewed in the fire; and declination can give us another view on all this.

Although the Sun annually peaks at its southernmost point of declination at 23S26 around 21st December on our calendar, it actually resides in this same degree, the 24th degree South, for 21 or 22 days from approximately December 11th to January 2nd. The number of 'days' will differ slightly each year depending on what time of day the moment of solstice takes place at your particular location in the world. But the interesting point is that if you count the day of the solstice as One, you can count approximately twelve more days backwards and forwards on either side and find the Sun still residing in the 24th degree South. With the solstice as its pivot, the Twelve Days of Christmas are therefore mirrored before, as well as after, the Sun's lowest point.

This bonds with the ancient idea of honouring the Sun at the solstices by giving something back to it in thanks for its life-giving power throughout the year. In the song **The Twelve Days of Christmas**, gifts are given in increasing numbers each day.

The old rhyme with its gifts of turtle doves and pear trees etc. may be symbolically related to quite different days to those most commonly used. We have been accustomed to the first day of Christmas beginning on Christmas Day or the day after, but it would be more correct to say that the first day of Christmas starts on December 21st at the solstice. And the Five Golden Rings - the Fifth Day of Christmas - which is the climax of each verse as it is sung, would now fall on Christmas Day itself. (The fifth day from the solstice). An astrological Sun symbol of golden rings is very appropriate for the *Sol Invictus*. And "Twelfth Night" is now January 1st.

If we count the twelve days backwards from the solstice like antiscion degrees, December 10th is twelve drummers drumming, or its many variants, December 11th is eleven piper's piping etc., and the five golden rings appear again on December 17th. The first day of Christmas meets up again on December 21st at the solstice.

The Birds in the Juniper Tree

Although the gift on the First Day of Christmas, the solstice, is commonly known as "a Partridge in a Pear Tree", some researchers contend that this was originally a Juniper Tree, "a part of a Juniper Tree". The Juniper has an ancient reputation as a rejuvenating tree and its branches were once laid on solstice fires and sacrificial altars to provide the pungent smoke of purification. Old belief in its life-giving power can be evidenced in the fairy tale collected by the Brothers Grimm called *The Juniper Tree*. In this story a dead boy buried beneath the tree is reborn in a burst of flame as a glorious bird with a ring of pure gold feathers around his neck. This phoenix-like ability to purify and recreate itself in fire and gold is also that of the Sun at the winter solstice. And in our Christmas song, all the first seven days - apart from the Five Golden Rings - describe different kinds of birds, which presumably came to rest on the Juniper Tree.

7 Swans a-swimming
6 Geese a-laying
(5 Golden Rings)
4 Colley Birds or Calling Birds
3 French Hens
2 Turtle Doves

It has even been speculated that the five golden rings might originally have been five goldspinks or goldfinches, although as in all choral traditions early written evidence of roundelay songs is virtually non-existent.

The popularity of birds at this time of year has a long history. The hunting of the wren on St Stephen's Day and declaring it the King of Birds is a tradition that survived into quite recent times. The legend of The Parliament of Birds in which all feathered species gathered to grant leadership to the one who could fly closest to the Sun, may also have had an influence. And in Shakespeare's *Hamlet* the following belief is extolled:

> "Some say that ever 'gainst the season comes
> Wherein our Saviour's birth is celebrated,
> The bird of dawning singeth all night long:
> And then, they say, no spirit can walk abroad;
> The nights are wholesome; then no planets strike..."
> [Hamlet, Act 1 Scene 1]

The gifts in the remainder of the Days from Eight to Twelve are mostly describing people rather than birds: Maids a-milking, ladies dancing, lords a-leaping etc. But this no longer makes any real sense in terms of gifts given to someone at Christmas, and is probably a memory of the mummers carnival in courts and cities. Mummers were dancing revellers dressed in colourful masks and disguises who paraded in matching groups or pairs bearing gifts for the king or the lord of the house.

In other words the song's gift of "nine ladies dancing" for example, does not mean that the nine ladies themselves were the gift but is referring to the manner in which the nine gifts were being presented. Seen in this light, the French hens and colley birds, doves and swans etc. could equally be gifts of seasonal fare intended to be roasted and eaten at the Christmas table.

Alternatively, as there are more variations to be found in the different versions of this song concerning the last six gifts than there are in the first six, perhaps there were once twelve different sets of birds, or rather eleven that came to rest on the Juniper Tree, the tree itself counting as One. This might also refer to the Halcyon Bird, which was supposed to nest on the sea at the winter solstice.

All the birds are attracted to come to the tree bringing their gifts. When the song is sung today we forget that there is a reflection of the whole thing in the eleven days before the solstice. These daily solstice points count down the gifts in reverse order so perhaps we give their energies to the Sun in thanks before the solstice and then receive them back renewed after. After the solstice it is Capricorn time where Saturnian energy, strictly speaking, allows us to receive only what we have earned.

Another odd factor about the song is that it lists the gifts "my true love gave to me" rather than the gifts the singer might have given. So it is in general a receiving rather than a giving song. This suggests that these are cosmic or spiritual gifts connected with the revitalisation of the Sun at the winter solstice. The "true love" could also be the Sun. (See *Gawain and the Green Knight*).

Conclusion

We should try and give something to the Sun by placing a small offering on a Christmas crib or Yuletide altar every day starting from approximately December 10th. Symbolically twelve items or offerings as this will be the Twelfth Day of Christmas. The following day we add eleven different items of our choice, the next day ten, and so on until the solstice itself when ideally we give a piece of juniper. We can then remove them from the board in reverse order as we count the Twelve Days of Christmas forward from the solstice. Each 'day' can be perceived as a zodiac month of the year that has just passed and of the year still to come.

The Twelve Days of Christmas
(In its most well-known form)

"On the first day of Christmas my true love gave to me
A Partridge in a Pear Tree
On the second day of Christmas my true love gave to me
Two Turtle Doves and a Partridge in a Pear Tree
On the third day of Christmas my true love gave to me
Three French Hens, Two Turtle Doves and a Partridge in a Pear Tree
On the fourth day of Christmas my true love gave to me
Four Calling Birds, Three French Hens, Two Turtle Doves and a Partridge in a Pear Tree
On the fifth day of Christmas my true love gave to me
Five Golden Rings
Four Calling Birds, Three French Hens, Two Turtle Doves etc
On the sixth day of Christmas my true love gave to me
Six Geese a-laying

Etc.
On the seventh day of Christmas my true love gave to me
Seven Swans a-swimming
Etc.
On the eighth day of Christmas my true love gave to me
Eight Maids a-milking
Etc.
On the ninth day of Christmas my true love gave to me
Nine Ladies dancing
Etc.
On the tenth day of Christmas my true love gave to me
Ten Lords a-leaping
Etc.
On the eleventh day of Christmas my true love gave to me
Eleven Pipers piping
Etc.
On the twelfth day of Christmas my true love gave to me
Twelve Drummers drumming
Etc."

Gawain and the Green Knight

A solstice allegory

The Sun in midwinter is like the dying heart of a stag. Caught in a Celtic knotwork of bare tree branches it reddens the sky, ebbing life, pulsing slow at its standstill. Soon it will die and be born again and, as in the solstice story of *Gawain and The Green Knight*, we sense it is part of an eternal design.

Gawain and The Green Knight is an anonymous tale dating from around 1400 in written form and regarded as a gem of Middle English literature. It is a snow-covered story with action taking place both within the warmth of castle walls and outside on the hard and lifeless earth. It seems to combine the figures of Jupiter and Saturn in its main character The Green Knight, who is both the huge and hoary winter man demanding his due, and the genial host and sporty husband of the lady who is special to Gawain. Let us review the story:

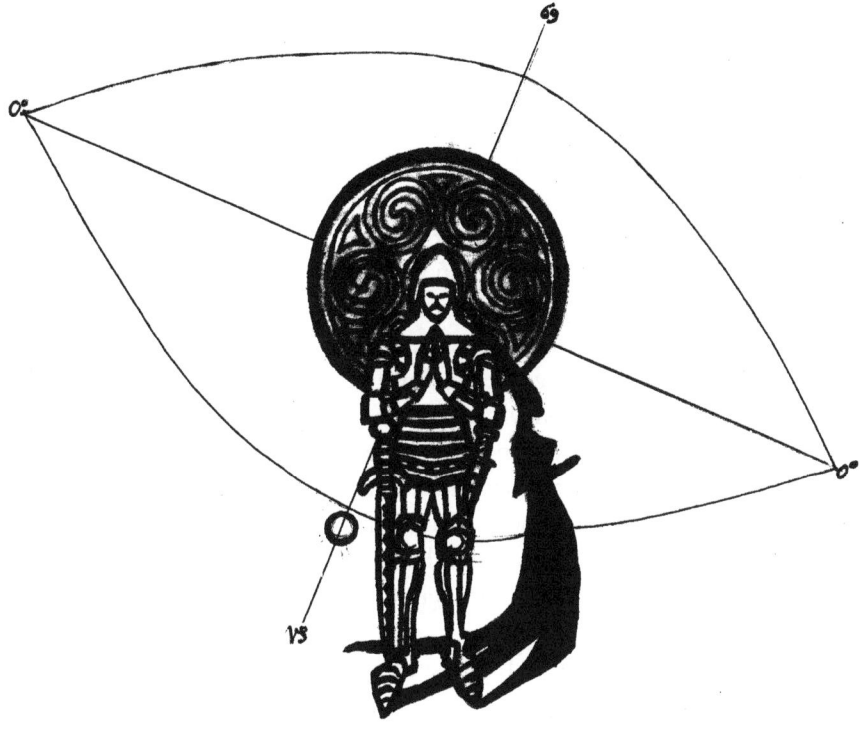

The Knight and Lady

It is Christmastide in Camelot, the season of Saturn and the rebirth of the Sun, when suddenly a huge green man rides into the feasting hall wielding an axe. He roars out a challenge daring anyone present to strike his head with the axe, provided he may return the stroke at the next winter season. Young Gawain accepts and beheads the giant with one blow. But the applause soon dies when the giant picks up his head, sets it on his shoulders and rides away, instructing Gawain to meet him for the return stroke at The Green Chapel in a year and a day.

This trade of a blow for a blow is very Saturn-like, especially as there is a long wait involved for Gawain. Yet the Green Knight in most accounts is quite cheerful and broad built and to be honest seems more like the Jolly Green Giant than the Grim Reaper.

Gawain is honourable and does not run from his fate. He spends most of the year trying to locate "The Green Chapel", of which no one appears to have heard. By the next Christmas he has wandered far and seems none the nearer. With his spirit as low as the winter sun he finally arrives at a remote castle.

The Lady

Now the scene becomes more radiant for the Lady of this house is warm and beautiful and generous to Gawain. Her husband also heartily invites him to stay. They both appear to have heard of The Green Chapel, which they say is close at hand. The jovial lord of the house is Jupiter indeed and a gambler too, lavishly encouraging Gawain to enjoy the bounty of his household while he (the lord) rides out every morning to hunt. They make a sporting deal to share whatever the day might bring and in this warm lull between the evening festivities Gawain finds himself increasingly alone with the Lady.

They flirt courteously; Gawain side-stepping her increasingly romantic invitations without causing offence, but under the quaint rules of courtly love he must honour his lady's request - and what she requests is a kiss. With little prompting Gawain obliges. Later in the afternoon when the husband returns and greets Gawain with great cheer, the spoils of the day's chase are laid out ceremoniously. The steaming carcasses of boar and deer will ensure good feasting for the castle. But when the cheerful master asks Gawain what he has gained throughout that day, the knight can only chivalrously admit, "a kiss".

Surprisingly the merry host seems content and the ensuing night of banqueting and Yuletide games is as hearty as the first. In the frosty morning light the lord sets out again for the hunt leaving Gawain and the Lady together once more. This time, in a highly romantic atmosphere, two kisses are won, although an old woman hovers in the long shadows like a dark guardian watching every move. Once more Gawain admits his prize to the host on his return.

On the third day, which the courtly lovers know must be their last; Gawain's willpower is weakening. Aware that his life may soon end abruptly with the fall of a green axe, his last day of inspiration with the radiant lady is even more to be savoured. The Lady secretly gives him a band of green silk as a magical protection to save him from the Green Knight. He accepts the favour but does not mention it to her husband as a prize he has gained throughout the day. Perhaps he is beginning to suspect that his ebullient host and the Green Knight may be one and the same. In any event he mentions only that he has gained more kisses.

The Beheading

The fateful day of the beheading game arrives and Gawain rides alone to the Green Chapel to meet his due. The Green Knight is already there, axe in hand, and Gawain bows his head to accept the stroke. But the Green Knight stops the blade just a hair's breadth from the young knight's neck. Once, twice, he does the same. Then on the third stroke he lightly nicks the skin to draw a bead of blood. Laughingly he reveals that he is indeed the Lord of the Castle and each of the three strokes relate to Gawain's three days with the Lady. The final cut was for concealing the truth about the gift of the magic silk, much to Gawain's shame. Otherwise the quest was won, the tests completed and Gawain a hero, free to go.

Although he had passed some kind of test, Saturn lingered, and Gawain remained tinged with guilt for not admitting to the Lady's gift. In compensation he vowed to wear the band of green as a mark of his shame until he died. At least that was his official explanation. Viewed in a different light the magic silk may indeed have saved his life. Without it he might have been beheaded at the first stroke. So now perhaps he wore it as a personal life-saving talisman, much as Arthur bore Excalibur.

The Blessed Green

In the green world of spirit Gawain had flirted and bargained with life and death in the persons of the lord and lady. His had been a shamanic journey to the otherworld on behalf of Arthur's court. Wrestling and gambling with Death was once the accepted way of maintaining life for the collective whole by shamen in tribal societies the world over. But the timing had to be right.

The Green Chapel is a time not a place, the Green Man's axe is Saturn's scythe, and the time is midwinter when physical life is least active and spiritual life is most active. It is the Yule tide; the winter solar standstill; the Twelve Days of Christmas; the Light in the Dark. And boundaries of any kind, time or place, must be perpetually rehonoured.

The Green Knight is a mixture of both Jupiter and Saturn. He is a Christmas Man, a composite of the signs that Jupiter and Saturn rule and that straddle the winter solstice. This Green Man is also possibly the Holly King who was crowned annually at the summer solstice and sacrificed (or beheaded) at the winter solstice to make way for the Oak King. In alchemy the *benedicta viriditas* (the blessed green) symbolised the start of the reanimation process. Green is the colour of nature, the transcendent state, the self-renewing life force within.

And the Lady is the Sun. The "true love" who gives gifts at Christmas. She is the Sun in winter, reborn at the solstice, while the dark old maid who shadowed her was the old year in decay. The great requirement of courtly love was to be perpetually in love and falling in love has a lot to do with the Sun and the astrological fifth house and the opening of the heart chakra. By 'kissing the Sun', Gawain made a mystical union with it.

The story ends with all guilt expunged. The secret magic silk given with love in the dark of the year was a creative gift from the twilight world to be borne with pride. On Gawain's return to Camelot he joyfully finds that the whole of Arthur's court have also donned a band of faerie green in his honour and all applaud him for facing the giant of winter and returning with the Sun. The life force has been renewed, the light has arisen, and the Green Knight can retire again ready to roar out his challenge to another initiate at the turning point of another year.

The Royal Arch

This diagram, after a seventeenth century Masonic document, lays claim to a revered and ancient architectural concept based on the declination of the Sun. What it represents is The Royal Arch, sometimes also referred to as the Royal Arch of Enoch. It was built of seven blocks on two pillars, which in Masonic lore represented the two pillars at the head of Solomon's Temple.

The Royal Arch

The seven stone blocks of the archway evoke the Sun's course from Aries to Libra, from spring to autumn equinox, and therefore the seven mystical grades or steps to be taken by an initiate. The seven stars below the keystone reiterate this number.

Seven, always regarded as a mystical number, was also the original number of planets. In Mithraic rituals the candidate for initiation was shown the face of the Seven Lords of the Universe, and bidden to answer: "I too am a planet; I too am a wandering star". He was then buried holding a scroll containing the words: "I am the child of Earth and of the Starry Heavens…"

The two equal suns in the picture are said to be illustrative of the equinox points.

The keystone of the Arch is the northern solstice, the Sun at the height of its power and the central principle on which everything depends. Such a Sun was also commonly depicted in occult symbolism as an all-seeing Eye streaming with rays. A keystone or *clef de voûte* is the central and highest stone which carries the weight and perfect balance of an archway vault. It was and is a basic principle of masonry both in a straightforward building sense and in a secret symbolic sense. Here we see that the symbol for Cancer leaves us in no doubt that this is the Sun at its mightiest time.

A coat-of-arms displaying the four Fixed signs: bull, lion, eagle and man, the emblems of the cross quarters, was often included within the arch in engravings like these, alongside compasses and other Masonic symbols.

> "…the imaginary arch made in the heavens by the course of King Osiris, the Sun, from the vernal to the autumnal equinox. The signs through which he passes in forming this semicircle, including those of the equinox, being seven, the number of grades or steps required to be taken by the Mason to entitle him to the honours of this degree." [24]

In his book *The White Goddess* Robert Graves comes to the same conclusion over dolmen arches albeit by a different route. In his analysis of the ancient bardic poem *The Song of Amergin* he concludes that a dolmen arch serves as an alphabet calendar "with one post for Spring, the other for Autumn, the lintel for Summer…"[25]

---

24. From a nineteenth century commentary on this design quoted in *Freemasonry* by Alexander Piatigorsky, Harvill Press, London. 1999.
25. Robert Graves, *The White Goddess*, Faber, London, 1999 (originally published 1948)

Juliet at Lammas Eve

"Come Lammas Eve at night shall she be fourteen"
[Shakespeare *Romeo and Juliet*, Act I, Scene 3]

According to the Nurse in *Romeo and Juliet* Juliet turned fourteen on the eve of Lammas. In that case one half of literature's most famous "pair of star-cross'd lovers" was a Leo. It may all be academic but we could construct a full birth chart for Juliet if we tread carefully. This is the relevant passage in more detail:

Juliet: How now, who calls?
Nurse: Your mother.
Juliet: Madam, I am here. What is your will?
Lady Capulet (Juliet's mother): This is the matter - Nurse, give leave awhile, we must talk in secret.
Nurse, come back again, I have remember'd me, thou's hear our counsel. Thou knowest my daughter's of a pretty age.
Nurse: Faith, I can tell her age unto an hour.
Lady Capulet: She's not fourteen.
Nurse: I'll lay fourteen of my teeth - And yet, to my teen be it spoken, I have but four - She's not fourteen. How long is it now till Lammas-tide?
Lady Capulet: A fortnight and odd days.
Nurse: Even or odd, of all days in the year, come Lammas Eve at night shall she be fourteen.

Lammas is usually celebrated on August 1st, so Juliet's birthday is probably July 31st, and the name Juliet means July. Like the other annual cross quarter days few of these occasions excite much comment amongst the general populace today, but Lammas in Shakespeare's time was an important solar festival.

As the above passage shows, ordinary people in the sixteenth century did base their notion of passing time from these special days rather than from actual calendar dates. As the festival halfway between the summer solstice and the autumn equinox, Lammas, calculated by the Sun, should be at 15 degrees Leo (16 N Dec). Juliet was born just before this.

We could therefore construct a full chart for Juliet Capulet if we are prepared to be a little pliable. We know when she was born, approximately: at night on the eve of Lammas. (The nurse, who says she knows the time to

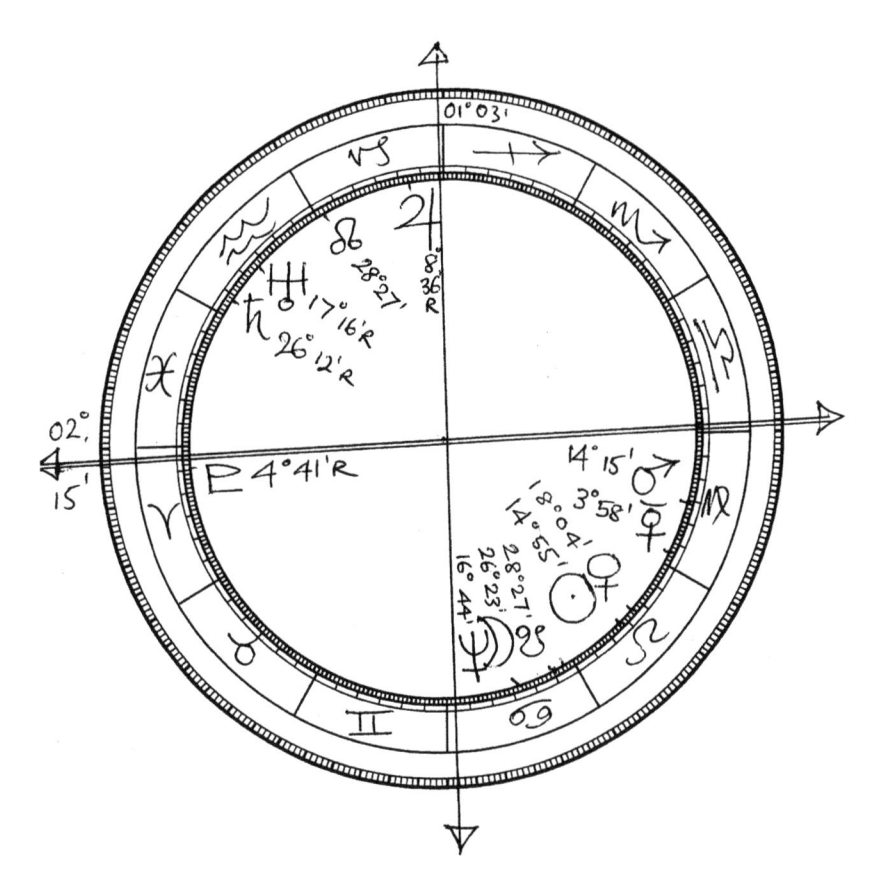

Chart of Juliet. 28 July 1581. 9pm. Verona, Italy 45N27 11E00.
No source. This is a symbolic chart.

an hour, unfortunately does not actually state the hour). We also know *where* Juliet was born: it was in "fair Verona", Italy. It is only a case of determining what year she was born.

Shakespeare does not give a specific year in which his version of *Romeo and Juliet* is set. He borrowed the basic theme of the story from folklore so we are unlikely to turn up any real birth data on Romeo and Juliet. Although the Verona tourist trade might insist otherwise, we must conclude that Romeo and Juliet are universal semi-mythical lovers. Under the name and story that we know therefore, William Shakespeare's Juliet is his own creation and we can only date her existence from the playwright's mind.

As *Romeo and Juliet* was one of Shakespeare's earlier plays, written and first performed in 1595 according to the most scholarly sources, we could be justified in saying that the action in the play takes place contemporarily in 1595. If Juliet turned fourteen in 1595 then she was born in 1581. If we speculate a time of 9pm for her birth (simply because this is about halfway through the evening) we arrive at a rather pleasing and interesting chart: Sun conjunct and parallel Venus in Leo, Sun exactly contra-parallel Uranus (16N24 16S24), Pluto rising in Aries and the Moon conjunct its South Node in Cancer. (To arrive at this chart one needs a date of: 28 July 1581 9pm LMT, Verona, Italy).

Juliet: Natal declinations

SUN	16N24
MOON	21N07
MERCURY	10N50
VENUS	16N43
MARS	07N01
JUPITER	23S28
SATURN	14S19
URANUS	16S24
NEPTUNE	21N48
PLUTO	13S48
NORTH NODE	20S31
SOUTH NODE	20N31

NEPTUNE	21N48
MOON	21N07
SOUTH NODE	20N31
VENUS	16N43
SUN	16N24
MERCURY	10N50

PLUTO	13S48
SATURN	14S19
URANUS	16S24
NORTH NODE	20S31
JUPITER	23S28

"It is the east and Juliet is the sun!"

Appropriately Romeo greets the sight of his Leo lover with the above words, likening her to the Sun that has suddenly arisen as she appears at her window. Her Sun contra-paralleling Uranus reflects this sudden quality and the contrast between dark and light in the structure of the play. Although Romeo likens her sudden appearance to the Sun, it is night-time when this balcony scene takes place, as it is in almost every scene that Romeo and Juliet come together as lovers. The juxtaposition of the forces of dark and light, of Juliet being the unexpected Sun in a Moon-ruled world, is a deliberate part of the story's setting. An ominously encroaching darkness can also be felt in our Pluto rising chart, and will conclude in the tomb where Romeo and Juliet take their lives.

On Juliet's chart both the Sun and the Moon are strong by conventional astrology: the Sun is in Leo in the fifth house, the Moon is in Cancer in the fourth. The Moon however is conjunct its South Node, making it weaker or at least more hidden, and could be interpreted as a difficult ancestry for Juliet or karmic obligation to her family. Indeed it is precisely because of her family's ancestral feud with Romeo's family, the Montagues, that the tragedy of Romeo and Juliet occurs and it will take her death (and Romeo's) to end the "ancient grudge" between the two households. That Juliet is the Sun - conjunct Venus - that strives to shine throughout this heavy destiny is evidenced at the play's end when both the families accept equal blame, and Romeo's father promises that he will raise a statue to Juliet in pure gold.

Like a Leo, Juliet's love is fixed and true throughout the story. She is the constant Sun around which the more mutable Romeo dances. She embodies the spirit of the lovers at Lammas, the hottest time of the year, the beginning of harvest, the time Italians called the "lion heat". But her Sun in its summer northerly declination is exactly shadowed by the unpredictable Uranus in the south. Things at cross-purposes, unexpected twists and mishaps, all conspire to confuse and eventually obliterate her Sun. The on-and-off flashing light analogy of Uranus is never more fatal than in the scene in the tomb, where Romeo takes his life because he thinks Juliet is lying dead before him: "her beauty makes this vault a feasting presence full of light...." He even muses at this point over what he calls "a lightning before death". In fact Juliet has only taken a sleeping draught and will wake again soon after Romeo has poisoned himself. Acting on a similarly sudden impulse Juliet then kills herself, piercing Romeo's dagger to her heart, and all light is extinguished.

Life and death, Sun and night, light and dark. All have flickered on and off in Juliet's brief but all-consuming love affair. *Romeo and Juliet* is an example of a Shakespeare play that seems to have been consciously set around one of the year's solar turning points (another obvious one is *A Midsummer Night's Dream* and to a lesser extent *Twelfth Night*). The Elizabethan masques were often performed at such festive occasions, and playwrights wrote especially for them. There is of course much else in *Romeo and Juliet* but it is beyond doubt that Shakespeare deliberately used the time of year with its hot bright summer days in contrast to dark black nights as his background setting, and created a dual world for the two main characters to inhabit. She was a Leo by day, but it was in the lovers' special night-time world that Juliet was the Sun.

The Sword in the Stone

Easter and Pentecost: the Solar-Lunar festivals

We have already speculated that the three-month run from an equinox to a solstice is a powerful one. In the northern hemisphere the spring months from March to June are particularly potent because the Sun is growing in strength each day and it is at this time of year that two more annual festivals are set. They are both based on the Sun but this time with the collaboration of the Moon: Easter and Pentecost.

The Arthurian image of the Sword in the Stone is a difficult riddle to penetrate but it has the promise of kingship or selfhood when accomplished. We might liken this joining of unrelated elements to squaring the circle or to understanding the union of Sun and Moon.

The eight-part year of the Sun based on its declinational positions (equinoxes, solstices and the midpoints between) has been subjected in our history to these two other great annual festivals based on the merging of Sun and Moon. Easter and Pentecost add a lunar flavour of flux and change to the solar year, not least as their calendar dates can be over 30 days different annually. Easter Sunday can fall anywhere from March 22 to April 25, and Pentecost, which is derived from the date of Easter, from May 10 to June 13.

The spring celebration of Easter is still the most important festival in the Christian Church and is based on a calculation involving the union of Sun and Moon. Easter is the Equinox Full Moon, or more precisely Easter Sunday is the first day of the Sun (Sunday) following the first Full Moon that follows the spring equinox. One can see how both the Sun and the

Moon are emphasised in this calculation with their symbols everywhere in the traditions of Easter: Christ as the risen Sun, the lunar Easter eggs and so on.

In Christian theology the crucified Christ was reborn on Easter Sunday and many dates in the Christian calendar derive in turn from this annual marker. The Ascension of Jesus is officially acknowledged on a Thursday, 40 days after Easter Sunday, and Pentecost or Whit Sunday takes place ten days after Ascension Day. Pentecost is then seven weeks after Easter, or as its name suggests, 50 days (approximately) after Easter Sunday. (Pentecost is the old Jewish harvest festival held 50 days after Passover). In the Christian story it was at Pentecost that a gathering of Jesus's followers were visited by rushing winds and tongues of flame, an event described as a visitation by the Holy Spirit. This is sometimes held to be the true beginning of the Christian Church.

Pentecost at Camelot

In Arthurian times (and certainly in the 15th century when Thomas Malory's *Morte D'Arthur* was published) it is clear that Pentecost was one of the biggest celebrations of the year. It is at Pentecost that Arthur is originally crowned king and later it is always at the feast of Pentecost when large numbers of lords and ladies gather at the Round Table for important quests to begin. We are told it was a custom of Arthur's court not to "sit at their meat" and begin the Pentecostal feast until some strange adventure had presented itself. The following is typical:

> "At the vigil of Pentecost, when all the fellowship of the Round Table were comen unto Camelot and there heard their service, and the tables were set ready to meat, right so entered into the hall a full fair gentlewoman on horseback, that had ridden full fast, for her horse was all asweat...."[26]

In this instance the adventure leads to a sword in a stone floating in a river, the arrival of Galahad and the appearance of the Holy Grail, whose vision through the hall has many similarities to that of the Holy Ghost:

> "Then anon they heard cracking and crying of thunder...(and) in the midst of this blast entered a sunbeam more clearer by seven times than ever they saw day...Then began every knight to behold other, and either saw other, by their seeming, fairer than ever they

---

26. Sir Thomas Malory, *Le Morte D'Arthur Volumes 1 and 2*, Penguin English Library, London, 1976.

saw afore...Then there entered into the hall the Holy Grail covered with white samite, but there was none might see it, nor who bare it. And there was all the hall fulfilled with good odours, and every knight had such meats and drinks as he best loved in this world."

The sword in the stone floating in a river, which in this instance is pulled out by Galahad, is not the same as the famous sword in the stone pulled out by the young Arthur to establish his kingship. And this again is not the sword that Arthur later accepts from the hand of the Lady of the Lake, although Malory says that both were called Excalibur and burned "as bright as thirty torches". But the story of Arthur's sword in the stone is surprisingly different in detail to that which is usually remembered. Particularly so as the sword is always pulled from the stone on a day of solar (or solar-lunar) significance.

According to Malory, Arthur first pulls the sword from the stone during the long Christmas festival. It appeared by magic outside a church on Christmas Eve when several people had unsuccessfully tried to claim it. On New Year's Day a tournament was held and the young Arthur was sent home to fetch a sword for his half-brother Kay who had mislaid his own. On the way Arthur sees the sword embedded in an anvil on a stone in the empty churchyard and innocently pulls it out to take to his elder brother. When his foster father realises that this is the Sword in the Stone with the wording:

> "Whoso pulleth out this sword of this stone and anvil, is rightwise king born of all England"

he drops to his knees and explains to Arthur his true lineage. Arthur replaces the sword and pulls it out again but there are not enough witnesses to substantiate his kingship. On hearing the story the Archbishop decrees that the whole event should be replayed at Candlemas (Imbolc).

At Candlemas Arthur proves once more that he is the only person who can pull the sword from the stone and many immediately hail him as king, but there is still dissension among certain barons and it is agreed to put off the majority decision until Easter. The same thing happens at Easter until it is finally agreed that Arthur will pull the sword from the stone for the last time at Pentecost, which is when he is unanimously accepted and crowned as king.

What this passage tells us apart from anything else is that the commonly celebrated festivals from winter to summer at that time were Christmas, Candlemas, Easter and Pentecost. Two solar festivals, two solar-lunar ones. Easter is definitely a form of the spring equinox celebration and Pentecost being a month and a half later would appear to substitute in some respects for the Beltane cross-quarter. May Day was certainly a day of importance in its own right however and is mentioned in Malory when Queen Guinevere goes a-maying, but for the Arthurian Court it did not have the significance of Pentecost it seems. Of course with an early Easter, Pentecost could also come as early as May 10th, although a late Easter would push it back to something like June 13th.

Because Easter is calculated as the first Sunday following a Full Moon it follows that the Moon will always be waning on Easter Sunday. It will either be the day immediately after a Full Moon or it will be up to seven days after a Full Moon. The Moon phase will range from Full to Last Quarter, mostly encompassing the Disseminating phase. The Moon waning prior to Easter Sunday falls in line with Holy Week, a period of inner reflection in anticipation of new growth. As Pentecost is always seven weeks (49-50 days) after this, the Moon phase will remain more or less standard too. Pentecost will always fall at the time of a waxing Moon, centred somewhere around the First Quarter.

This means that Pentecost has the same energy of Growth and Challenge (First Quarter phase) every year, no matter what its calendar date. In contrast the solar festivals of Equinox, Solstice and Cross-quarter are determined by the declination of the Sun - our constant seasonal marker - but the Moon's phases on these dates will always be different.

There do not appear to be any other great Arthurian feast days beside Easter and Pentecost that are determined by both Sun and Moon together. And this is most telling because, as mentioned before, Easter and Pentecost both fall in that quarter of the year when the Sun in the Northern Hemisphere is at its most youthful and vigorous, between the spring equinox and the summer solstice. None of the other nine months of the year has one festival, let alone two, that take heed of the Moon in collaboration with the Sun.

Easter and Pentecost will also have parallel days in the second quarter of the year between summer solstice and autumn equinox, when the Sun's declination will be at an equivalent height. These dates will differ each year of course and the Moon's phases will not always be the same. An early Easter with the Sun's declination not far above zero will be mirrored by a late antiscion for the Sun in September close to the autumn equinox, whereas a late Easter in April would have its antiscion in the latter part of August. Pentecost in May or June would be mirrored in dates from July to early August.

Pentecost is therefore high summer. With its possible date between May 10 and June 13, the Sun's declination would be between 17 North and 23 North. And if we take account of the antiscia the special time would run for a period anywhere between two weeks (June 13 to June 29) to almost three months (May 10 to August 2) - the midpoint being the summer solstice in all cases.

3

Beyond the Steps: Planets Out of Bounds

The Golden Sun not only gives us life on Earth but is unfailingly constant in its heavenly movement. The Sun, which marks the boundaries of our seasons, moves within its own designated limits and can therefore never be 'out of bounds'. Most of the other planets however do occasionally tip over the Sun's boundary lines in either northern or southern declination. Most commonly a planet that is out of bounds will be in the zodiac signs bordering the solstices, that is Gemini or Cancer, Sagittarius or Capricorn, because the solstices are the farthest boundaries of the Sun. These four signs have Mutable and Cardinal qualities, not dissimilar to the animated and restless energy of the out-of-bounds pattern.

As a general rule you can insert any or all of the following adjectives in front of the normal astrological keywords for a planet to arrive at its additional meaning when it is out of bounds:

> unrestrained
> extreme
> independent
> wild
> awkward
> vulnerable
> privileged
> magnified

'Feral' is another good word. For example an out-of-bounds Moon could display wildly developed instincts in general plus an intuitive ability to assess public taste. An extreme awareness of atmosphere may at times be a privilege but at others a vulnerability. With independent emotions and feelings that can swing wildly from agony to ecstasy, the out-of-bounds phenomenon can be an awkward as well as a privileged gift.

We should remember that as all out-of-bounds planets are beyond the reach of the Sun they remain immune to any hand of authority and do not have any commonly accepted yardsticks with which to assess themselves.

OOB Tales: Tarzan of the Apes
Mercury and Mars out of bounds

Mercury rules literature and Mercury rules apes, so it is interesting to find that Mercury was out of bounds when Edgar Rice Burroughs wrote his famous tale of Tarzan the Ape-man in 1911.

Burroughs was a Sun Virgo (1 September 1875, time not known), and he meticulously noted both the time that he started and the time that he finished working on the manuscript that would eventually make him world-renowned. He began writing *Tarzan of the Apes* in Chicago on 1 December 1911 at 8pm and completed it on 14 May 1912 at 10.25pm. As he began his famous work Mercury was out of bounds South at 25S51 and appropriately it was a Mercury hour. Mercury was almost at its farthest OOB position at that time and would peak at 25S52 the next day (2 December 1911), before gradually returning to an inbounds position about a week before Christmas. It then moved up through the southern declinations until it crossed the zero line three months later in March (1912). The plot and the bulk of the work had by then been clearly established and the last two months saw Mercury hovering up and down in northern declinations to finish at 07N47 as Burroughs completed the story on 14 May. His own natal Mercury was close to this at 05N39.

The journey of Mercury through the southern declinations during that winter can relate symbolically to an exploration through the inner realms that produced a gripping fantasy tale of darkest Africa. It spoke of a human child (Mercury) lost and abandoned beyond normal civilization (Mercury out of bounds South) who is adopted and brought up not by lunar wolves or cats but by chattering Mercurial apes. The child learns to stand on two feet, like an ape, and later as a young man - in a cleverly contrived piece of plotting presumably to make him look more human - he shaves his face with a knife so that he still resembles an ape. He is also famous for his cry, the sound he makes from his mouth (Mercury), his ape-call. This unique piece of communication would become more famous in the Tarzan movies to follow, but in the original book Tarzan's first spoken language is not even English but French. He learns to speak from a Frenchman he rescues in the jungle, although Tarzan has already taught himself to read and write in English from some books left behind in the cabin of his parents Lord and Lady Greystoke.

> "...the strange little bugs which covered the pages where there were no pictures excited his wonder and deepest thought..."

So the ape-man never actually said "Me Tarzan - You Jane" when he first met his future love, and language was to prove unusually challenging for him. He was in the peculiar position of being able to speak in French but to read and write (but not speak) in English. Quite a mercurial dilemma. If it seems an unnecessary complication to introduce a convoluted language sub-plot into a straightforward action adventure story, with Tarzan writing notes to the Frenchman in English who then has to translate them back into French, then write them back in English, then attempt to teach the ape-man to speak in French etc., we should remember that Burroughs was writing with an eye to serialised publication. This was originally a story composed of many parts. In later adaptations of the tale the complex language mix-up is conveniently ignored, but of course Mercury was out of bounds when the original was being written.

In Burroughs' birth chart however, it was Mars rather than Mercury that was natally out of bounds (Mars: 27S22). Although Burroughs' Mars was further beyond the boundary than the Tarzan Mercury (25S51) it was still close enough to make the OOB Mercury a significant transit in 1911. The combination of Mars and Mercury beyond normal limits describes the Tarzan character quite well: an intelligent action-man in his own world outside the normal world. Maybe Burroughs had always harboured fantasies of living the life of a noble savage himself, and with natal Mars out of bounds his vital masculine energy would have naturally been wild and adventurous. (It is recorded that at the age of 15 he had enlisted in the Seventh Cavalry but was discharged when it was discovered he was under-age). Transiting Mercury out of bounds obviously allowed him to commit the force of his wild Martian energy to written form, creating a hero who was both a muscular savage and a potentially intellectual human being. But Tarzan was not the first of his literary creations. The same OOB Mercury transit had taken place the winter before in December 1910 when Burroughs, having failed in business and desperate for cash, tried his hand at writing a pulp magazine story under the pseudonym of Norman Bean. The hero of this story, John Carter, was an ex-cavalry captain who travelled to Mars. This was accepted for publication in 1911 and fired Burroughs' confidence as a writer. With natal Mars out of bounds he would become prolific in writing adventure stories of exploration into unknown places, not only with further adventures of Tarzan in the jungle but also with different characters on other planets. Not surprisingly these often took place on Mars itself, and his first published story was called *Under the Moons of Mars*. (Later re-titled *A Princess of Mars*).

In terms of transits of course, Mercury had been in the habit of going out of bounds South, and thereby approaching his Mars, many times before the winters of 1910 and 1911. But it had not encouraged him to lift his pen and gain immortality. So was there another timer?

Indeed there was. If we progress his natal planets from birth we find the Moon had moved to 27 degrees South, conjunct his natal Mars, at his age of 34/35 years (in 1910/1911). And it remained progressed at this extreme declination for approximately the following three years. As an almost literal illustration of this, (progressed Moon conjunct natal Mars), Burroughs was moved to write *Under the Moons of Mars*, and his destiny was underway. But it was *Tarzan* that rocketed him to fame, selling in book form by the million and being translated into almost every language on Earth. The first Tarzan movie appeared a few years later in 1918 and by 1920 Burroughs was a millionaire.

Acknowledged today as one of the great early science fiction and fantasy writers, Edgar Rice Burroughs wrote about sixty books during his lifetime and died on March 19, 1950 at the age of 74. Meanwhile the force of his out-of-bounds Mars lives on.

> "As I stood thus meditating, I turned my gaze from the landscape to the heavens where the myriad stars formed a gorgeous and fitting canopy for the wonders of the earthly scene. My attention was quickly riveted by a large red star close to the distant horizon. As I gazed upon it I felt a spell of overpowering fascination—it was Mars, the god of war, and for me, the fighting man, it had always held the power of irresistible enchantment. As I gazed at it on that far-gone night it seemed to call across the unthinkable void, to lure me to it, to draw me as the lodestone attracts a particle of iron..."
>
> [From his first published story *Under the Moons of Mars*]

Tarzan of the Apes
Birth of the manuscript
1 December 1911. 8pm. [27]
Chicago, USA 45N52 87W39.

SUN	21S47
MOON	04N28
MERCURY	25S51 (OOB)
VENUS	06S37
MARS	21N29
JUPITER	19S01
SATURN	13N57
URANUS	21S21
NEPTUNE	20N50
PLUTO	16N56

MARS	21N29
NEPTUNE	20N50
PLUTO	16N56
SATURN	13N57
MOON	04N28
VENUS	06S37
JUPITER	19S01
URANUS	21S21
SUN	21S47
MERCURY	25S51 (OOB)

---

27. Source: Irwin Porfes, *The Man Who Created Tarzan*, Brigham Young University Press, 1975. Quoted by Lois Rodden in *The Mountain Astrologer*, April 1997, page 111.

Edgar Rice Burroughs
1 September 1875. Chicago, USA 41N52 87W39. [28]
(Positions shown for noon)

SUN	08N16
MOON	00N38
MERCURY	05N39
VENUS	11N38
MARS	27S22 (OOB)
JUPITER	10S10
SATURN	15S41
URANUS	16N21
NEPTUNE	10N48
PLUTO	04N40
URANUS	16N21
VENUS	11N38
NEPTUNE	10N48
SUN	08N16
MERCURY	05N39
PLUTO	04N40
MOON	00N38
JUPITER	10S10
SATURN	15S41
MARS	27S22 (OOB)

OOB Tales: The Ruby Slippers
Mars out of bounds

MGM's famous movie **The Wizard of Oz** went on public release on 25 August 1939. This date had nearly all planets in northern declination except the Moon and Mars, with Mars far out of bounds in the south (27S04). With such a focus on the outgoing energies of northern declination, plus Jupiter critically positioned just above zero, the plot easily falls into the category of

---

28. Source: Lois M. Rodden, 'The American Book of Charts', ACS San Diego, 1980. This quotes a speculative birth time of 7am.

The Wizard of Oz theatrical movie release
25 August 1939. Hollywood, California, USA 34N06 118W21.
Source: www.classicentertainment.com. Positions shown for noon

SUN	10N52
MOON	17S30
MERCURY	15N40
VENUS	13N10
MARS	27S04 (OOB)
JUPITER	01N35
SATURN	09N24
URANUS	17N57
NEPTUNE	04N08
PLUTO	23N09
PLUTO	23N09
URANUS	17N57
MERCURY	15N40
VENUS	13N10
SUN	10N52
SATURN	09N24
NEPTUNE	04N08
JUPITER	01N35
MOON	17S30
MARS	27S04 (OOB)

a Quest. A heroic band are travelling to reach an objective goal. Judy Garland looks upward and outward when she anticipates the future, singing "Somewhere over the rainbow, skies are blue..." Later, via the Yellow Brick Road, Dorothy, Scarecrow, Tin Man and Cowardly Lion, are off to see the Wonderful Wizard of Oz with optimism and hope in their step. Yet Mars, the planet of dynamic masculine energy, is in the South - and out of bounds. Why?

One of the strange facts about this ever-popular tale is that all the male characters are impotent. The Scarecrow, the Tin Man and the Lion, are three 'men' all lacking some vital quality and this makes them feel incomplete. The Scarecrow wants a brain, the Tin Woodsman wants a heart and the Cowardly Lion wants courage. They readily look to Dorothy to lead them to the Wizard of Oz and the attainment of their missing qualities. Dorothy is also seeking the help of the Wizard, but only to find her way home to Kansas; unlike the men she is not lacking any essential personality characteristic. In fact it is she who wears the Ruby Slippers (Mars) throughout the adventure, signifying that she is directing the masculine drive.

But the Wonderful Wizard of Oz (another man) turns out to be a phoney. He has no mighty powers at all. For his own protection the Wizard of Oz has hidden himself away in a fortified city where he magnifies and emphasises fearful aspects of himself in Martian fashion, but he is basically out of reach of others (out of bounds). Psychologically he is deep within himself, walled off from the outer world. He occasionally overreacts with wild bursts of smoke, flame and energy when and if anyone comes too near. All this seems to represent Mars out of bounds in the far south; his basic energy has been misunderstood and misplaced but he has got away with it and people fear him. In truth the Wizard is an ingenious and inventive man, the equivalent to the "Professor" in Dorothy's home town. All the main characters in the technicolor world of Oz had their human doubles in the everyday black-and-white world that opens and closes this film. The Wizard will eventually provide clever substitute gifts for our heroes: a brainy diploma for the Scarecrow, a courageous medal for the Lion, a mechanical ticking heart for the Tin Man, although to be honest these are simply a cop-out as far as most children watching the film are concerned.

The author of *The Wonderful Wizard of Oz*, L.Frank Baum (born 15 May 1856. Chittenango NY [29]) had natal Mars only 16 minutes below the critical zero line (00S16), which inclines one to wonder if the unconscious impetus behind his story-telling was the attempt to understand and claim his own emerging masculinity. There is no doubt that it is the female characters in the story who own the power: the good and bad witches, and to a large extent Dorothy. Yet until the later scenes all the characters believe that the strongest person in the land is the Wizard. As the heroine of the tale is a girl it is only right that the most powerful figures in her inner world are correspondingly female, but unlike the traditional female-heroine fairy story there is no wise king or handsome prince hovering in the background here. The surprising conclusion has to be that there are no helpful males for Dorothy in Oz.

---

29. Source: http://en.wikipedia.org/wiki/L._Frank_Baum.

Jupiter, which could represent a magnanimous king or a wonderful wizard, is critical and unstable. The Sun is parallel Saturn in northern declination, and may relate more to the hard-won efforts that Dorothy achieves for others (especially on a Sun-Saturn road of yellow brick), rather than any help given directly to herself. Dorothy reorganises and improves a lot of lives in Oz, intentionally and otherwise, but she gains no tangible reward other than to return home to a place she originally wanted to escape from, with little more than some half-baked philosophy about finding your heart's desire in your own back yard. This, plus the movie's tendency to be slightly overlong, all sounds rather Saturnian to me.

Of course it is the movie's chart we are talking about here, and it is the date of the film's general release rather than its separate and earlier premiere that is being examined.[30] The Sun-Saturn vibes do not necessarily apply to the book, nor to the chart of its author. Baum was a writer born with the Sun conjunct Uranus on the tropical zodiac plus Mercury out of bounds by declination. The 1939 *Wizard of Oz* movie appeared almost exactly on its author's Uranus Return (only a month adrift by both declination and zodiacal longitude), although he was not around to see it - he died in 1919. But both the book and the movie began with that classic Uranian symbol, a whirlwind, and Baum named his heroine Dorothy *Gale*.

Judy Garland, who played Dorothy Gale, has far more links to *The Wizard of Oz* movie chart than does Baum, which is just as we might expect. Most powerful perhaps is her Mars, her Ruby Slippers, which like the movie's Mars is out of bounds in the south (25S56). Whatever else this meant for her personally, it enabled her to harmonise naturally with the 'lost men' theme, bringing credibility to her character's interaction with the Scarecrow, Lion and Tin Man. Her acquisition of the Ruby Slippers in the plot is revealing as they originally belong to the Wicked Witch of the East, a character who gets flattened when Dorothy's house lands on her at the start of the tale. Dorothy wears "wicked" slippers but on her feet their magic is transformed from evil to good. It all illustrates the extremes at which a southern Mars out-of-bounds can operate. Dorothy steps into the shoes of a previously powerful figure who was also female, and continues this strange Mars heritage, but this time she uses its exalted energy (Mars in Capricorn)

---

30.   I have found that when a movie premiere predates the date of its general release by a noticeable gap - in other words when the premiere does not immediately mark the birth of the film to the public - the chart for the premiere does not describe or explain the nature of the film, nor responds to later transits, as noticeably as the chart of its date of public release.

beneficially to aid the men. Also, and this is one of those trivial things that would seem inconsequential where it not for the revelations of astrology, the Ruby Slippers were one of the few details that were changed when the book was turned into a movie. In Baum's original they were called Silver Shoes. It was the film and the actress, whose charts unconsciously demanded ruby rather than silver energy, that added a special dimension to the story. Today anyone who knows anything about *The Wizard of Oz* remembers the Ruby Slippers, which have since become one of the most famous and sought after items of movie memorabilia of all time.

Judy Garland also had a natal Venus out of bounds (23N49) which when brought back inbounds conjuncts *The Wizard of Oz* Pluto. Significant yes, but one suspects her OOB Venus to have more personal repercussions. Her whole chart declination-wise is subject to extremes with Mars OOB in the south, Venus OOB in the north, and two planets close to zero including Saturn in north declination at 01N55 and southern longitude at 00 Libra 51. This disturbance bonds with *The Wizard of Oz* Jupiter at 01N35 and mirrors her own Jupiter at 02S17. Almost certainly it was Judy Garland who managed to turn this potentially Saturnian film into a heart-warming Jupiter experience. But could she have done it without the Ruby Slippers?

Judy Garland
10 June 1922. 6.00am Grand Rapids, Minnesota, USA 47N14 93W31
Source: From birth registry (Edwin Steinbrecher)

SUN	22N59
MOON	18S27
MERCURY	21N46
VENUS	23N49 (OOB)
MARS	25S56 (OOB)
JUPITER	02S17
SATURN	01N55
URANUS	07S11
NEPTUNE	16N50
PLUTO	20N13
ASCENDANT	23N00

VENUS	23N49(OOB)
ASCENDANT	23N00
SUN	22N59
MERCURY	21N46
PLUTO	20N13
NEPTUNE	16N50
SATURN	01N55
JUPITER	02S17
URANUS	07S11
MOON	18S27
MARS	25S56(OOB)

OOB Tales: Two Astrologers

1. Ronald C. Davison - Moon, Mars and Mercury out of bounds

If three personal planets out of bounds indicates a unique individual then the astrologer Ronald Davison was a good case in point. He was born with the Moon, Mars and Mercury all out of bounds. Davison was a respected name in astrological circles for over thirty years yet possibly remains one of the more unsung of the twentieth century's astrology heroes.

Ronald C. Davison
10 January 1914. 08.44am. Bromley, Kent, England 51N24 00E02.
Source: The Astrological Lodge of London

SUN	22S04
MOON	28N24 (OOB)
MERCURY	24S20 (OOB)
VENUS	23S20
MARS	26N49 (OOB)
JUPITER	21S03
SATURN	20N38
URANUS	19S13
NEPTUNE	20N19
PLUTO	17N36
NORTH NODE	05S17

SOUTH NODE	05N17
ASCENDANT	20S00
MIDHEAVEN	20S36
MOON	28N24 (OOB)
MARS	26N49 (OOB)
SATURN	20N38
NEPTUNE	20N19
PLUTO	17N36
SOUTH NODE	05N17

NORTH NODE	05S17
URANUS	19S13
ASCENDANT	20S00
MIDHEAVEN	20S36
JUPITER	21S03
SUN	22S04
VENUS	23S20
MERCURY	24S20 (OOB)

Ronald Carlyle Davison (10 January 1914 - 22 January 1985) was President of the Astrological Lodge of London after Charles E. O. Carter for 26 years from 1952 - 1978. He was then honoured as President Emeritus from 1978 until his death in 1985 aged 71. He was editor of the long-running *Astrologers' Quarterly* magazine (again after Carter) for 25 years from 1959 - 1984.[31]

Like his contemporary John Addey, it seems a shame that Davison might only be remembered in a more sober fashion through his books and writings. While Addey is known for midpoints and harmonics, Ronald Davison gave us, amongst much else, the legacy of the 'Davison' composite chart - the midpoint in time between two birth dates, first suggested in his book *Synastry* (1977) - a valuable idea to work in declination (see later chapter devoted to this). Yet both these men had a reputation for the inclusion of humour in their work. John Addey had his witty Mercury and a fair talent for cartooning, but Ron Davison with Mercury, Mars and the Moon out of bounds was likely to jump from the sublime to the ridiculous in mid-speech or paragraph as befits a man who started his career with the burning desire to become a vaudeville comedian.

---

31. To see further tributes to Charles Carter please visit the award-winning website: www.charlescarter.co.uk

At the Lodge

He never became a vaudeville comedian, his twelfth house Capricorn Sun no doubt over-rode his rising Jupiter on that issue, but Davison's humour always crept in somewhere. One of my favourite illustrations of this comes from a 1947 *Astrology Quarterly* magazine when Davison was in charge of the magazine's "At the Lodge" section which gave brief write-ups of the lectures that had taken place at London's Astrological Lodge during the preceding three months. One of these lectures, a presentation with lantern slides on 'Zodiacal Physiognomy' by someone who called himself *Regulus*, attempted to match facial features to the signs of the zodiac. Unfortunately the post-war deprivations meant that the available magic lantern was so ancient that practically every image looked the same - a ghostly blur; and everyone depicted on screen, whether male or female, appeared to be wearing a beard. Describing this farcical situation Davison wrote:

> "From the rather scanty visual evidence provided by the slides the writer was left with the impression that most Aries types produce an abundant crop of hair on all parts of the face and that the qualities of courage, forcefulness, and initiative which most of them display were first stimulated and developed through their own whiskers, in order to catch a glimpse of the world outside. This theory was rather knocked on the head when the lecturer came to the sign of Taurus and the images of further bearded citizens were thrown upon the screen, and the death-blow was delivered when it was seen that Gemini was not without its due proportion of shaggy bearded visages..." [32]

Mercury out of bounds is a rogue Mercury and combined with the wilful OOB Mars (the two planets also closely opposed by longitude) accounts for Davison's love of inflicting puns on an innocent audience. This was all part of playing to the crowd (Northern OOB Moon) and in personal interactions he was respectful and kindly. Mars, Mercury and Moon in excess often came out in his book reviews (forceful, critical and funny). Following are some typical extracts:

> "...There are a series of short essays on the planets, which are rather stereotyped in their presentation. A prominent Jupiter, for example, is accused of going round slapping people on the back as a kind of hobby. Your reviewer, with Jupiter rising, has never indulged in this pastime, reserving such action for extreme cases when food might have lodged in the wind-pipe...."

---

32. *The Astrologers' Quarterly*, Volume 21 Number 4. December 1947.

> "...The first chapter starts promisingly with a few potted biographies, though Margaret Thatcher is stated as having Sagittarius rising, Scorpio rising and Libra rising in the short space of twenty-one lines. Allowing for the fact that politicians seldom allow themselves to be pinned down, this kind of presentation must be confusing for beginners..."

And on a book about astrology and sex:

> "...I have no hesitation in stating that I am completely unqualified to judge the accuracy of the descriptions given. Were I in a position to do so my wife would most certainly want to know the reason why."

Power struggles

When Charles Carter retired from the position of President of the Astrological Lodge in 1952 it seems there was something of a power struggle to direct the future course of astrology in Britain. Geoffrey Cornelius, in his obituary to Davison, aptly described this as "a period of rising personalities".[33] Besides Davison, the rising personalities included John Addey, Brigadier Firebrace and Margaret Hone, and it was the latter trio especially who wanted to sever the Lodge more drastically from its Theosophical roots. But it was Ronald Davison, standing more for the middle ground that Carter had established, who won the members' vote and became the third president of the Lodge (after Bessie Leo and Charles Carter) on 10 November 1952, 8.17pm, London. Although the early days of Davison's presidency sometimes had to weather stormier seas than Carter's, Davison and Addey had always shared a mutual respect and relationships were cordial between them.

This period coincided with several progressions in declination becoming active on Davison's chart, especially his Mars. He was born when Mars was at 26N49 and heading farther out of bounds. For the following 17 days (17 years by progression) Mars continued on its OOB journey until it reached a maximum of 27N11. It then retraced its steps arriving back at its natal position about 38/39 days from the start. Hence at Davison's age of almost 39 years (November 1952) his Mars was at full power, firing on all cylinders.

---

33. Geoffrey Cornelius 'In Memory of Ronald C. Davison', *The Astrologers' Quarterly*, Spring 1985.

The first encounter

Ronald Davison was one of those comparatively rare individuals who could name the date, place and time of his first encounter with astrology. It was a library in Croydon, near London, he was aged 29 (a couple of months past his Saturn Return), his progressed Moon was parallel his out-of-bounds Mars and - in his own words:

> "My own 'first moment' occurred when I visited the local Public Library in order to choose some books on philosophy and comparative religion, subjects in which I was beginning to develop a special interest. I noticed on adjoining shelves textbooks on astrology and the thought came to me: 'Why shouldn't I be my own astrologer?' It was only a few days later that I learned from the textbook I had chosen that the moment of starting an enterprise was all-important. It was not difficult to work back and estimate the moment when the idea first came to me as my Saturday afternoon visits to the library followed a fairly consistent pattern...It never occurred to me until fairly recently that the angles (of this First Moment chart) are almost identical with Charles Carter's natal angles - hardly surprising since in terms of Lodge history I followed in his footsteps. Also it was not until fairly recently that I realised that 17 Libra (the ascendant of this chart) ...is the antiscion of 12 Pisces...(and therefore) had very good claims to be considered as an astrological degree..."[34]

Here we see that Davison was experimenting with the use of antiscia and the "astrology degree" to which he refers is one of those quoted by Carter in *An Encyclopaedia of Psychological Astrology*.

Davison's inaugural moment into astrology occurred on 3 July 1943 (2.51pm, Croydon), during the time of World War 2, and one may perhaps wonder why this able-bodied 29-year-old man was not serving in uniform somewhere. Mars in Cancer usually produces a patriotic fighter, one who will fight to protect his homeland, but this Mars was out of bounds. Davison was a conscientious objector. His beliefs, which encompassed the Buddhist view of non-violence, led to his decision; a difficult and unexpected stance to take in those times and an apt illustration of the reliance on his own truth plus the strength to go against the herd shown both by his Aquarian ascendant and his three personal out-of-bounds planets. Whether the fact that his first four years of life were concurrent with the 1914-18 War had

---

34. Quoted by Davison a few months before his death in 'Here, There and Everywhere' *The Astrologers' Quarterly*, Summer 1984

any bearing on this, and/or whether his family suffered at that time or raised him with a particular outlook, I do not know. As his Moon was out of bounds, early emotional imprints could have been strong. Davison's father served in France during the First World War and during this time Ronald was taken by his mother to stay in Somerset at Weston-super-Mare, a coastal town on the west of England where the mother and father had been married. Throughout his life Davison would periodically return to this spot as if he gained spiritual sustenance from it.

In his book *Synastry* he refers obliquely to this place as "a certain seaside town" that had played a prominent part in his destiny. He also mentions that the horoscope of the town made several favourable aspects to his natal chart. If that horoscope is the same as the one Harold Wigglesworth recorded it has its Sun within one minute of an exact contra-parallel to Davison's natal Venus and it was at this town that he met Marian, his future life partner.[35]

The shy astrological giant

Davison's early wish for a touch of showbusiness never entirely left him. His first ever public lecture was titled 'Stage and Screen Talent' (18 February 1946) and his first major written piece was on the astrological significators of Jazz. As a Sun Capricorn he had eventually taken a safe pensionable day-job in the Civil Service with the Ministry of Agriculture and Fisheries, but the rest of his life was devoted to astrology.

Almost alone amongst the elite of mid-twentieth century British astrology, Davison was a great advocate of degree symbols - an intuitive, imaginative shade of the art that he had no problem integrating with the more traditional rules of astrology. Without the benefit of Declination we might have said it was the blend of Capricorn and Aquarius on his chart that allowed him to be both ancient and modern, but with the additional knowledge of his three out-of-bounders it is not surprising that he should take a larger-ranging and unconventional view. As Charles Harvey put it:

> "Ron was always ready to entertain, indeed introduce, new heresies, yet ever ready to remind us of the larger, richer, and more truly mysterious picture if we should show signs of straying too far into particular or overly narrow views".[36]

---

35. Weston-super-Mare. 51N20 02W59. Modern date of Municipal Corporation: 28 June 1937, 00.00 hours. Source: Harold Wigglesworth, *The Astrology of Towns and Cities*, Astrological Association, London, 1973.
36. Charles Harvey 'In Memory of Ronald C. Davison', *The Astrologers' Quarterly*, Spring 1985.

His other main astrological specialisms included medical astrology and the pre-natal epoch.

This "shy astrological giant" (to use Ken Gillman's phrase) saw his first textbook *The Technique of Prediction* published in 1955, his more well-known *Astrology* in 1963 and *Synastry* in 1977. The international sales of these books made Davison a welcome visitor to North America in his later years and he made several successful coast-to-coast lecture tours, which in turn gave him more fuel for expanded insights and anecdotes to deliver to his audiences back in London. (Rising Jupiter ruling midheaven and tenth house).

Ronald Davison's death when it came was sudden, unexpected but peaceful. He had not long passed his 71st birthday and died in his sleep only hours after delivering another of his lectures at The Lodge. No one present that evening recalled him being in the slightest bit different to his familiar "twinkly-eyed" self. His three personal out-of-bounds planets plus the Uranian/Aquarian ascendant probably ensured that his exit would be as sudden and unexpected as his initial discovery of astrology in the first place, leaving those who had shared his presence just hours before, startled, shocked and not a little bemused.

OOB Tales: Two Astrologers

2. John Addey - Mercury out of bounds

The astrologer John Addey (15 June 1920 - 27 March 1982) is probably most well-known for the work he left for posterity on midpoints and harmonics. As one of the founders of the Astrological Association of Great Britain in 1958, and for some years the editor of its Journal, his astrological reputation was - and is - secured. But Addey was not a stuffy academic; he was a man of impish wit and agile mind who dared to be trivial on the speaker's platform or in the sober pages of his magazine. In particular he had an abiding fascination with the astrological significance of the names of roads and streets. Not surprisingly really, as his natal Mercury was out of bounds.

John Addey

15 June 1920. 8.15am. Barnsley, England 53N33 01W29.
Source: The Astrological Association of Great Britain

SUN	23N18
MOON	19N29
MERCURY	24N36 (OOB)
VENUS	22N52
MARS	09S20
JUPITER	17N06
SATURN	10N58
URANUS	10S09
NEPTUNE	17N52
PLUTO	19N41
NORTH NODE	16S23
SOUTH NODE	16N23
ASCENDANT	18N51
MIDHEAVEN	04N32

MERCURY	24N36 (OOB)
SUN	23N18
VENUS	22N52
PLUTO	19N41
MOON	19N29
ASCENDANT	18N51
NEPTUNE	17N52
JUPITER	17N06
SOUTH NODE	16N23
SATURN	10N58
MIDHEAVEN	04N32
MARS	09S20
URANUS	10S09
NORTH NODE	16S23

John Addey was strongly Geminian (Sun and Moon in Gemini), and his mind skated across a variety of ideas, some deep some shallow. "We are always inclined to underestimate the power of ideas", he once said. He was always fascinated in finding the cosmos in the ephemera of everyday life and, with Mercury out of bounds, roads and highways led him to some strange places.

He once recorded for instance that the *Avenue Churchill* in Paris was officially dedicated to the memory of the wartime leader on a date when Winston Churchill's own natal Mercury was being activated. On another whim he once scoured the Atlas of Greater London (a city which is traditionally ruled by Gemini) to search out every zodiac reference he could find in the street-names of the capital. This allowed him to produce an Aries to Pisces list that stretched from 'Ram's Gate' to 'Fish Street Hill'. He also amused himself by drawing up the following list of names for imaginary zodiac roadways:

> "Aries *Drive*, Taurus *Gardens*, Gemini *Walk*, Cancer *Crescent*, Leo *Court*, Virgo *Lane*, Libra *Approach*, Scorpio *Alley*, Sagittarius *High Road*, Capricorn *Square*, Aquarius *Embankment* and Pisces *Cloisters*."[37]

But these were all lightweight Mercurial brainteasers compared with the mysterious microcosm he was to discover on his very doorstep.

One day, as John Addey was walking around the block from his home in Cheam Road, Surrey, he noticed a perfect order that could only be apparent to an astrologer. All the zodiac symbols were right there in the colours, names, gardens and inhabitants of the houses he passed - beginning with his own home as Cancer - and each followed the other in the correct zodiac order. Cheam Road was a miniature cosmos.

There had always been some controversy amongst British astrologers in those days on the subject of Earth Zodiacs. The claimed antiquity of the Temple of the Stars at Glastonbury in Somerset was not everyone's cup of tea. (The Glastonbury Zodiac or Temple of the Stars is a circle thirty miles round whose natural geographical features form the shapes of the signs of the zodiac). Like Cheam Road it is a real place, but like the Cheam Road Zodiac it seemed it was only a real place to some when the light was right and the mind attuned.

Typically Addey deduced that if the zodiac on his doorstep was as real as the zodiac in his mind, then it would respond in the same fashion if he

---

37. From the Tailpiece in *The Astrological Journal*, London, Spring 1966. Volume VIII Number 2

changed it. So a few days later he deliberately traversed the block starting from a different sign, counting his own house as Aries this time, and was excited to notice that a completely different yet equally valid zodiac now opened up before him. (Instead of the twins who lived in the house next door he now noticed the fish pond etc).

Unfortunately although he recounted this tale in public as a humorous episode he never recorded his deeper thoughts about it.[38] I think he would have avoided the glib statement that if you are looking for Earth Zodiacs you can find them anywhere, because his Mercury was too far-reaching - saw too many options - for him to believe in simple mind games. Mercury beyond the borders is in another land altogether, yet because of the nature of Mercury it must fly back to base and report its findings, if only spasmodically. This possibly makes an out-of-bounds Mercury different to any other out-of-bounds planet, for Mercury is the messenger between heaven and earth, the god who is obliged to set up lines of communication. Like any planet out of bounds he can operate freely, beyond restraint and convention, but unlike other planets he must periodically return like a homing pigeon, allowing the mind to grasp and grapple with what it has found. Mercury OOB can build a road from the Twilight Zone rather than just be a resident in it.

When John Addey died in 1982 he was saluted not only as a great astrologer but also as a teacher of severely physically disabled children, his main profession for many years. He had empathy with their plight because he had himself been struck down by an acute form of rheumatism in his early twenties and never properly regained the use of his legs and back for the remainder of his life. Originally a sporty and athletic man he eventually refound a form of mobility with the use of walking sticks, but for eighteen months he was on his back unable to move or read.

---

38. This throwaway tale of The Cheam Road Zodiac has started to gain a life of its own, almost threatening to become as famous an anecdote when the name of John Addey is mentioned as anything he wrote on midpoints and harmonics. Addey never committed the Cheam Road story to writing at all. It was first mentioned in published form by Charles Harvey in *Mundane Astrology* (1984), a couple of years after the actual incident, where a full page was devoted to it in a chapter titled 'The Search for the Earth Zodiac'. Geoffrey Cornelius discussed it in *The Moment of Astrology* (revised edition 2003) in a chapter titled 'Appearances: The Symbol in Context', finishing with the sentence: "Perhaps John Addey's inspired Cheam Zodiac has more truth to it than we care to admit." Meanwhile I had published the above account in the Declination SIG Journal in Spring 2002. There may of course be other references in astrological periodicals of which I am unaware, as this is the kind of story that is guaranteed to

Here is the other more disturbing side of this tale of a man with Mercury out-of-bounds: Mercury energy was so extreme that all mobility was suddenly lost and his life forced into a different turn. Mind then became superior to body. Mercury, the ruler of triviality, forced his life to become less trivial. Addey by his own admission saw the physical tragedy as an order from fate to keep him still for long enough to reflect on his life and work out what he was really supposed to do with it. From then on he became a dedicated researcher into astrology and mentor to the young and handicapped.

OOB Tales: The Lunar Ranger

Moon out of bounds

An avenging hero who masks his identity while fighting on the side of truth and justice has a long cinematic and literary pedigree. Well-known examples include The Scarlet Pimpernel, The Lone Ranger, Zorro and Bat Man. What all these fictional characters have in common - particularly the last three - is the need to wear an actual mask to protect their private identity, for without this mask they could not act so freely, nor in so revolutionary or humanitarian a fashion. In other words by being Scorpionic they become more Aquarian. A nice touch of antiscia.

This time we are looking at The Lone Ranger, a surprisingly lunar figure who called his horse Silver and inherited his wealth from a silver mine. Without many reliable birth dates to examine, for this hero stretches back into the early days of comic books and cinema, I have taken the chart of his famous television series that ran throughout the 1950s. This gives us an exact date and time to work with and, appropriately, has the Moon out-of-bounds.

---

provoke debate amongst astrologers. Also, in Britain, there is something about the name "Cheam Road" that lends it a humorous slant. "Cheam" is a funny word, not least as it has associations with the great comedian Tony Hancock who supposedly lived in East Cheam. But when something is funny for no rational reason we have entered the same zone that gives meaning to things that can not be conventionally measured, yet are undeniably relevant - like the Cheam Road Zodiac itself.

82   *Declination in Astrology*

The Lone Ranger - Television premiere
15 September 1949. 7.30pm. New York, NY. USA 40N45 073W57.[39]

SUN	02N52
MOON	28N22 (OOB)
MERCURY	10S14
VENUS	12S31
MARS	19N56
JUPITER	22S08
SATURN	08N51
URANUS	23N36 (OOB)
NEPTUNE	04S08
PLUTO	23N00
NORTH NODE	06N39
SOUTH NODE	06S39
ASCENDANT	02N10
MIDHEAVEN	23S25
MOON	28N22 (OOB)
URANUS	23N36 (OOB)
PLUTO	23N00
MARS	19N56
SATURN	08N51
NORTH NODE	06N39
SUN	02N52
ASCENDANT	02N10
NEPTUNE	04S08
SOUTH NODE	06S39
MERCURY	10S14
VENUS	12S31
JUPITER	22S08
MIDHEAVEN	23S25

---

39.   Source: Tim Brooks & Earl Marsh, *'The Complete Directory to Prime Time Network and Cable TV Shows'*, Ballantine, NY. 1999.

Among the fortuitous elements of this birth chart we find the Sun and the ascendant in parallel at 2° North. This is a feature that only becomes apparent through declination, for the Sun is not on the ascendant by longitude. On the zodiac chart the Sun is in Virgo in the sixth and the ascendant is Aries, but in fact they hang together here over the zero line representing a noticeable new outer image. There can be little that remains hidden with this conspicuously forthright arrangement, which in view of the character's need to maintain a hidden identity is somewhat strange. Like the Aries ascendant, The Lone Ranger's outer face is quite open. One wonders why he bothers to wear a mask. With spotless suit, shiny guns and a magnificent white horse, his outward persona couldn't be more instantly recognisable if it tried.

The Moon being out of bounds in the north means that this masked man is certainly a 'ranger' in the sense of ranging wide beyond boundaries, instinctively searching outwardly for goals. But he is hardly a lone ranger as he is almost always accompanied by his trusty Mohawk friend Tonto. Let us review the actual legend of The Lone Ranger, which would have been enacted in the first episode of the television series:

A band of six Texas Rangers are ambushed and shot by an outlaw gang and left for dead in the underbrush. One of them survives thanks to a friendly Indian (Tonto) and is nursed back to health. This lone ranger then buries his five companions but marks out six graves so that his own survival will be unknown to the murderers. He later dons a mask to hide his former identity and becomes a kind of rogue vigilante devoted to righting wrongs and defending the weak, while all the time hunting down his original attackers.

Although The Lone Ranger is fictitious, it is interesting to see that his chart ties in to that of the Lone Star State of Texas primarily through that critical Sun and ascendant just above zero. Texas has a Mars-Uranus parallel in virtually the same place. (Lone Ranger Sun: 02N52, Asc: 02N10, Texas Mars: 01N48, Uranus: 01N54). The tale of The Lone Ranger seems to access the revolutionary excitement (Mars-Uranus) present at the birth of Texas into the Union of the United States.

Texas - Natal Chart
29 December 1845. Texas, USA 38N53 77W00 [40]
(Positions shown for noon)

SUN	23S13
MOON	17S38
MERCURY	20S32
VENUS	14S15
MARS	01N48
JUPITER	10N38
SATURN	16S56
URANUS	01N54
NEPTUNE	13S58
PLUTO	07S01
NORTH NODE	16S25
SOUTH NODE	16N25

SOUTH NODE	16N25
JUPITER	10N38
URANUS	01N54
MARS	01N48
PLUTO	07S01
NEPTUNE	13S58
VENUS	14S15
NORTH NODE	16S25
SATURN	16S56
MOON	17S38
MERCURY	20S32
SUN	23S13

In some ways the Texas chart is more appropriate to the Lone Ranger than his own. With the majority of planets including the Sun and Moon in double figures in south declination there is more of a hidden aspect here. And apart from Jupiter at 10 degrees north, the only other northern planets are Mars and Uranus in parallel just above zero. As mentioned above this

---

40. Source: *Horoscopes of US States and Cities*, Carolyn R. Dodson, AFA, 1975.

may indicate an explosive burst of youthful energy as Texas finally broke away from its previous ties to Mexico.

In comparison The Lone Ranger chart has most of its planets (including the Sun and the Moon and a just out-of-bounds Uranus) in the north, yet its Jupiter is far south at 22S08 close to the Texas Sun. One way or another the two charts have some interesting links and The Lone Ranger's out-of-bounds Moon may in part refer to this revolutionary ancestral heritage. The Texas Rangers were formed some years before the state's acceptance into the Union to help protect new settlers from raiding Mexicans, Indians and other lawless opportunists while the area was gradually organising itself for independence from Mexico. They remained a separate unit of the law until well into the twentieth century.

Another aspect of the out-of-bounds Moon in The Lone Ranger's personality is the rogue element previously mentioned. The Lone Ranger is no longer an official Texas Ranger, he is now operating as a law unto himself. He is an unknown quantity. Who is that masked man?

Tonto certainly knows who he is, as presumably does Silver, The Lone Ranger's horse. Both of these figures have lunar connections: Silver - (obviously), and Tonto who was played throughout the long-running television series by the actor Jay Silverheels. Clayton Moore, who played The Lone Ranger, celebrated his 35th birthday one day before the television series premiered, so by one degree his natal Sun was conjunct and parallel the Lone Ranger Sun. (Clayton Moore: 14 September 1914 [41]). Even more arrestingly, the actor's own natal Moon was out of bounds beyond the northern limits. The potential for public empathy was magnified.

Remarkable synastries wherever you look helps to confirm why this particular character and the television show named after him achieved its near legendary status.

---

41. Source: www.wildwesterns.com

OOB Tales: A Photograph of the Beatles

The Moon out of bounds squaring Pluto and Nodes

Of all The Beatles' album cover sleeves there was probably none more famous than *Sergeant Pepper's Lonely Hearts Club Band* - and rightly so for the amount of thought and work that went into it. Messages were read into that cover, but then messages were put there to be read. The same is not true of their second most famous album cover *Abbey Road*, intended to be one of the simplest of ideas showing the four Beatles in a line crossing the road outside the E.M.I. Abbey Road recording studios in London in 1969. Yet this also became a much-imitated image and possibly gave rise to more speculation over hidden meanings than any other Beatles' record.

The Abbey Road Photograph
Friday 8 August 1969. 11.35am. London, England 51N32 00W12.

SUN	16N08
MOON	28N26 (OOB)
MERCURY	11N48
VENUS	21N45
MARS	24S54 (OOB)
JUPITER	00S25
SATURN	12N04
URANUS	00N03
NEPTUNE	17S35
PLUTO	16N31
NORTH NODE	03S17
SOUTH NODE	03N17
ASCENDANT	07S00
MIDHEAVEN	21N24
MOON	28N27 (OOB)
VENUS	21N45
MIDHEAVEN	21N24
PLUTO	16N31
SUN	16N08
SATURN	12N04

MERCURY	11N48
SOUTH NODE	03N17
URANUS	00N03

JUPITER	00S25
NORTH NODE	03S17
ASCENDANT	07S00
NEPTUNE	17S35
MARS	24S54 (OOB)

Because the original *Abbey Road* cover image is a photograph it captures a specific moment in time that we can examine astrologically. This is particularly so as it was an outside shot rather than an interior studio one and it had to be taken quickly. Mark Lewisohn in *The Complete Beatles Chronicle* records a time of 11.35am on 8 August 1969 for the picture.[42] This was when the photographer Iain Macmillan balanced on a stepladder and fired several shots at The Beatles from his camera as they walked back and forth across a zebra crossing while a policeman held up the traffic. The resultant astrology is interesting indeed.

The Moon is well out-of-bounds by declination at this moment (28N26, almost at its maximum extremity), and exactly squaring Pluto and the Lunar Nodes by longitude. The wild and transformative psychic field thus created could be seen as linking pasts and futures together: as the individual Beatles stepped from black to white and white to black on the zebra crossing, the photograph captured an instant when every one of them had a foot in both worlds. Appropriately the Moon was in Gemini, the ascendant Libra and the North Node Pisces. All the dual signs were covered.

Zodiac-wise, the Moon at 23 Gemini was only a few degrees from Paul McCartney's natal Sun, and the Sun on this day was conjunct his Leo Moon. So it was Paul McCartney above all whose picture on this photograph was the most scrutinised. (And it was he who chose this particular photograph out of several other options). Strangely, although perhaps not altogether surprisingly with all the Moon-Pluto-Node tension, it also fuelled contemporary rumours that he was dead.

Mars out of bounds in the south may have also added to this lost man quality. In the photograph McCartney, who as an interesting aside has every

---

42. Source: Mark Lewisohn, '*The Complete Beatles Chronicle*', Chancellor Press, London, 1996.

88   Declination in Astrology

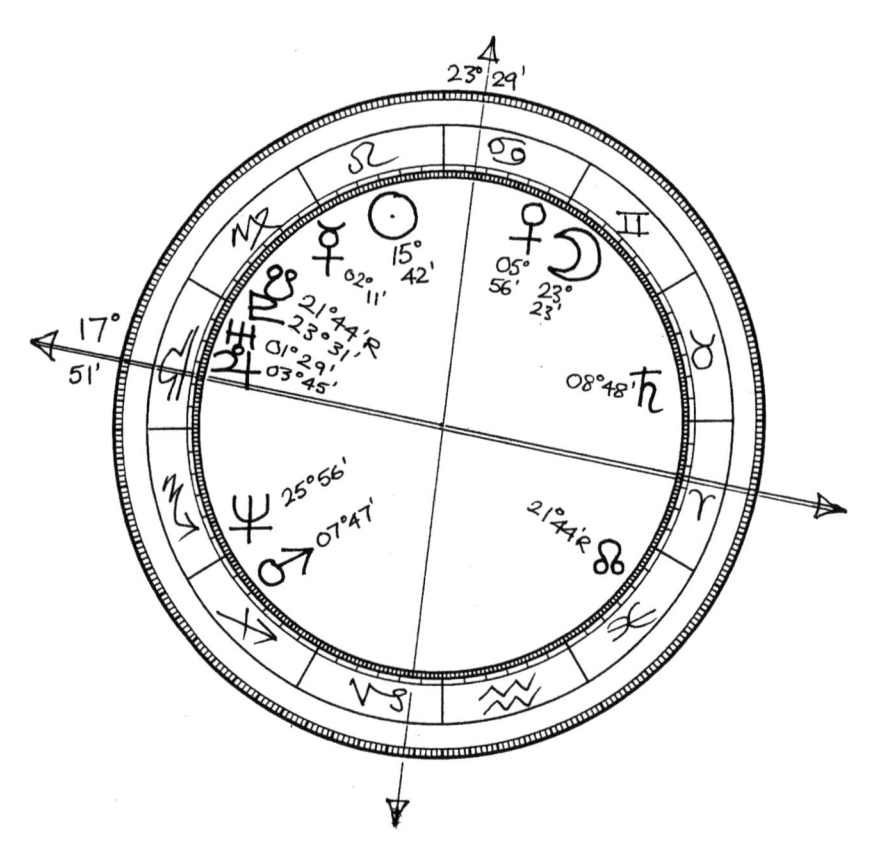

Abbey Road Photograph
8 August 1969. 11.35am London 51N32 00W12

planet in his chart in northern declination, is pictured walking out of step with the others. He has no shoes. He is odd. He could be perceived as being ill-fitting or out of place like Mars and the Moon. But the whole procession of The Beatles was open to interpretation here according to their dress. As some saw it at the time: John Lennon, leading the procession, was all in white as an angel; Ringo Starr, next in line, was all in black as the undertaker, then came Paul McCartney barefooted as the dead man followed at the rear by George Harrison in jeans as the gravedigger. A car parked in the background had the clearly visible licence-plate *28 IF* - implying to some that Paul would have been 28 years old *if* he had lived.

Maybe such dark and heavy messages were read because this image carried an imprint of an exact Moon square Pluto, an intense need to destroy or cut off the past. As Pluto was also conjunct the Moon's South Node this is doubly true. The celebrated photograph is reflecting a moment when something is required to die so that karma can be transformed and the soul move on.

Strangely enough the Paul-is-dead rumour spread the unlikely idea that he had died in a car accident as far back as 9 November 1966. How this specific date was plucked from the ether is debatable, yet on astrological examination this is another highly nodal moment. On 9 November 1966 the Moon's South Node was exactly conjunct the Sun and Venus at 16° Scorpio, which moreover was exactly conjunct Paul McCartney's natal Part of Fortune.[43] The declination of the Sun-Venus-South Node conjunction at the date of the phoney accident was 16 South, parallel Neptune and exactly contra-parallel the Sun and Pluto on the Abbey Road photograph. Both Suns (for accident and photograph) were square each other at the mid-degrees of Fixed signs close to the powerful activations of Lammas and Samhain. The solar identity with such deep and dark features as Pluto, the South Lunar Node, Halloween etc. may reflect the doppelganger effect of a supposed double who - rumour insisted - had secretly taken McCartney's place in the group since 1966.

By hindsight we know that this last album picture of the famous foursome together does indeed mark the death of The Beatles. They were all individually experiencing or fast-approaching their Saturn Returns and *Abbey Road* was their last creative work as a group. Although even they had not admitted it to each other in as many words, in their hearts they knew their time was up. The last musical track on *Abbey Road*, which was partly recorded later that same day when they returned to the studio, was titled suitably *The End*. The Beatles were increasingly starting to branch out into solo projects. Exciting new expansive futures and times of great change were on the horizon (Jupiter and Uranus at zero).

The Sun on this chart makes a powerful declination parallel to Pluto (Sun: 16N08, Pluto: 16N31). In other words: death of the old self, transformation and release. The Sabian symbol for the Sun is "Sunshine after a storm", another Sun-Pluto image suggestive of rebirth.

The astrology of *Abbey Road* touched all the Beatles' individual charts quite strongly. As already mentioned its Moon was conjunct Paul's Sun, he may have felt comfortable here; he loosely took charge. The ascendant at 17° Libra was conjunct John's Sun at 16° Libra, he is the star in front; he

---

43. Paul McCartney: 18 June 1942. 2pm. Liverpool, England. 53N25 02W55. Source: Frank C. Clifford, *British Entertainers*, Flare, London. 1997.

leads the procession. The Sun is conjunct both Ringo and Paul's Moons and George's midheaven; the picture involved all of them and is still one of the most famous of the four together in the late 1960s and probably always will be. Lastly the chart's Pluto/South Node combination touches everyone's Neptune, the end of a collective dream.

The little islands of separate yet collective unity that the *Abbey Road* album cover portrays were reflected in the music of that album. Its seamless progression of one tune into the next gave the appearance of a band united, especially after the disjointed and more individual tracks on their previous White Album (*The Beatles* 1968). The tensions apparent in the film *Let It Be* had eased a little by this time as each of the Beatles was ready to step into his own future. And this is what the *Abbey Road* photograph also displays, The Beatles striding towards an unknown destination on the other side of the street. (Jupiter/Uranus at zero). Although perfectly in line, none of them appears to be looking at the others. Their faces bear an air of inward contemplation. They are somewhere else. (Moon out-of-bounds). They are all facing the same direction but they are not looking at the same thing.

In later years you might have been hard pressed to find a time to traverse Abbey Road at that famous zebra crossing in London when there was not a stream of tourists photographing each other doing the self-same thing. Without doubt it must be the most venerated pedestrian crossing in the British Isles, but back in 1969 it was merely an innocent little piece of road marking and had no idea that it would one day become a site of international pilgrimage.

For The Beatles back then, this brief and convenient photo-shoot was a relief from what could have been a more longwinded and exotic affair. At one time the *Abbey Road* album had been conceived under the working title of *Everest* with the possibility of the four of them having to travel to the Himalayas for the cover photographs. But the heights of Everest were suddenly ditched (Jupiter and Uranus again?) and instead the boys just stepped outside the door and it became simply *Abbey Road*, honouring the name of the place that had always captured their creative genius on record. But now the heavens had colluded with their unconscious needs to let things die and start anew. It was time to cross the road and walk away.

OOB Tales: Extreme Venus

Venus out of bounds

What kind of woman might have an out-of-bounds Venus? Would it manifest as an almost over-the-top feminine image as in - say - Dolly Parton? Would it be an unreachable, mysterious Venus as in the persona of Greta Garbo? Or the more sassy femininity of Mae West? Would it perhaps be a woman whose name was synonymous with perfume and fashion as in Coco Chanel? Or someone famed as a "Pretty Woman" as was/is Julia Roberts? Was Venus OOB at the birth of that controversial every-little-girl's-companion, the Barbie Doll? The answer is "No" every time. Not one of the above-mentioned examples was born with Venus out of bounds, although surprisingly Mars was out of bounds in each and every case.[44]

What about famous feminists, do they have Venus out of bounds? The answer in every example I could find was "No".

So let's ask another question. Bearing in mind that Mars has been twice as likely to be out of bounds than Venus in the past hundred years, we might ask what kind of *man* has Venus out of bounds?

The two famous examples that I found of men with an extreme feminine side are the subject of this piece, and in a sense they couldn't be more different: Rudolph Valentino and Liberace.

---

44. Dolly Parton: 19 January 1946. 8.25pm. Locust Ridge, Tennessee, USA. Source: Birth certificate (Frank Clifford).
Greta Garbo: 18 September 1905. 7.30pm. Stockholm, Sweden. Source: From birth record (Ivan Wilhelm, Roscoe Hope) - Frank Clifford.
Mae West: 17 August 1892. 10.30pm. Brooklyn, New York, USA. Source: Frank Clifford.
Coco Chanel: 19 August 1883. 4pm. Saumur, France. Source: From birth certificate (Frank Clifford).
Julia Roberts: 28 October 1967. 00.16am. Atlanta, Georgia, USA. Source: 'American Astrology' January 1977. Gary Nowell quotes birth certificate.
The Barbie Doll: 9 March 1959. 09.00am. New York, USA. Source: maxpages.com/mainshome/The_Birth_of_Barbie. Time of 9.00 am is speculative.

Rudolph Valentino
6 May 1895. 3pm Castellaneta, Italy 40N37 16E57.[45]

SUN	16N26
MOON	04S14
MERCURY	16N54
VENUS	24N59 (OOB)
MARS	24N39 (OOB)
JUPITER	23N27
SATURN	09S59
URANUS	16S52
NEPTUNE	21N07
PLUTO	11N40
NORTH NODE	03S44
SOUTH NODE	03N44
ASCENDANT	00N26
MIDHEAVEN	23S27

VENUS	24N59 (OOB)
MARS	24N39 (OOB)
JUPITER	23N27
NEPTUNE	21N07
MERCURY	16N53
SUN	16N26
PLUTO	11N40
SOUTH NODE	03N44
ASCENDANT	00N26

NORTH NODE	03S44
MOON	04S14
SATURN	09S59
URANUS	16S52
MIDHEAVEN	23S27

---

45. Source: From birth certificate. Lois M. Rodden, 'The American Book of Charts' ACS, San Diego, 1980. There are many sources for Valentino's data, most quoting entry in family log or direct from him to an astrologer. The birth times are consistently 2.30 - 3.00am.

Liberace

16 May 1919. 11.15pm West Allis, Wisconsin, USA 43N01 88W00. [46]

SUN	19N05
MOON	21S37
MERCURY	09N18
VENUS	25N35 (OOB)
MARS	18N42
JUPITER	23N00
SATURN	15N35
URANUS	11S38
NEPTUNE	18N31
PLUTO	19N24
NORTH NODE	20S55
SOUTH NODE	20N55
ASCENDANT	23S21
MIDHEAVEN	12S05

VENUS	25N35 (OOB)
JUPITER	23N00
SOUTH NODE	20N55
PLUTO	19N24
SUN	19N05
MARS	18N42
NEPTUNE	18N31
SATURN	15N35
MERCURY	09N18

URANUS	11S38
MIDHEAVEN	12S05
NORTH NODE	20S55
MOON	21S37
ASCENDANT	23S21

---

46. Source: From birth certificate. Lois M. Rodden, *'The American Book of Charts'* ACS, San Diego, 1980

We know of course that one of these men was heterosexual and the other was homosexual. Before he became a film star Rudolph Valentino made his living as a professional dancing partner. Liberace hid his homosexuality until later years but he was promiscuous and died from AIDS. For both men Venus was rampant, though in some way detached.

In their private lives Venus operated beyond the rules of convention. Valentino (can you get a more Venusian name?) was once a gigolo, a rare species of man. Liberace, whose name sounds like 'Libra' or the Latin *liberalis* or *liberatio* (meaning 'gracious' and 'freedom') was gay, at a time when being gay was regarded by many as sinful and despised. In keeping with the evidence that an out-of-bounds planet is awkward as well as power-giving, these Taurean men would have known from early on that in the Venus department they were different from the average.

Venus is out of bounds in the north on both charts and this together with other factors thrusts it more into the public eye. Rudolph Valentino, the dark latino dancer, whose Mars was also out of bounds, became a smouldering love-god of the silent screen. Liberace, the sensitive musician, charmed television audiences in the early black and white days of that new medium. More accurately, we should say that these men charmed and galvanised the *females* in their audiences in a way that quite surprised the viewing menfolk.

Liberace oozed Venus in a very different way to that of Valentino. Liberace's out-of-bounds Venus in Cancer (conjunct Pluto in longitude) prompted a deep-felt motherly response from his adoring female fans. He was such a nice young man, a man (unlike Valentino) who you could proudly take home to the family. He spoke predominantly through his music - that gentle, sensitive, piano music that was not raucous or threatening. He dressed immaculately in evening wear and his smile was sincere. Later his elegance would become flamboyance as Venus urged him further over the top and it was obvious he would never make a perfect husband, yet he retained a dedicated army of female followers to the end. With comically over-sized rings and jewellery, gaudy candelabra, pastel clothes and coiffeured hair, he had become a caricature of his wild Aphrodite. As an old man he looked like an old woman.

Rudolph Valentino, who died aged 31 at the height of his fame, did not look like a woman. At least he didn't in his time. Today, with his eye make-up and silk pantaloons, we might think otherwise. But fashion, which is ruled by Venus, cannot be judged from a different age. Valentino's out-of-bounds Venus was in Gemini - interesting for a silent star. His attraction came from his looks and the way he moved, sensuously and rhythmically like a dancer. With the volatile OOB Mars in addition he was the embodiment of sex appeal: graceful and dangerous at the same time.

In the early 1920s Valentino's manhood was once publicly questioned by a film critic, who called him a "powderpuff". Incensed, Valentino instantly challenged the critic to a boxing match (Mars out of bounds) but the accuser backed down. From that time the silent star deliberately commissioned a series of fan photographs showing himself barechested to emphasise his manly physique. This man with Venus out of bounds was one of the first masculine pin-ups.

When Rudolph Valentino died he was mourned by women the world over: his funeral was Venus over the top. Flowers and females rained in on all sides and several women committed suicide.

Our two examples of Venus out of bounds were admittedly special cases, famous people, but it seems clear that an out-of-bounds planet, being magnified, attracts its own kind. The women quoted at the beginning with Mars beyond the normal boundaries may have attracted men, whereas these two men had an extravagant Venus - attracting women. And we should not forget that Liberace and Valentino were naturally talented in other Venusian arts, namely music and dancing, before they became famous. (As an aside it is not surprising to find that many famous artists and painters have Venus out of bounds. The list includes Rosetti, Magritte, Durer, Toulouse-Lautrec, Rodin, William Blake...and Picasso who had Venus at zero).

While a man or woman's personal sexual orientation cannot be read from an out-of-bounds Mars or Venus in either combination, the attraction of their gender does seem to be highlighted. Perhaps the subtle message picked up by others is of an energy available and unrestrained. Venus (or Mars) is conveniently obtainable. It does not follow of course that an out-of-bounds Venus or Mars is a necessary prerequisite for sex appeal, but as these two planets are the eternally oppositely attracting gender poles their magnification is bound to have an effect on those whose sex they symbolise.

Footnote: Clint Eastwood

As a footnote to this piece it is interesting to observe the case of another famous show business personality with Venus out of bounds, the film star Clint Eastwood.

Eastwood not only has Venus out of bounds but also the Moon. In other words both the female planets on his chart are emphasised. It is certainly true that he falls into the sex symbol bracket, attracting women, but the screen persona for which he became famous could hardly be more violent and macho. The strong, silent killer would seem a million miles from such a 'feminine' man, although his gift of "dynamic lethargy" - as fellow actor Richard Burton described his talent - is a very good description of the wildness of the out-of-bounds condition as it relates to the passive planets. (Another entertainer with a similar OOB Moon and Venus "dynamic lethargy" was the actor/singer Dean Martin).[47]

It has also often been noted that Clint Eastwood had an uncanny instinct to make career moves successfully timed to public taste. This would be the influence of the Moon, especially as it is almost exactly parallel to the benefic Venus. To quote the man himself: "Everybody has to have an edge and my edge is instinct".[48]

As a life-long music lover (Venus) the first film that Eastwood directed and starred in himself was built around a song: *Play Misty for Me* (1971), the story of a man harassed and stalked by a woman. Like almost all the movies he chose to direct, in contrast to those in which he was directed, he ensured strong roles for female characters. (Moon-Venus). He later fulfilled a long-held ambition to direct a film in which music played an even more central role. *Bird* (1988) was in homage to the jazz musician Charlie Parker.

---

47.   Dean Martin: 17 June 1917. 11.55pm CST. Steubenville, Ohio, USA. Source: Rodden 'A' rating.
48.   Clint Eastwood in an interview with Douglas Thompson, quoted in Thompson's book *Clint Eastwood Sexual Cowboy*, Smith Gryphon, London, 1992.

Clint Eastwood

31 May 1930. 5.35pm. San Francisco, California, USA 37N46 122W25 [49]

SUN	21N56
MOON	24N49 (OOB)
MERCURY	15N10
VENUS	24N44 (OOB)
MARS	10N00
JUPITER	23N04
SATURN	22S18
URANUS	05N04
NEPTUNE	11N46
PLUTO	22N07
NORTH NODE	12N15
SOUTH NODE	12S15
ASCENDANT	17S22
MIDHEAVEN	12N11

MOON	24N49 (OOB)
VENUS	24N44 (OOB)
JUPITER	23N04
PLUTO	22N07
SUN	21N56
MERCURY	15N10
NORTH NODE	12N15
MIDHEAVEN	12N11
NEPTUNE	11N46
MARS	10N00
URANUS	05N04

SOUTH NODE	12S15
ASCENDANT	17S22
SATURN	22S18

---

49. Source: From birth certificate. Lois M. Rodden, *'The American Book of Charts'* ACS, San Diego, 1980.

OOB Tales: A Most Unusual Mouse

Mickey Mouse:
Moon, Venus and Mars out of bounds. Uranus at zero.
Cartoon characters are an interesting study. Taking their first screen appearances in public as their dates of birth we find that strong-arm Popeye was born with Mars out of bounds, spluttering Donald Duck had Mercury out of bounds, Pluto the loveable family dog had the Moon out of bounds, and so it goes on.[50] But Mickey Mouse, the most famous of them all, has an intriguingly complex chart with the Moon, Venus and Mars, all out of bounds. This strangely makes him the least knowable of all these humorous caricatures.

Mickey Mouse
First public showing of *Steamboat Willie*
18 November 1928. The Colony Theater, New York City, NY. USA
40N45 73W57.[51]
(Positions shown for noon)

SUN	19S18
MOON	23S43 (OOB)
MERCURY	13S07
VENUS	25S17 (OOB)
MARS	24N54 (OOB)
JUPITER	11N05
SATURN	21S45
URANUS	00N48
NEPTUNE	11N32
PLUTO	21N31
NORTH NODE	20N16
SOUTH NODE	20S16

---

50. Popeye: 11 April 1929 (comic strip). Source: Internet.
    Donald Duck: 9 June 1934. Source: as for Mickey Mouse below.
    Pluto: 18 August 1930. Source: as for Mickey Mouse below.
51. Mickey Mouse. Chart taken for 12 Noon. Source: Astrological Association data section quotes "official Disney archives". *The Astrological Journal Newsletter*, London, May 1992.

MARS	24N54 (OOB)
PLUTO	21N31
NORTH NODE	20N16
NEPTUNE	11N32
JUPITER	11N05
URANUS	00N48

MERCURY	13S07
SUN	19S18
SOUTH NODE	20S16
SATURN	21S45
MOON	23S43 (OOB)
VENUS	25S17 (OOB)

In *Steamboat Willie* and other early film appearances Mickey is quite an assertive Mars-like action-man character - or action-mouse character - rescuing his girlfriend Minnie, who also shares the same birth date, in the melodramatic fashion of the day. Both the out-of-bounds Venus and Mars are on full display in the exaggerated sexual archetypes of Mickey and Minnie as masculine and feminine principles. From an audience's point of view there were three potent unconscious out-of-bounds hooks here. While the powerful OOB Moon provided general public popularity, the OOB Venus and Mars brought specific male and female fascination. We have already speculated that people with personal planets out of bounds provide easy targets for the unconscious projections of the opposite sex that they symbolise and here are those factors in abundance.

Later in his film career Mickey Mouse became more of a straight man to the comic antics of Pluto and others, but we can see from the astrology that Mickey had the successful potential of being virtually anything to anybody. Millions of children over the years have projected a personality on to their Mickey Mouse toys and dolls in a way that is perhaps not quite so possible with others like Donald Duck etc., who already have strong identifiable characters. Mickey is obligingly flexible in this regard. Although he is massively famous he can still be personally available to each and every one. Either that or we feel we do not know him at all.

Another declinational feature of Mickey Mouse's birth is Uranus just above the zero line. Similar in certain ways to his Aquarian Moon, there is something distinctly original about Mickey Mouse that in his wider context as the figurehead of an organisation, represents pioneering innovation and new modes of seeing. In this and in other ways he is tied to the genius of his creator Walt Disney.

Walt Disney
5 December 1901. 01:35am
Chicago IL. USA 41N52 87W39 [52]

SUN	22S18
MOON	06S31
MERCURY	18S35
VENUS	22S48
MARS	24S16 (OOB)
JUPITER	22S48
SATURN	22S26
URANUS	22S51
NEPTUNE	22N15
PLUTO	13N37
NORTH NODE	15S51
SOUTH NODE	15N51
NEPTUNE	22N15
SOUTH NODE	15N51
PLUTO	13N37
MOON	06S31
NORTH NODE	15S51
MERCURY	18S35
SUN	22S18
SATURN	22S26
VENUS	22S48
JUPITER	22S48
URANUS	22S51
MARS	24S16 (OOB)

---

52. Source: Astrological Association data base. Time of birth "speculative".

Walt Disney also has a striking declinational chart. The artistic abundance of an exact Venus parallel Jupiter is also in the same degree as his Sun. Whatever disputes there may be over his actual time of birth[53] it does not alter the facts displayed here. There is only the one out-of-bounds planet, Mars at 24S16, midway between Mickey's OOB Moon and Venus, but there are no less than six planets all situated in the same degree, the 23rd South - as is Mars if it is brought back inbounds, thereby making seven. Moreover all of these southern boundary energies are contra-parallel a solitary Neptune in the 23rd degree North. An extremely powerful weight of organised inspiration finds outer expression through the artistic and imaginative Neptune.

---

53. After writing this piece I found that Charles Jayne had examined Disney's chart some years ago in *Parallels: Their Hidden Meaning* as an example of how much would be lost in interpretation without the declination view. He used a time of birth of 00.30am CST.

4

The Two Hemispheres

The equator that divides our globe is of paramount importance in the study and measurement of declination. By extending it into space we will measure all stars and planets in distances north or south of this line; the northern and southern divisions will have characteristics of their own.

The northern declination signs of Aries to Virgo were once called the Commanding signs[54] while Libra to Pisces were the Obeying or Obedient signs. Northern hemisphere signs were also known as 'boreal' signs after Boreas the Greek god of the North Wind.

Boreas, son of the Dawn and the Stars, was a straightforward character, a model in that respect of the direct and external attributes of North declination. In mythology he was unable to woo Orithyia, the nymph he loved, because he lacked the necessary subtlety and gentleness. Eventually he carried her off by force. Had he possessed more the qualities of Auster, the South Wind (South declination), he might perhaps have found her more amenable to his advances.

North and South declination are not simply extravert and introvert respectively but the idea of the outreaching forthright energy of Aries, which begins the Sun's journey, and the musing meditative Pisces which ends it, can sum up the different meaning of the hemispheres. In 1941 Horicks and Michaux suggested that North declination was more "dynamic" and South declination more "stable"[55]. Dane Rudhyar in his essay *The Latitude Cycle* equated North to cosmic power and South more to the biological and emotional energy[56]. John Willner related North declination to outgoing energies with effects on others and South Declination to incoming energies and effects on oneself.[57] He also likened Northern and Southern declinations to the upper and lower hemispheres in longitude. Just as astrology has equated

---

54. Ptolemy. *Tetrabiblios*.
55. Quoted by Geoffrey Dean in *Recent Advances in Natal Astrology* 1977. Quoted by Karen Christino in *The Other Dimension*, Spring 1999.
56. Dane Rudhyar, *Person Centred Astrology*, Aurora Press, New York, 1980.
57. John Willner, *Considerations, Volume XI number 4*, New York, 1996. and *The Powerful Declinations*, AFA, Tempe, 1998.

the daylight half of the birthchart (the upper area of houses 7 to 12) with worldly objective experience and the lower night-time area of houses 1 to 6 as more inward and subjective, so the upper and lower hemispheres in declination are somewhat similarly defined.

The line of zero declination that divides the two hemispheres, the equator, is an important demarcation. It relates to the ingress into Aries, the beginning of cycles, and the bringing of new things into reality. C.C. Zain suggested that "when a planet moves from south declination to north declination there is a definite change of polarity which marks itself in the astral substance which environs the world"[58] and he likened the new cycle to a "birth"[59]. Planets close to the zero line therefore represent new energies impatient to burst into being.[60] Nelda Tanner has likened them to energies needing development "like teaching a baby"[61]. The slower-moving planets are more generational in this respect, hovering around the same place for months if not years and therefore affecting the wider course of human history, but the seven traditional planets from Sun to Saturn hold a personal importance when situated near zero. There is a magnification of the particular energy involved and a new cycle of influence regarding the factors associated with that planet.[62] The equator can also be called a life-and-death position in a regenerative sense, because it represents the birth of the Sun at the Spring Equinox or the ebbing of its power after the Autumn Equinox.

---

58. C.C.Zain, *Mundane Astrology*, Church of Light, Brea, California, 1999. Originally copyright Elbert Benjamine 1935.
59. See above.
60. Zain says a planet crossing the zero line "tends to bring a response from the physical environment".
61. Nelda L.Tanner specifically addressed research to the zero point and solstices and published her conclusions in 'Introducing the Life Diagram', The Other Dimension, Vol.1, No.3, October 1996, 'How to Read Life Declination Graphs' and 'Data Time Watch' both in The Other Dimension Spring 2003, multiple taped lectures from 1987-2001 and articles for AFA Today's Astrologer in the 1980s and 90s.
62. C.C.Zain, *Mundane Astrology* Church of Light, Brea, California, 1999. Originally copyright Elbert Benjamine 1935.

Science Fiction and Soap Opera

North versus South

As the cosmos speaks through events as well as people, what follows is an examination of the effect of the declinations of planets north, south and out of bounds at the birth of television shows - the first public broadcast of a series taken as the relevant chart.

Two possible out-of-bounds television genres immediately stand out: Soap Opera and Science Fiction, both of which go beyond the norm in some way. In Soap Opera it is emotion that reaches extremes, whereas in Science Fiction it is more the imagination that takes flight. In both cases one might expect to encounter out-of-bounds planets especially perhaps an OOB Moon. As Science Fiction is always going somewhere while Soap Opera usually remains in one setting finding the drama and intrigue within itself, the difference between southern and northern declinations might also become apparent.

In fact we find this to be true when we examine the first known examples of Science Fiction and Soap Opera on television. Neither of these TV programmes may be particularly sophisticated examples of their art by today's standards, but they were prototypes and as such should be relevant to their categories as a whole.

The first TV Soap Opera: *Faraway Hill* [63]
2 October 1946. 9pm. New York City, NY. USA 40N45 73W57.

SUN	03S40
MOON	25S13 (OOB)
MERCURY	08S59
VENUS	23S16
MARS	13S29
JUPITER	11S05
SATURN	18N54
URANUS	23N16
NEPTUNE	02S00
PLUTO	23N10

---

63. Source for all American shows in this section: *The Complete Directory to Prime Time Network and Cable TV Shows*, Tim Brooks & Earl Marsh, Ballantine, NY. 1999.

URANUS	23N16
PLUTO	23N10
SATURN	18N54

NEPTUNE	02S00
SUN	03S40
MERCURY	08S59
JUPITER	11S05
MARS	13S29
VENUS	23S16
MOON	25S13 (OOB)

(Moon out of bounds, 7 out of 10 planets - including all personal planets - in southern declination)

The first TV Science Fiction: *Captain Video*
27 June 1949. 7pm. New York, USA 40N45 73W57

SUN	23N19
MOON	26N00 (OOB)
MERCURY	19N11
VENUS	22N30
MARS	22N29
JUPITER	20S35
SATURN	12N17
URANUS	23N39 (OOB)
NEPTUNE	03S26
PLUTO	23N38 (OOB)

MOON	26N00 (OOB)
URANUS	23N39 (OOB)
PLUTO	23N38 (OOB)
SUN	23N19
VENUS	22N30
MARS	22N29
MERCURY	19N11
SATURN	12N17

```
NEPTUNE              03S26
JUPITER              20S35
```

(Moon, Uranus and Pluto out of bounds, 8 out of 10 planets - including all personal planets - in northern declination).

It will be noted that both of these programmes had the Moon out of bounds. In the first example the OOB Moon was in southern declination, in the second example it is in the north.

Faraway Hill

A chart for the short-lived series *Faraway Hill* shows Neptune conjunct and parallel the Sun in Libra, a fitting signature for the fantasy/relationship element of Soap Opera. Yet the Sun and Neptune were also close to the zero line and squaring an out-of-bounds Capricorn Moon in the seventh house, so harsher realities and extremes of emotional heartache were on offer too. Plenty of passion and jealousy came from a Scorpio Venus and Mars, and Venus contra-paralleling Uranus from high and low extremities spelt out some unexpected relationship twists (Venus: 23S16, Uranus: 23N16). In all it was a pretty good formula for the tangled web of a doom-laden weepy. But it is the wild southern out-of-bounds Moon that over-rides it all, going beyond expectancy into uncharted realms of sensitivity and emotional excess.

The focus on southern declination here seems to confirm a more inward karma-resolving search[64], and how the depicted events affected the feelings of one woman in particular (the fictional character Karen St John). One of the unusual features of this show was the ability of this main female character to speak her innermost thoughts aloud on screen behind the normal action and dialogue. While this was obviously because early TV was still following the way it had worked on radio, it might also reflect the delving into the workings and motivations behind outer reality with which southern declination is more concerned.

---

64. See Helen Adams Garrett, *Karma by Declination*, AFA, Tempe, 1982.

Captain Video and his Video Rangers

This show began with the Sun and Moon in high declinations in Cancer and its theme music was Wagner's *Flying Dutchman*.[65] Cancer is the solstice height with any occupying planets in this sign usually on or beyond the northern boundary. The *Captain Video* Moon at 26°00' North was certainly beyond the boundary, and this plus the Sun conjunct Uranus (and Sun parallel OOB Uranus and OOB Pluto), brought in a futuristic as well as a powerful inventive energy to the proceedings. As well as a somewhat quirky one.

Captain Video embodied all these high declination planets (especially Sun/Uranus/Pluto), as an action-man, a gifted scientist and a guardian of the world. He dressed in a uniform that looked suspiciously like an ex-US military cast-off from the 2nd World War, and with his young sidekick and other Video Rangers he played spaceman on the screen for the benefit of a whole generation of American children. (Emphasis again on the Moon). It was by all accounts a crazy mix of old cowboy films, all-American values, evil-genius enemies and the cheapest budget possible for special effects, (Jupiter's not riding high with the rest on this chart). But children loved it and it ran for six years until 1955.

With its northerly declinations and out-of-bounds planets *Captain Video* demonstrates a futuristic shot into the outer limits. There is a forward-looking, future-building energy, and alongside plenty of action Captain Video is concerned with events that affect others (or that affect the entire population of the world even), as opposed to the southern declination (Soap Opera) focus on how events affect the self.

In declination the zero line of the equinoxes shares an energy of power and change with the high degrees of the solstices. These are all critical zones. We find that some of the most celebrated science fiction TV shows mirror the *Captain Video* extremes by choosing starting dates that either have out-of-bounds planets or planets crossing the zero line.

Please note it is easier to identify those television programmes in the Science Fiction category than it is in Soap Opera. The latter, though just as popular on television, tends to be indigenous to its area or country and does not export or travel well, so few titles are internationally known. Science Fiction on the other hand has a broader multicultural appeal, and we examine a few well-known examples over the page:

---

65.   Holland is traditionally ruled by Cancer.

Science Fiction

The Twilight Zone, (2 October 1959. 10pm. EST. New York) was truly born in the twilight zone with the burst of a New Moon in Libra just south of the zero boundary. (New Moon earlier that day at 8°34' Libra). Part of its regular opening spoke of "the middle ground between light and shadow" - which is precisely where it was. But this show had much more of a focus on southern declination than north, more like the Soap Opera, with 7 out of 10 planets - including Sun and Moon - in the south. Unlike the basic science fiction of *Captain Video*, the stories in *The Twilight Zone* were rarely set in the future, concentrating instead on the strange dimensions to be accessed in the human mind from a starting point of the present. Very often this was how the world seemed through the inner eyes of one particular person. Whenever the phrase 'psychological thrillers' can be applied, we appear to be more in the province of southern declination.

The Outer Limits, (16 September 1963. 7.30pm EST. New York), had the Sun, Mercury, Venus and Jupiter all clustered in parallel and contra-parallel above and below the zero line. The count of planets in northern and southern declinations here were more or less equal (6 north, 4 south). "We will control the horizontal. We will control the vertical", boomed the voice of control each week. Accordingly some stories were definitely set in the future while others impinged back on the present.

Star Trek, (8 September 1966. 8.30pm. EST. New York), follows the classic futuristic science fiction pattern with 8 out of 10 planets in northern declination including an out-of-bounds Moon. Captain Kirk and his crew were firmly off in Star Date three thousand and something "to explore strange new worlds...seek out life...and boldly go" etc. As this is now regarded as the most famous television *sf* series ever, its chart could also be taken as a template. Accordingly its declinations are given below:

SUN	05N34
MOON	26N37 (OOB)
MERCURY	07N36
VENUS	12N33
MARS	19N02
JUPITER	20N57

SATURN	03S25
URANUS	04N44
NEPTUNE	16S02
PLUTO	17N47
MOON	26N37 (OOB)
JUPITER	20N57
MARS	19N02
PLUTO	17N47
VENUS	12N33
MERCURY	07N36
SUN	05N34
URANUS	04N44
SATURN	03S25
NEPTUNE	16S02

(Moon out of bounds, 8 out of 10 planets - including all personal planets - in northern declination)

Doctor Who, (23 November 1963. 5.16pm. London [66]), also follows the out-of-bounds pattern with three personal planets (Mercury, Venus and Mars) all beyond the Sun's boundaries. But this time the direction is south, and the limits being broken here are those of Time itself. Unlike *Captain Video* and *Star Trek* this quest is not only set in the future but also in the past. The Time Traveller of the title has come back to the Earth *from* the future, and 7 out of the 10 planets (including the Sun and Moon) are now in southern declination. The sense of mystery, an element that appears to be a hallmark of southern declinations, is also captured in the title of the show. And the ability of the Doctor to change his physical appearance periodically is helped by an out-of-bounds Mercury and the general mutability of his birth chart.

The Invaders, (10 January 1967. 8.30pm. EST. New York), also had planets out-of-bounds south: Moon 26S00, Mercury 24S11, as did **The Prisoner**

---

66. Source: Howe, Stammers and Walker, *'Doctor Who: The Sixties'*, Virgin, London, 1993. Actual time of first broadcast quoted as 5:16:20 pm.

(29 September 1967. 9.30pm. London [67]) with an OOB Mars at 24S01. Both of these popular shows could be termed psychological thrillers playing on irrational fears and secret menace, and both were seen through the eyes of just one character who appeared to be alone in a desperate need to unmask the truth, (southern declination dilemmas). Both stories were also set in the present rather than the future.

We could no doubt continue with many more examples and still have barely scratched the surface, but there is another interesting point to be considered regarding north and south declination. Remembering that any planet situated in the tropical signs Aries to Virgo will most likely be in north declination, and any planet in Libra to Pisces in south declination, there will be times when all three outer planets are in the south. (For example 1988 to 2010). If in addition we are examining a birth date that falls between late September and late March, when the Sun is between Libra and Pisces, there is a good chance that at least half the ten planets or more will be in southern declination at any time, and this is obviously intensified when the Moon is below the zero line.

What I am saying is that some periods - some decades - are more likely to produce a mindset of futuristic optimism (a *Star Trek* mindset), than others. In the late twentieth century and early twenty-first century the energy of working through the tangled and complicated webs of interaction and results of past deeds are connected with the southern declination focus. From the time of Pluto's discovery, both Pluto and Uranus were in northern signs for at least four decades from the 1930s to the 1960s (inclusive). Pluto would finally cross the line south in the late 1980s. Neptune was also in northern declination for the first half of the twentieth century until it crossed the line into the south in 1943. So at least two out of three of the heavyweight generational planets were still giving the human race a basically progressive and rosy belief in the future throughout the 1930s, 1940s, the 50s and the 60s.

After that time, and again this would be intensified according to the time of year, the future did not seem so straightforwardly open to conquest as it once did to either Captain Kirk or Captain Video. The typical example of a successful television science fiction series in the latter years of the twentieth century is illustrated by **The X Files** (10 September 1993. 9pm.

---

67.   Source: '*Six of One*', The Prisoner Appreciation Society, P.O.Box 66, Ipswich, IP2 9TZ, England.

EST. New York) - concerned with secret files and cover-ups - where we find 6 out of 10 planets in the south. Also, though more strictly labelled Fantasy than Science Fiction, **Buffy the Vampire Slayer** (10 March 1997. 9pm EST. New York) is definitely a southern declination phenomenon, with 7 out of 10 planets in the south. This is an interesting declination chart with all personal planets hanging above or below the life and death zero line.

As for the television programmes that people watch, the chances are that most new series will continue to premiere between September and March (between the Autumn to Spring Equinox). And if so the Sun at least will be inclined towards the inner mysteries of the human condition as it travels the southern dimensions. We can therefore be sure that plenty more of the entertainment that pleases the public will continue to be on offer.

Omar Khayyám and the Seven-Ringed Cup

> Iram indeed is gone with all his Rose
> And Jamsh'yd's Sev'n-ring'd Cup where no one knows
> But still a Ruby gushes from the Vine
> And many a Garden by the Water blows.
> (Omar Khayyám) [68]

Jupiter on zero
Iram was a fabulous garden planted in Arabia in the earliest of times and Jamsh'yd was a mythical king who was said to have reigned for 700 years. His intriguing "Seven-ringed Cup" in Omar Khayyám's verse refers to the divining qualities of the seven planets that were once held in perfect understanding. "Where is that Cup?" now asks the eleventh-century Persian sage, who seems to be looking back on a lost art with nostalgic regret. Omar Khayyám infers that his present day astrology held only a shadow of its former glory in terms of divination.

But this lost art apart, the celebrated astronomer-poet takes heart in life's more immediate pleasures. Omar Khayyám resigns himself to the passing

---

68. Quoted verses of Omar Khayyám in this passage are from the first, second and fifth edition of *The Rubáiyát of Omar Khayyám* by Edward FitzGerald, 1859, 1868 and 1889 respectively. The whole collected in *The Rubáiyát of Omar Khayyám, Khorasan Edition*, edited by George F.Maine, Collins, London, 1969.

of that time of a paradise on earth when the planets spoke directly and unambiguously to us and instead he suggests we grasp the salve of the present moment. "The ruby still gushes from the vine, and many a garden by the water blows".

Many of Omar's verses suggest that having searched hard for life's meaning at lofty levels like "the seventh throne of Saturn", and subsequently failed, he has turned back to the wisdom of the here and now, which in his case usually encompasses the pleasures of the Vine.

> Up from Earth's Centre through the Seventh Gate
> I rose, and on the throne of Saturn sate,
> And many a Knot unravel'd by the Road;
> But not the Master-knot of Human Fate

To my mind, one of the keys to Omar Khayyám, and to his Victorian translator Edward FitzGerald (1809-1883), is not so much Saturn as Jupiter. The great planet of the solar system (Jupiter) is mentioned by name in one of the verses under the Arabian name of *Mushtari*, and of course the poet's whole philosophy is concerned with the aspects of eat, drink and be merry, plus the deeper questioning of life itself. Omar questions his God. He believes in him but does not offer him much admiration when he doesn't act like Jupiter. He rails against Saturn at every turn:

> What! Out of senseless Nothing to provoke
> A conscious Something to resent the yoke
> Of unpermitted Pleasure, under pain
> Of Everlasting Penalties, if broke!

More typical of Old Omar is a verse like:

> Dreaming when dawn's left hand was in the sky
> I heard a voice within the tavern cry,
> Awake, my little ones, and fill the cup
> Before life's liquor in its cup be dry.

Omar Khayyám's birth date is difficult to substantiate. A birth chart is given for him in B.V Raman's *Notable Horoscopes* [69] with sources that certainly seem ancient. This chart with a birth date of 18 May 1048 is

---

69. B.V.Raman, *Notable Horoscopes*, published in Delhi, 1995. The birthdate of Omar Khayyam quoted by Professor P.S. Sastri in *The Astrological Magazine* December 1945 is from information given by Zahiruddin Abdul Hassan in his *Fatimma Siwan Al Hikmat*. Ascendant rectified to 3 Gemini by Swami Govinda Thirta in his book *Nectar of Grace*.

predominantly Air (Sun, Moon, Ascendant in Gemini) with Uranus at zero declination (in Air) trining Jupiter (in Air) trining a triple conjunction of Sun-Venus-Mercury (in Air), with Jupiter contra-parallel to Mercury (in Air). Freedom of thought and a radical wide-ranging outlook is attributable. Jupiter in Aquarius as part of a Grand Air Trine suggests tolerance and confidence in humanity with little time for restrictive religious codes. It is suggestive of the broader philosophy that would seep into European sensibility in the high medieval renaissance of the early 12th century and it all seems to fit the image of Omar Khayyám as a Jupiter-man.

We are on safer ground with the birth date of Edward FitzGerald (31 March 1809), without whom it must be said we would hardly be acquainted in the English-speaking world with Omar Khayyám at all. FitzGerald's renderings of the eleventh and twelfth century quatrains were far more than translations, they were a labour of love, capturing the spirit of the originals in a wholly poetic way. And it is no wonder that FitzGerald was especially attracted to the eat-drink-and-be-merry side of Omar's philosophy because he (FitzGerald) was born with Jupiter conjunct the Sun. More than that, Jupiter was crucially placed just above the zero line at 00N19. The entire exercise of expanding and reworking the multiple layers of meaning in the verses can be counted as much a life's work for FitzGerald as it was for Omar Khayyám. To Edward FitzGerald it was both an uplifting and a learning experience, illustrative of the meaning of Jupiter in this critical zero degree position. Jupiter was the ardent new energy eager to be expressed.

Edward FitzGerald
31 March 1809. Woodbridge, Suffolk, England 52N06 01E19. [70]
(Positions shown for noon)

SUN	04N06
MOON	05S21
MERCURY	08S15
VENUS	23N09
MARS	06S07
JUPITER	00N19*
SATURN	18S48
URANUS	13S59

70. Source: George F.Maine's essay on Edward FitzGerald the Man in 'The Rubáiyát of Omar Khayyám', Khorasan Edition, Collins, London, 1969.

NEPTUNE	19S50
PLUTO	18S58
NORTH NODE	12S36
SOUTH NODE	12N36
VENUS	23N09
SOUTH NODE	12N36
SUN	04N06
JUPITER	00N19*
MOON	05S21
MARS	06S07
MERCURY	08S15
NORTH NODE	12S36
URANUS	13S59
SATURN	18S48
PLUTO	18S58
NEPTUNE	19S50

Edward FitzGerald was born into a wealthy family and the need for his poetry to make money was never an issue. Neither, strangely, did he seek public recognition for his considerable literary talent as he published his various versions of The Rubáiyát anonymously and none would become famous until after his death. He was a popular person in life with many friends and wealth meant little to him. He lived simply, as a bohemian and rather eccentric figure. In material terms his extravagance was generally for the benefit of others less fortunate and he found ways of distributing money quietly to those in need. Biographers called him a "generous and big-hearted man"[71]. In this we see clear evidence of Jupiter the philanthropist.

FitzGerald certainly succeeded in manifesting the energy of Jupiter to the world both in the sense of his material generosity and more indirectly in the publishing of philosophical verses that would eventually bring pleasure to millions. These Jupiterian impulses were both undertaken with as little outward fuss as possible and fame and glory on the world stage did not come into it. In fact he seemed happy to avoid it.

If handled correctly, which means to continually work with it and learn from it, the zero line planet can enrich one's life but it is as much an

---

71. ibid.

inner energy working outward as an outer energy working inward. FitzGerald's Jupiter did not bring him the outer "luck" of having a large publisher swoop on his verses and insist on distributing them immediately to all corners of the globe. Instead in an uncharacteristically pessimistic moment Fitzgerald once wrote to one of his friends: "I hardly know why I print these things, which nobody buys; and I scarce now see the few I gave them to...."[72]

In terms of the enrichment to his life however, the quest and immersion in mystic Sufi philosophy and his ability to render it so warmly and buoyantly, is the true Jupiter gift. It is also typically Jupiterian that Edward FitzGerald did not make acquaintance with the work of Omar Khayyám until middle-life. He discovered an obscure manuscript of Omar Khayyám's 158 quatrains (written in purple ink on yellow paper and powdered in gold) at the Bodleian Library at Oxford. Jupiterian too is the fact that the only literary work he ever published under his own name was a translation of *Spanish* poetry.[73]

The seven-ringed cup is the pure distillation of the planetary energies from which we could once drink and be enlightened. It is a Grail. The verses in the Rubáiyát are fond of images of cups and clay urns but these vessels are generally found to be wanting in the enlightenment department, as in the following:

> Then to the Lip of this poor earthen Urn
> I lean'd, the secret Well of Life to learn:
> And Lip to Lip it murmur'd - "While you live,
> Drink! - for, once dead, you never shall return".

This of course can be read in two ways. On a straightforward level it could be saying don't waste your life searching for answers, drink the wine and enjoy today. But on a different level it suggests that we should never stop searching for answers, we should never stop drinking from the Well of Life. In the end it all depends what we understand the Cup in this verse to contain.

Jupiter on the line of zero declination is certainly an invitation to learn about life at the Tavern. And a tavern in early times was not just a drinking hole, the equivalent to the modern-day bar or pub, it was an inn - a place where pilgrims and travellers rested on their journeys. In Persia it was a caravanserai, a place where caravans halted for the night. Symbolically

---

72. Extract from a letter to Edward Byles Cowell dated 27 April 1859. Quoted in *The Rubáiyát of Omar Khayyám, Khorasan Edition*, edited by George F.Maine.
73. *Six Dramas of Calderon* 1853. Spain is traditionally ruled by Jupiter.

these are stages on life's journey where we stop and imbibe the inner philosophy of the spirit. To both Omar Khayyám and Edward FitzGerald life was understood as a continual pilgrimage to higher ground, a Jupiterian philosophy that FitzGerald tackled with humility and humour. His is an apt and positive illustration of Jupiter on the celestial equator.

Omar Khayyám

18 May 1048. Near sunrise. Naishápúr, Persia. 36N13 58E45

SUN	20N45
MOON	18N35
MERCURY	19N28
VENUS	22N25
MARS	12N16
JUPITER	19S13
SATURN	22S17
URANUS	00S27
NEPTUNE	03N44
PLUTO	26S33 (OOB)
NORTH NODE	03N37
SOUTH NODE	03S37

VENUS	22N25
SUN	20N45
MERCURY	19N28
MOON	18N35
MARS	12N16
NEPTUNE	03N44
NORTH NODE	03N37
URANUS	00S27
S.NODE	03S37
JUPITER	19S13
SATURN	22S17
PLUTO	26S33 (OOB)

But things can be very different when a zero-line planetary energy is not acknowledged, as we will see in the following account.

Cat People

A story of Neptune on the line

For all its astrological intangibility Neptune is quite regular and well behaved declination-wise. Apart from its retrograde wobbles it keeps a steady movement and it never goes out of bounds. Within the frame of the twentieth century Neptune began (in 1900) at 22 North, which was as far north as it could go, and slowly and surely moved southwards to reach 22 South (as far south as it could go) during the 1980s. By the end of the century it was at 19 South gradually moving upwards again.

For our purposes the most interesting time was just before the middle of the twentieth century when Neptune crossed the zero line. For a planet that cannot go out of bounds this should have marked one of its most noticeable manifestations.

Neptune hovered backwards and forwards over the zero line, positioned less than one degree either way, from November 1942 - March 1943, from September 1943 - September 1945 and lastly in June 1946, having gradually changed its position from north to south declination. Most of this coincided with a period of global conflict and is easy to equate with the meaning of collective ideals forced into the light, clashing and changing. But the beginning of this period (November/December 1942) saw two specific events that in symbolic and actual form could be described as illustrative of this. One is trivial the other is historic. The historic one was the splitting of the atom on 2 December 1942. The symbolic one was the release of a movie-film called **Cat People**.

Cat People, which premiered in New York on 6 December 1942, was credited to the combined work of a few creative souls but nevertheless sprang to life from a totally blank page. The director Val Lewton was given the title "Cat People" by his RKO bosses and required to make a black and white film of it, quickly and cheaply, to rival the success of Universal Studio's *The Wolf Man*. Yet instead of a silly horror movie the result was a superior psychological thriller that rescued RKO from going bankrupt and is widely honoured today as a Hollywood classic, especially in the *film noir* genre. Like all great art that falls into place quickly and easily it encompassed archetypal themes and it is not too far-fetched to suggest that it tapped into a major event that was entering the collective unconscious at this same time. As Zain says, a planet crossing the line marks its energy onto

118   Declination in Astrology

the world [74] and symbolically the movement of Neptune can be seen in *Cat People* as the unreal becoming real. We might learn more about the meaning of Neptune crossing the celestial equator by examining this film.

Cat People (First showing of movie)
Sunday 6 December 1942.[75]
The Rialto Theatre, New York, USA 40N45 73W57.
(Time of first showing unknown. Noon chart positions given below)

SUN	22S29
MOON	14S05
MERCURY	24S09 (OOB)
VENUS	23S13
MARS	18S33
JUPITER	21N28
SATURN	19N50
URANUS	20N26
NEPTUNE	00N29
PLUTO	23N23
NORTH NODE	12N07
SOUTH NODE	12S07
PLUTO	23N23
JUPITER	21N28
URANUS	20N26
SATURN	19N50
NORTH NODE	12N07
NEPTUNE	00N29
SOUTH NODE	12S07
MOON	14S05
MARS	18S33

---

74.   C.C.Zain *Mundane Astrology* Church of Light, Brea, California, 1999. Originally copyright Elbert Benjamine 1935.
75.   Source: Various movie reference books and sites. Kim Newman in '*Cat People*', British Film Institute, London, 2001, gives a date one day later (7 December 1942) as the film's first public showing. Whichever date is taken however the astrology pertinent to this analysis remains unchanged.

SUN	22S29
VENUS	23S13
MERCURY	24S09 (OOB)

We can see that apart from Neptune's critical position, Mercury is out of bounds. This helps to explain why this is primarily a film of the mind and why it is far from conventional in its depiction of psychiatry. The psychiatrist in the story is a rather untrustworthy character and is in many ways more of a rogue element than his patient - the woman who believes she can turn into a cat. The five personal planets Sun to Mars are all in southern declination bringing us into the labyrinthine undercurrents of the inner worlds and their emphasis on a search for the self. A further dimension is hinted through the use of declinational midpoints. The contra-parallel of the Sun and Pluto finds its exact midpoint at 00N27, two minutes away from Neptune. We can suspect that such striving for power may have a hint of martyrdom as it absorbs itself into this already powerfully positioned Neptune.

In essence *Cat People* is the haunting story of a woman who metamorphoses into a big cat (a black panther, as far as the shadowy Neptunian images reveal) when her emotions are significantly aroused. Like a planet close to the zero line, she is strongly influenced by these urges but is less than open about it (Neptune). This Neptune is splitting consciousness in a deceptive way. Irena Dubrovna, the cat woman character, is an immigrant artist from the Balkans who meets and falls in love with an American architect soon after her arrival in New York. The young couple get married but Irena is unable to consummate the marriage dreading that at the height of her emotion she will transform into a cat and tear her husband to pieces. At his suggestion she visits a psychiatrist, the first person to whom she confides her fear that she has inherited a curse that has run through her family for generations (since an event in European history when cats were slaughtered in the name of God). But the psychiatrist is too sophisticated to believe all this and tells her that she only thinks she turns into a cat and that it is all in the mind. The movie is made in such a way that at first we might be confused about this too.

The two wild energies on this chart are Neptune and Mercury and these can represent the characters of Irena, the artist, and Dr Judd, the psychiatrist, respectively. Like their planets neither of these two people are stable. Ideally Irena, representing Neptune near the zero line, needs to develop her energy in a positive fashion. The nocturnal, hunting, killing instincts of a cat are not the only feline options available here. The cat's legendary sixth sense could perhaps have been a better option to pursue, although with the intruding influence of the Sun-Pluto contra-parallel it has to be said that it might have been difficult for her to find power in other less intense ways. But her husband, perhaps inevitably with their sexual estrangement, starts to find a sympathetic female ear in one of his colleagues at work and this arouses Irena's jealousy and triggers the beast in her. Dr Judd meanwhile continues to act as if everything is in the head (Mercury) assuming that Irena's fear of intimacy has a textbook explanation. But he is an unethical character and is fatally attracted, as a logical mind might be, to his illogical Neptunian patient and unwisely he tries to ravish her. (We see shades of the Sun-Pluto tension again). The desire to dominate comes to the surface, arousing Irena's retaliatory anger and her need to unleash power. Accordingly she transforms into a cat and kills him, but not before he has wounded her badly in the fight. As a result she also dies soon after.

What this film illustrates about Neptune - or any planet within one degree of the zero line - is that its qualities are close to the surface of physical response and simply cannot be ignored. On one level Neptune, the planet of imagery on film, produced a stunning piece of visual art whose whole ambience blurs the edges of reality while sharply engaging the feelings of the viewer. But on another level the story itself challenges assumptions of what is real and what is unreal and highlights the danger of not allowing an unknown energy to be openly discussed or taken seriously. In the real world The Splitting of the Atom was a seminal moment as it opened a new dimension to life on Earth. Nothing could be quite the same again. Because this happened in wartime Science was in the hands of the few, and scientific breakthroughs and discoveries were necessarily kept secret and hidden from the public. The eventual result was that a general mistrust or fear of Science slowly began to spread. As Barbara Hand Clow says in her book *Chiron. The Rainbow Bridge*: "When the atom was split, you were split".[76]

Cat People is about someone who was literally split between human and feline. The fantastic dreamlike truth of this is something that even the main character in the story tries to deny, with the result that it all ends in tragedy. A planet on zero must be allowed its expression because its compulsion to prominence is unfaltering. One of Neptune's keywords is 'belief' and at this uncertain time in the 1940s many people's beliefs were

---

76. Barbara Hand Clow, *Chiron: Rainbow Bridge Between the Inner & Outer Planets*, Llewellyn, St Paul, 1988.

enhanced or shattered according to their experience of war. Prayers, seances and occult dabblings were intensely magnified and practised around the globe. And yet another religion on the rise was Science itself. In Neptunian fashion the possible positive benefits of events like Splitting the Atom would be largely dissolved and mistrusted in the public mind after the horrors of its use as a bomb.

This confusion over belief, in the story of *Cat People*, is evidenced in the fact that some viewers and commentators on the film today will still insist that the story is purely psychological and that we are intended to believe that the main character never does turn into a cat at all. This is Neptunian deception on a large scale, as there are certain cinematic elements that cannot be wished away, like a tracking shot of paw-prints gradually turning into a woman's shoe-prints, and certain indoor items clawed to shreds. The filmmakers were not producing a documentary report, they were telling a story, allowing fantasy into an everyday setting. It is understandable that an intellectual movie critic would not want an intelligent film to descend to the level of a cheap horror movie, but the story is a Neptunian one and should be taken at face value and in that spirit.

Lastly it is interesting that *Cat People* is set in New York, although this is not necessary to the plot and it could be any urban city. In fact the location is hinted rather than made specific, almost as if this was New York in another dimension. (Because of budget constraints the entire movie was actually shot indoors in Hollywood so there is an inevitable unreality about it). But the City of Kong, as we might term the Hollywood version of New York, has always been a magnet for the irrational. Its awe-inspiring skyscrapers, testifying the high-reaching intellect of Man, have been the perfect backdrop for invasion by monsters from the darker side of existence, like King Kong or The Beast from 20,000 Fathoms. Civilised New York has always attracted Neptune and it is not surprising that a film of this type should choose to be set there. Whether that will remain so in the future, after 2001 when the unreal did become real, is open to question.

Liverpool: Scorpionic City of Dreams

Venus and Neptune at zero

We turn now to a different port and city, across the Atlantic from New York. The declinations of the birth chart of the City of Liverpool are shown below, highlighting both Venus and Neptune in contra-parallel astride the zero line.

Liverpool - Natal Chart
28 August 1207. 12:00 noon (LMT +0:12)[77]
Liverpool, England 53N25 03W00.

SUN	07N24
MOON	14S04
MERCURY	01N50
VENUS	00N26
MARS	12S42
JUPITER	22N07
SATURN	22N09
URANUS	13N09
NEPTUNE	00S23
PLUTO	25N59 (OOB)
NORTH NODE	11S26
SOUTH NODE	11N26
ASCENDANT	17S47
MIDHEAVEN	07N15
PLUTO	25N59 (OOB)
SATURN	22N09
JUPITER	22N07
URANUS	13N09
SOUTH NODE	11N26
SUN	07N24
MIDHEAVEN	07N15
MERCURY	01N50
VENUS	00N26

---

77. Source: Traditional Quoted by Zadkiel and earlier. See footnote 78.

NEPTUNE	00S23
NORTH NODE	11S26
MARS	12S42
MOON	14S04
ASCENDANT	17S47

Traditionally the City of Liverpool is ruled by Scorpio. The etymology of the name Liverpool - *lifer-pool* in Old English - is said to mean "a muddy pool". Similarly, though not etymologically, a lifer-pool suggests a pool of life. The Scorpio rulership of this regenerative city seems justified as the sign of Scorpio also rules dark pools and muddy transformational places. Murkily similarly is *scouse*, an adjective describing the Liverpudlian people

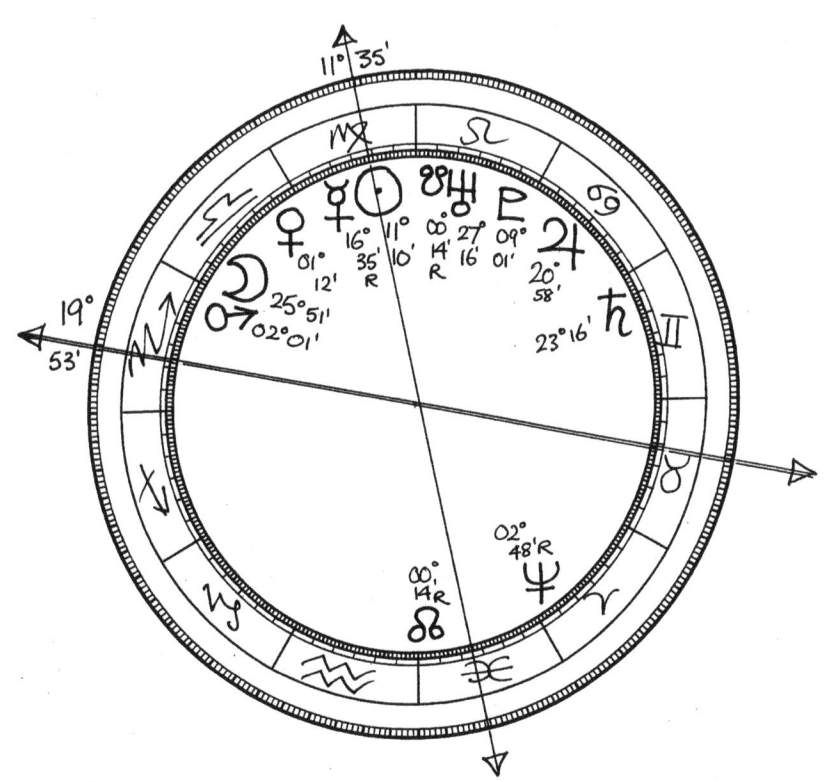

Chart for Liverpool. 28 August 1207. Noon

and their accent. The word is short for *lobscouse*, a thick soup native to the area. Once again we find ourselves peering into unclear waters.

Charles Carter quotes the Scorpio rulership of Liverpool in *An Introduction to Political Astrology*, giving H.S.Green as his direct source. But the tradition goes way back to Liverpool's borough foundation chart: 28 August 1207, local noon, which has a Scorpio ascendant.[78]

The Scorpio rising chart with the Moon in Libra and the Sun on the midheaven in Virgo is relevant to a study of the history of the city, but declination gives us an additional picture. Venus and Neptune immediately stand out as critical influences, their placement less than one degree from the equinoctial zero line. If you ask anyone who doesn't actually live there "What is Liverpool famous for?" they will most likely reply "sea trade" (Liverpool had eight miles of docks) or "The Beatles". The connection with the sea is obviously Neptune; the connection with music and artistry is Venus.

Both these planets are not only close to zero, they are also contra-parallel to each other - almost exactly. Venus is positioned above the equator (00N26) but in a southern zodiac sign (1°12' Libra) while Neptune is positioned below the equator (00S23) but in a northern sign (2°48'R Aries). The sympathetic pair are tied together in an unusual dynamic that, given the nature of the two planets and the ever-present influence of the Scorpio ascendant, leads to an intense self-containment, an imaginative idealism or delusory romanticism.[79] There is inspiration in the depths but it shifts and is difficult to grasp. A typical example is Joseph Williamson, the so-called "Mole of Edge Hill", a wealthy Victorian philanthropist who instigated the building of a vast underground system of tunnels and chambers beneath parts of Liverpool, which he then bricked up as soon as they were built. These labyrinths led nowhere and the chambers housed nothing and no one has ever been certain that they had any purpose at all. Williamson had made his money through tobacco (Neptune) and may have planned his underground mazes with a similar Neptunian aim - this time simply a

---

78. Correspondence in *The Astrologers' Quarterly*, Winter 1970, states that Liverpool's Scorpio rising horoscope "has been known since medieval times and it was Cmdr Morrison who in the mid 19th century publicised it in his writings" [Letter from R. Marshall Harmer]. Commander R.J.Morrison was better known as the astrologer Zadkiel.
79. "Deranged idealism seeps into the water table of Liverpool, bubbling up in the spurts of left-wing utopianism". Matthew de Abritur, on Liverpool in *Crap Towns*, Boxtree, London, 2003.

compassionate one - of providing years of paid building work for the unemployed.

In more modern times Liverpool's fortune and reputation continues to ebb and flow dramatically. In the 1960s by conventional astrology the mighty Uranus-Pluto conjunction was activating the Virgo Sun and midheaven of the Liverpool chart, while the third outer giant, Neptune, was transiting its Scorpio ascendant. All three outer planets were affecting this horoscope in the same period as Liverpool's diminishing importance as a sea port was giving way to a revolutionary new reputation as a musical city of dreams. Declination backs this up. In 1964 and 65 Uranus was at 7 degrees North transiting the Liverpool Sun while Neptune was hovering at 14 degrees South transiting the Liverpool Moon.

The glamour of the 1960s was short-lived and Neptune and Venus soon seemed a passing reverie. A decade later unemployment was biting hard and Liverpool's traditional industries continued to downturn. By the time that Pluto entered Scorpio in the 1980s Liverpool was at one of its periodic low ebbs. At the end of that decade transiting Pluto by declination had reached the life-and-death zero line and was hovering back and forth over the celestial equator activating Venus and Neptune directly, and indirectly through their midpoint. In the spring of 1989, as Pluto touched Neptune for its last short run before moving away to the south, a profound collective emotion was triggered. To an astrologer the outer illustration of the Pluto transit was apparent when two million local people covered the Liverpool football ground at Anfield in wreaths to commemorate 96 football supporters who had died in a terrace crush accident in a game away from home. At this shrine to the dead (Pluto-Neptune) the soul of the city lay stark and bare with grief and was obvious for all to see (zero-line = "response from physical environment" [80]).

Then came the rebirth. From the beginning of the 1990s as Pluto transited the degree of the Scorpio ascendant, the city started to regenerate. Venus and Neptune are highly artistic planets and their critical positions demanded to be taken seriously. During the following years, amongst other social rejuvenation, Liverpool Airport was renamed John Lennon Airport ("above us only sky"), Paul McCartney's boyhood home was purchased and opened as a site of national importance, while cultural tours of the city, "Magical Mystery" and otherwise, became a flourishing business. An annual Beatles Week in the last week of August began attracting huge numbers of

---

80. C.C.Zain.

visitors, and how apt that this celebration should take place each year on the anniversary of the Liverpool birth date, thereby recharging its solar return batteries in the process.

At last Liverpool was officially accepting its art. The critical planets were being acknowledged and by the early twenty-first century the phoenix had risen so far that Liverpool had won the coveted title 'European Capital of Culture'.

The Elephant Man

Pluto at zero

Joseph Merrick, the hideously deformed Elephant Man, was born on one of the only five days in the nineteenth century when Pluto stood exactly on the line of zero declination. With dark rough skin erupting from his misshapen body he was later diagnosed as having the most extreme form ever known of *Proteus syndrome*, a disease named after the god who would take a variety of different shapes as he transformed himself.[81] Perhaps nothing more drastically illustrates the personal expression of a zero-line planetary energy than this case.

There is no surviving record of the actual hour of Merrick's birth in Leicester, England on 5 August 1862 but using seconds of arc Pluto was precisely on the celestial equator at 00°00'00" declination for approximately three hours during the morning of that day centred around 10am. We can only speculate whether Joseph Merrick entered the world at that particular hour but in any event it was a highly Plutonian day.

To put the rarity of this measurement into perspective: although Pluto wobbled up and down over the zero line five times between 1862 and 1864, it would not reach zero again until well over a hundred years later (in the late 1980s). In the twenty-first century it will not reach zero at all; and its next activation of this kind is in 2107.

Merrick was born on the second of Pluto's five short passes across the equator; which meant that Pluto was retrograding back from north to south

---

81.   "Proteus...resorted to his arts, becoming first a fire, then a flood, then a horrible wild beast..." A description of Proteus in the story of Aristaeus the Bee-Keeper, from *Bulfinch's Mythology*, Spring books, London, 1964.

on his birth date although the overall direction of Pluto was south to north after a stay of 130-odd years in southern declination.[82]

Obviously being born with Pluto on zero does not make you an elephant man but it impels some kind of drastic transformation into the light. Joseph Merrick was unknowingly an outer symbol of an underground Pluto emerging and temporarily returning to its unknown realm of nightmare. Merrick's disease worsened as he got older so it is possible that others born with a similar condition may have died in infancy and never been generally known to either the public or the medical establishment of the day. Joseph Merrick however did become famous in his lifetime and eventually found a measure of understanding and acceptance from the establishment after having suffered years of torment and social ostracism. Although he was naturally a friendly and cheerful soul he was forced into prominence as the embodiment of something dark and hideous (Pluto).

Joseph Merrick - The Elephant Man
5 August 1862. Symbolically timed at 10am. [83]
Leicester, England 52N38 01W05.

SUN	17N01
MOON	23S19
MERCURY	21N03
VENUS	22N19
MARS	01N33
JUPITER	02N35
SATURN	05N36
URANUS	23N06
NEPTUNE	00N08
PLUTO	00N/S00
NORTH NODE	23S20
SOUTH NODE	23N20

---

82. The cluster of five dates in which Pluto touched zero in the 19th century were 25 May 1862, 5 August 1862, 3 April 1863, 4 October 1863 and 20 February 1864. The approximate length of stay of slightly less than 130 years in each hemisphere is the equivalent to Pluto's complete zodiac cycle of twice this amount (248 years).
83. Source: Birth certificate. Quoted on 'QED' BBC Television, May 1997. Article 'John Merrick: The Elephant Man' by Wanda Sellar and Garry Heaton, *The Astrology Quarterly*, London, Spring 1998.

SOUTH NODE	23N20
URANUS	23N06
VENUS	22N19
MERCURY	21N03
SUN	17N01
SATURN	05N36
JUPITER	02N35
MARS	01N33
NEPTUNE	00N08
PLUTO	00N/S00
MOON	23S19
NORTH NODE	23S20

In addition to Pluto; Mars, Neptune and Jupiter are also quite close to zero, representing ingress-like birth positions and giving Merrick many new experiences to tackle in this life. Apart from the Moon everything in his chart is in the Northern Hemisphere so his destiny and character were naturally external and publicly oriented. Backing this up by longitude is a Grand Fire Trine between Sun, Moon and Mars on his chart. It seems that this otherwise unfortunate soul was ordained to make his mark on the world and not be allowed to quietly crawl into a hole and die. His resourcefulness and strength of spirit were remarkably strong and the latter years of his life, when he was looked after and treated with dignity and kindness by the physician Sir Frederick Treeves, were happy and rewarding. He died in his sleep at the age of 27. (11 April 1890).

The Moon's Nodes at his birth were also fairly close to other natal planets, in both longitude and declination. The Moon was conjunct the North Node and Uranus conjunct the South Node suggesting possible soul issues involving emotional security and alienation.

The Invisible Man

"...on the twenty-ninth day of February, at the beginning of the thaw, this singular person fell out of infinity into Iping Village...."

A hidden zero-line Pluto

The Invisible Man by H.G.Wells was first published in 1897, initially as a serialised story in a magazine called *Pearson's Weekly* in June and July of that year, then in book form in September.

I have been unable to find the actual date in June 1897 when the first weekly instalment of this magazine story appeared, so we must guess that it was within the first days of June 1897. This seems likely from an astrological point of view as the Sun would have been conjunct Pluto by longitude all that week (Pluto at 13° Gemini), though not conjunct by declination. "Invisibility" can be seen as Plutonian for several reasons. Firstly selfhood is blacked out, especially when Pluto is conjunct the Sun. Secondly the mythological Pluto had a helmet of invisibility. And thirdly, in 1897 the planet Pluto had not yet been discovered, hence it was culturally invisible.

For the first three days of June 1897 the Moon was out-of-bounds in the north, a beyond-the-solstice condition arguably adding to the unseen or invisible status. In fact in the first week of June 1897, eight out of the ten planets were in the higher region of northern declination: that is at or above 11° north. Only Saturn and Uranus were in the south.

If we take the date quoted at the head of the page above, *"the twenty-ninth day of February"*, as the appearance (so to speak) of the Invisible Man in the novel and look at the planetary data for this, we run into a couple of difficulties. Firstly Wells contradicted himself in this fictional detail, stating in the first chapter of his book that "The stranger came in early February...", then in the third chapter giving a more specific date in *late* February, the date quoted above. This is confusing enough but if we follow the February 29th date above we realise it is that vanishing day that occurs only in a leap year. 1897 was not a leap year and so contained no February 29th, but the previous year of 1896 did. As the story is being narrated as something that has happened in the recent past, we could allow ourselves to think that it was supposed to have happened in 1896, the year before the book was published. In this case we find that on 29 February 1896 the Piscean Sun was exactly square to Pluto, and by declination the majority of planets were in the south rather than the north. Perhaps this is our clue that "invisibility" was going to be anything but easy for the Invisible Man.

Invisible Problems

Following hot on the heels of H.G. Wells' huge success *The Time Machine* in 1895 (and *The Island Of Doctor Moreau* in 1896), *The Invisible Man* in 1897 was another of his scientific romances that took a magical idea and updated it to the era of science. Two years later he published *The War Of The Worlds* and three years after that *The First Men In The Moon*. Although he wrote much else besides, these were the early science fiction stories for which he is still justly best known. Yet *The Invisible Man* was not a great success at the time and as a story rather than an idea it remains possibly the least satisfactory of his science fiction tales today.

The problem with *The Invisible Man* is again threefold. Firstly the invisible hero is not a very nice piece of work, secondly there is no feminine element in the story and thirdly the scope and the sweep of the story seems too limited in the setting Wells chooses to put it. It takes place amongst the inhabitants of a small rural Sussex village, a locale that may have been chosen by the author to produce some comic moments: a community of God-fearing country bumpkins dealing with an irascible invisible man. But we have little point of reference with such a community today and their humour and expressions of speech are too far-removed in time. Unlike *The Time Machine* (which incidentally does include an important female character), the story of *The Invisible Man* has dated badly without retaining much historical interest. Like later film-makers we want to expand the idea of a man invisible on to a much larger geographical stage and into more meaningful areas of personal relationships.

To return to our other stated problem: the hero being an anti-hero, or worse an outright villain. The motives of the medical student Griffin (the Invisible Man) become corrupted in his pursuit of absolute power. This certainly sounds like Pluto. Wells was producing a cautionary tale emphasising that "with undreamt of power comes an unimagined price". It was a theme that would underlie a lot of Wells' early stories. In *The Invisible Man* the ill-tempered Griffin was unable to reverse his goal of invisibility and once achieved he could do little with it to gain the wealth and power he craved. While in theory he could slip into buildings unnoticed and steal whatever he wanted, in reality he could not sell such items or spend the money because he was stuck in invisibility. Even his stealing would raise suspicions if people saw items floating through the air. Most of the time he felt extremely cold as it was only his body that was invisible and not his clothes, and he had to resort to covering himself in coats, hats and gloves and any remaining parts in bandages (the familiar image of the Invisible Man). Ironically this made him look more conspicuous than ever.

Surprisingly many critics and readers also found that Griffin's alter ego in the story, the decent and upright Doctor Kemp, had little more claim as a satisfactory hero. As an afterthought Wells added an Epilogue that was not in the original serial publication, in which an old tramp called Marvel is seen to be the real benefactor of the Invisible Man's reign of terror. Although the tramp is much abused and mistreated in the story and certainly not educated enough to understand the invisibility formulae within Griffin's note-books, he is the one who ends up not only with these books but with a substantial amount of Griffin's money too. Thus some sort of karmic justice seems to have been attained after the death of The Invisible Man, although even this is not wholly satisfactory. The money that has come into Marvel's possession is almost certainly stolen, and the real treasure - the scientific note-books - are unlikely ever to be donated to the furthering of science or the world at large. Marvel keeps them secretly hidden and, as Wells' says in the novel's last line, "none other will know of them until he dies". Pluto reigns till the end.

Wells and Pluto

In this story the obsessive pursuit of science has become the equivalent of selling one's soul to the Devil. Although no specific Faustian bargain was made, the aggressive and frustrated Invisible Man does eventually meet a brutal end. Science was not always the enemy in H.G.Wells' stories but he often warned of the effects of science in the wrong hands. *The Island Of Doctor Moreau*, a tale that today we would put in the bracket of genetic tampering, is another good example. "With undreamt of power comes an unimagined price"...So what was H.G.Wells' astrological affinity to the yet undiscovered Pluto? As can be seen in Wells' natal chart, Pluto squares his ascendant, opposes his Venus and trines his Mercury, but it stands alone in terms of conjunctions with angles and planets. Only on the declinational read-out do further interesting factors come to light:

H.G. Wells

21 September 1866. 4.30pm LMT
Bromley, England 51N24 00E02.
Source: The Astrological Association

SUN	00N37
MOON	11S08
MERCURY	06N03
VENUS	18S50
MARS	23N32 (OOB)
JUPITER	22S10
SATURN	12S41
URANUS	23N29 (OOB)
NEPTUNE	03N11
PLUTO	01N13
NORTH NODE	01S07
SOUTH NODE	01N07
ASCENDANT	16S57
MIDHEAVEN	21S53

MARS	23N32 (OOB)
URANUS	23N29 (OOB)
MERCURY	06N03
NEPTUNE	03N11
PLUTO	01N13
SOUTH NODE	01N07
SUN	00N37

NORTH NODE	01S07
MOON	11S08
SATURN	12S41
ASCENDANT	16S57
VENUS	18S50
MIDHEAVEN	21S53
JUPITER	22S10

Immediately noticeable here is that the Sun, the South Node and Pluto are all parallel within two degrees of the zero line. (Sun: 00N37, Pluto: 01N13, South Lunar Node: 00N07). So Pluto *is* conjunct the Sun, by declination

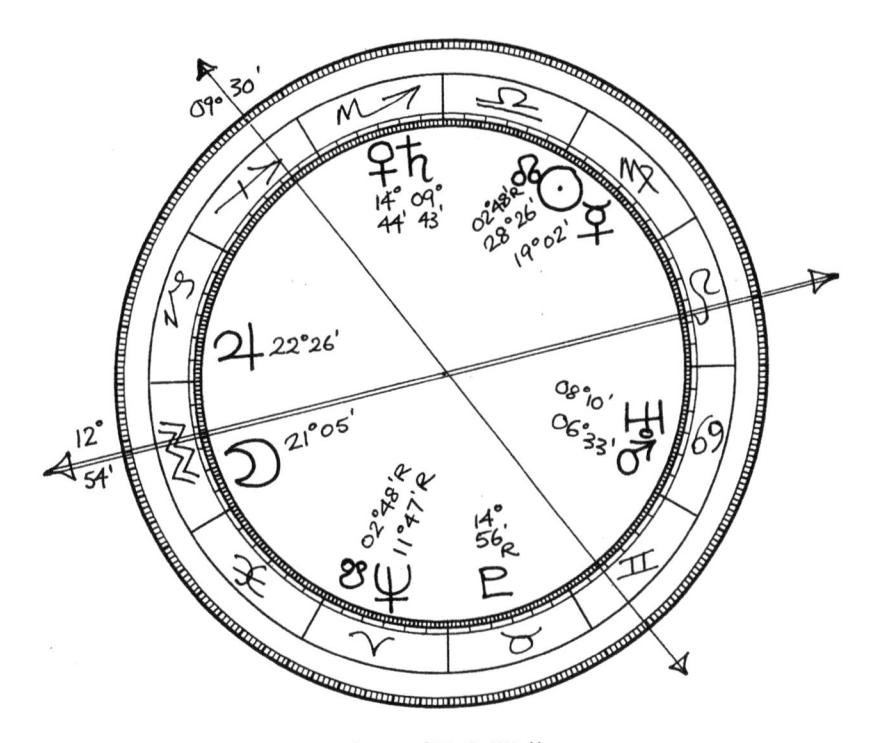

Chart of H.G.Wells

anyway, and stands on the zero-line. Little wonder perhaps that Wells took a new and expanding area like science as the backdrop to his fictional grapples with ancient life-and-death problems.

It is interesting that the Sun is closely conjunct the Moon's *South* Node by declination while it is conjunct the *North* Node by longitude. This is because the Sun is at the end of Virgo and the North Node at the beginning of Libra. While they are conjunct on the zodiac wheel they are separated in declination by the equator at zero degrees Libra. It is the *South* Node, which stands directly opposite at 2° Aries, that just tips into the northern hemisphere and is therefore parallel to the declination of the late-degree Virgo Sun.[84]

In interpretative terms the Sun is conjunct one of the Moon's Nodes whichever way you look at it, but the difference between longitude and

---

84. This also throws up the interesting observation that when the Moon's Nodes are positioned at zero degrees Aries/Libra by longitude they will both be at zero degrees by declination. Here perhaps is another explanation for that "sense of mission" suggested by Pamela Crane when the Aries Point coincides on both tropical and draconic. Pamela Crane, *Draconic Astrology*, Aquarian, Wellingborough, 1987.

declination is striking. By longitude H.G.Wells has the Sun conjunct the North Node, a fortunate combination suggesting a positive development and successful destiny in life. There can be no argument about this. Whatever his other personal trials, he enjoyed material success and worldly prestige throughout a long career. But by declination (and only by declination) his Sun is conjunct both the South Node and Pluto: here a less obvious and a darker side to things is glimpsed. New issues concerned with the pursuit of power (Sun parallel Pluto close to zero) align with old fears of Faustian intensity (Pluto parallel South Node). We also notice that Wells had two out-of-bounds planets almost exactly parallel by declination and conjunct by longitude: Mars and Uranus. With this wild energy of futuristic force it is not surprising that he made his name and will be ever remembered for speculations on the shape of things to come.

Critics of Wells have complained that his fictional characters were often:

> "peculiarly self-centred yet intellectually gifted individuals who believe themselves interested in the welfare of the masses they somewhat paranoically proclaim to represent..." [85]

This is a charge that could possibly be levelled at Wells himself with his accentuated Mars-Uranus, his Virgo Sun and Mercury, his Aquarian Moon in the first house, his midheaven-ruler Jupiter in the twelfth (we could go on and on here)...and especially his "invisible" Pluto falling out of infinity and onto his Sun by declination.

As in *The Time Machine*, the story of *The Invisible Man* illustrates a god-like power attained through modern scientific equations. Prospero's magic books are updated to the era of rational thought and reason. In a sense Magic is brought to the light (zero-line Sun conjunct Pluto). But in Wells' stories power comes with terrible warnings. He seemed particularly concerned about the consequences of modern scientific magic in the wrong hands.

Griffin, the Invisible Man, (his name is that of a hybrid monster) is not morally mature enough to deal with his power. Even the un-named Time Traveller in *The Time Machine*, a much more likeable person, observes in the far future how the Victorian world of rich and poor had mutated into two

---

85. Alfred Borrello, *H.G.Wells: Author in Agony*, Southern Illinois University Press, 1972, quoted in "Wells and his critics" by Macdonald Daly in an appendix to *The Invisible Man* reprinted in 1995.

entirely different species. To his dismay the underprivileged have now become the Plutonian underground masters.

The planet Pluto was unknown at the birth of H.G.Wells although it would come to light and be discovered during his lifetime.[86] But Pluto is invisible on his chart, as it might be on many charts, because its zodiac position differs considerably from its declination, and the very power of having Pluto conjunct the Sun might not otherwise have been recognised.[87] Added to all this is the personal importance of Pluto's zero-line energy. When Wells created his Invisible Man he was writing of his Pluto. He named him Griffin, the transformative monster (in that sense reminiscent of an elephant man), and he was a dark, awkward and unpleasant being. Like Pluto forced into the light, rising over zero and conjunct the Sun, he found his marvellous powers were compromised. It was as much a burden as an asset.

This is coarse and unprocessed zero-line energy coping with the realities of the world. As Wells himself once said:

> "Now and then, though I rarely admit it, the universe projects itself towards me in a hideous grimace." [88]

---

86. Wells died in 1946. Pluto was discovered in 1930.
87. We can find a similar situation on the chart of John Addey, whose natal declinations have been shown previously in the Out of Bounds section. In Addey's case it was his Moon that was closely conjunct Pluto by declination (Moon: 19N29, Pluto: 19N41) although by longitude this is not immediately apparent (Moon at 5° Gemini, Pluto at 6° Cancer). And Liberace also in the Out of Bounds section has Pluto conjunct his Sun by declination (Sun: 19N05, Pluto: 19N24) though not closely by longitude (Sun at 25 Taurus, Pluto at 5 Cancer). Liberace kept his sex-life secret for many years.
88. Source: H.G.Wells discussing his writing in the authorial preface to 'The Scientific Romances of H.G.Wells', published by Gollancz, London, 1933.

136   Declination in Astrology

The Return of the Ancient Mariner
A Voyage into Southern Declination

> At length did come an Albatross
> Through the fog it came
> As if it had been a Christian soul
> We hailed it in God's name

Samuel Taylor Coleridge's poem *The Rime of the Ancient Mariner* has haunted and delighted its readers for two centuries. Open to many interpretations, its plot hinges on the karmic mysteries of crossing the line (crossing the equator or the point of zero degrees of declination).

Helen Adams Garrett has written that natal planets in southern declination carry the implication of karma to be resolved or worked through. She mentions a belief that many avatars were born between 27° Sagittarius and 3° Capricorn (when the Sun is at its most southerly declination around the winter solstice), and suggests that the farthest declinations south indicate a peak of responsibility in karma.[89]

Historically it seems that those who lived in the Northern Hemisphere always viewed the Southern Hemisphere as a strangely different realm. A voyage of discovery to the opposite pole of the world was like the symbolic inner work of the alchemists and gnostics, reflecting the mysterious *via negativa* or inner road. And the medieval sea travellers with their tales of the Southern Cross hanging in the sky above them encouraged ideas of being closer to God, along with other wild stories of fabulous creatures inhabiting the uncharted southern shores. Of all the maritime traditions the one that exerts a perpetual fascination is the ceremony connected with crossing the zero line from one hemisphere to another.

Crossing the Line

The ceremony of Crossing the Line continues on many cruise ships to the present day, where those who have never passed across this boundary before may volunteer for a light-hearted initiation. Along with plastic seaweed, buckets of water and someone in costume presiding as King Neptune, this is now seen as a good-humoured piece of entertainment for passengers and crew. Yet it overlays a deeper feeling that some god has to be appeased, something of importance is taking place and a different world is being entered. As has been established by Nelda Tanner when describing the movement of a planet across the zero line of declination by transit or progression, a change of consciousness is triggered. [90]

In *The Rime of the Ancient Mariner* by Coleridge,[91] it is only after the old navigator crosses the equator and sails south that all the strange events mentioned in the poem begin to occur. He rashly kills an albatross far down in the South Sea after which all kinds of hallucinations and strange

---

89. Helen Adams Garrett, *Karma by Declination*, AFA, Tempe, 1982.
90. See previous reference to the work of Nelda Tanner.
91. Samuel Taylor Coleridge. Birth data: 21 October 1772. 11.00am. Ottley St. Mary, Devon. 50N45, 03W17. Source: Helene and Willem Koppejan in *The Zodiac Image Handbook*, Element, Shaftesbury, 1991 quote "11am" from Grimm's *Astrologie*. Alan Leo's *1001 Notable Nativities* gives an ascendant that equates with this time. Data Plus UK in 1998 suggest the time may not be so precise, quoting "one autumn morning" from a biography *Coleridge: Early Visions* by Richard Holmes, Hodder & Stoughton, 1989. None of this alters the basic fact that Coleridge had the Sun and Moon contraparallel by declination and a chart evenly spread between North and South.

happenings take place as a tutelary spirit of the southern regions decides to avenge the crime.

The Southern Albatross

Many superstitions attached to the albatross have a basis in fact. The seafarer's belief that to sight an albatross heralded a storm or at least brought hope of wind is of practical nature. The Wandering Albatross can have a wingspan upwards of twelve feet and is unable to fly without wind, so to those on sailing vessels its mighty silhouette in the distance was a gladdening sight. More esoterically every albatross was once believed to be the soul of a dead sailor, hence the taboo in killing one. As in the biblical story of Cain being physically marked and then banished for killing his brother Abel, so the Ancient Mariner was marked out for his crime by the other crew members and forced to wear the dead bird as a weight around his neck. If southern declinations in general represent karma being opened along with the need to face and resolve the energy, then crossing the zero line by progression or transit may force an awareness of this. Planets in southern declinations - especially in high declinations - could be described as an albatross around the neck (heavy karma). Let's examine a piece of The Ancient Mariner in more detail.

The Arrival of the Bride

The tale begins outside a church where a wedding guest is detained by an old "grey-beard loon" (the Ancient Mariner) and is obliged to listen to the old man's story. The Mariner tells how he began a sea journey sailing southward from his homeport. No actual geographical locations are mentioned but we deduce the southern direction from his poetic description:

> "The Sun came up upon the left
> Out of the sea came he!
> And he shone bright, and on the right
> Went down into the sea"

Everything was fine until the ship reached zero declination. Coleridge does not mention the equator by name, but his description of the actual movement of the Sun to become overhead at noon is suddenly interrupted by the wedding guest impatiently realising that the bride has just entered the church.

> "Higher and higher every day
> Till over the mast at noon -

> The Wedding-Guest here beat his breast
> For he heard the loud bassoon.
>
> The bride hath paced into the hall
> Red as a rose was she..."

When the Mariner is able to regain the attention of his impatient listener and continue the dialogue he returns to this auspicious moment of line-crossing to recount that a violent storm then arose and compelled the ship to race further south.

There are many poetic insights converging here. The obvious one is that as soon as the zero line is crossed, the world changes. Fair weather suddenly turns foul and one's vessel is temporarily out of control. There is a different phase of life ahead. For the Ancient Mariner this looks heavy, storm-laden and driven by Fate alone. (The sailors are barely in control of their craft). We might be reminded here of the neglected art of astro-meteorology or weather predicting. According to such lore, each planet represented a different weather pattern and declination played an important part. Planets exerted a strong influence when at a station or in parallel to one another, and changes in weather were expected when planets reached maximum declination or crossed the celestial equator.[92] This was the basis of a belief that weather patterns tended to change annually at the solstices and equinoxes.

Then there is the other theme interwoven into the poem about a Wedding, and (at this actual zero crossing point) the arrival of the Bride. The music strikes up inside the church and the Wedding Guest jumps up just as the Ancient Mariner speaks of reaching and crossing the line. The zero line then, also brings a Bride into manifestation.

The Universe is the Bride of the Soul

The starry universe can be seen as the soul's veiled bride, visible but as yet unknowable. Switching writers briefly from Coleridge to Emerson, we find the quote "The Universe is the Bride of the Soul" amongst one of Ralph Waldo Emerson's essays entitled *Experience*.

As astrologers we have a special understanding of the universe as the Bride (or Consort) to our soul, for we all share knowledge of destiny going hand in hand with the movement of the heavens. Remaining aware of the

---

92. Information from an article by Bernard Eccles, 'Weather Forecasting from the Ephemeris', *The Astrology Quarterly*, London, Spring 1998.

marriage to the stars and meeting it halfway, rather than being ruled by it or over-imposing our will on it is surely one of the goals of a good astrologer. *The Rime of the Ancient Mariner* has led us to consider that the moment of crossing the line is tied to the possibility of bringing forth the Bride or Bridegroom of the Soul. In plainer talk crossing the line brings the universe into a sudden relationship with us. We symbolically enter the marriage bed of the stars every time a personal planet progresses south, equating to a sojourn through Libra (the first southerly sign), leading onward and downward to the equivalent of Scorpio and the eighth house. The karmic play continues as the farthest southern declinations are reached.

Key lessons for the Ancient Mariner, including the nightmare experience of being the only soul alive amongst a ghostly crew, all take place on his return journey. We know that these things happen after the ship has changed direction from south to north at the farthest declinations south, and that they begin to happen after the shooting of the Albatross. Following the line " I shot the Albatross", the next line of the poem states:

"The Sun now rose upon the right…"

It would be astrologically appropriate if the arrow from the Mariner's crossbow killed the Albatross at the end degrees of Sagittarius (the farthest declination south).

The Nightmare Life-in-Death

After the shooting of the Albatross there is an initial burst of wind and the ship appears to be sent along a parallel into a different ocean where it is again becalmed. It is still seemingly stuck in the farthest declinations south; stuck possibly somewhere in Capricorn, stuck in the peak of responsibility in karma.

"As idle as a painted ship
Upon a painted ocean"

This is a most disconcerting time. The Mariner is perhaps starting to drift up towards the zero line or imagining that he has already reached it, even though the ship is not moving. He describes again that the Sun at noon is now right above his mast, but he says it was "No bigger than the Moon". He is surely hallucinating, yet at the same time is obviously nearing the equatorial regions from the descriptions of the unbearable heat:

Water, water, everywhere
And all the boards did shrink;

> Water, water, everywhere,
> Nor any drop to drink

We may now deduce that he has reached and is becalmed on or near the line of zero declination, waiting to cross it and travel north. Many strange things will now come into manifestation at this point including a shadow-image of the Bride. We met this distant feminine figure in the poem before when the Mariner crossed the equator south, but this time as he waits to cross from south to north she approaches him in darker guise on a phantom ship, throwing dice with a figure of Death. The prize they are both dicing for is the Mariner's soul.

Again we see the theme of wrestling and gambling with Death that we met in *Gawain and the Green Knight*. For life to be restored and maintained for all, a special initiate must "dice with death". But here it is not the Mariner who gambles directly with the figure of Death but a dark lady on his behalf. She is once more the universe as bride of the soul, but now she is the dark universe.

Clearly the zero line is a place of life and death decisions. Instead of symbolising the marriage bed as it did when crossing north to south (Virgo to Libra), this time it is a judgmental calling-to-account by the boundary keepers (Pisces to Aries). Death loses the dice-game to this frightening female apparition before the ghost ship sails away. But the Mariner himself gains little relief. While the souls of the other dead crew members now shoot off to heaven or hell, zinging past him like "the whizz of my cross-bow", the Mariner is not allowed to die. He has been won by the Bride, the consort of the soul, but she is described here as "the Night-mare Life-in-Death" and he is still required to live through some deathly experiences. He is now on the actual cusp of zero, for as the phantom ship hurries away the sun sets and the stars "rush out" and the poem says: "At one stride comes the dark". In other words there is no twilight because he is on the equator. He is now both alive and dead and poised for rebirth.[93]

After this, and still in a kind of zero-degree limbo, the Mariner takes the step that breaks the karma. Seeing what he describes as water snakes playing beneath his ship, a rush of happiness at their beauty and their joy at being alive causes him to suddenly bless them. This spontaneous and

---

93. Strictly speaking there is a short period of twilight at the equator. According to nautical almanacs, civil twilight lasts from the moment of the sun's disappearance until it is 6° below the horizon, and this can last for almost half an hour at zero degrees. But poetically it appears as if a light is suddenly blown out.

unmotivated act mirrors the way he had previously shot the Albatross - impulsively without thinking - and at this precise moment, again at the cusp of a Cardinal sign, the Albatross falls from his neck into the sea. A karma has closed.

From here on everything changes, including the weather. It rains and refreshes the atmosphere. A wind gets up, lightning flashes, and the ship moves on. Eventually the Ancient Mariner returns to his home port in the north but he is a changed man. He later becomes a kind of wandering teacher compelled to share the insights of his world and soul voyage with any who will listen to him.

Reactions to the Poem
When it first appeared in 1798, Coleridge's poem met with an unexpected degree of hostility from some quarters and he revised and tinkered with it subsequently. There are several variations published at different times and places and my quotes are from the most widely known 1834 version. One of the literary criticisms at the time was that the Mariner had no real identifiable character and that he did not act but was continually acted upon. Yet it is this degree of anonymity and openness to the designs of fate that makes the subject matter so amenable to studies such as this, where we are observing the forces of different declinations upon a moving body.

Although Coleridge has a reputation as a drug-taker, suggestions that *The Ancient Mariner* was all an opium-induced trip are without foundation. The poem was soberly planned during a walk on the Quantock Hills in collaboration with his friend and colleague William Wordsworth. The bare bones of the idea came from a strange dream recounted to Coleridge by one of his friends. It has not escaped modern interpretations either that the date of the poem coincides with the fight for the abolition of slavery. The theme of retribution inherent in the text is on a greater and perhaps unconscious level pricking the feeling of collective guilt over the maritime slave trade and those shameful voyages across the ocean from one continent to another. The majority of these voyages sailed from the African Congo and the Ivory and Gold Coasts to the islands and mainlands of the Caribbean and the Americas, centred along or close to the line of zero declination. When a ship is at sea and out of sight of land it is perilously unearthed and normal realities can slip away. Who knows what inhuman sufferings are still impressed into the psychic atmosphere around the equator?

Conclusion

We all have planets that will cross the line of zero declination by progression during our lifetime, or we may have natal planets situated there or in southern declinations generally. For most of us it is the Moon that is the most constant timer, as it crosses the zero line twice in a lunar month. By day-to-a-year progression this means that roughly every 14 years of life a great change is indicated. The strongest of these by far would be if a lunation took place on or near the line, especially a New Moon or Solar Eclipse (beginning a new progressed Moon cycle), and obviously any other strong planetary movements that might coincide. The days of sailing ships and undiscovered countries have passed, but the journey of life is as new and full of surprises as ever. All astrologers are navigators who use maps to chart life's course, and as all lone navigators must, they use the stars to guide them. The Ancient Mariner whose "soul hath been alone on a wide wide sea" is an aged Saturn figure at the end, yet his "eye is bright". He has endured the voyage into southern declination and ultimately triumphed to tell the tale.

5
Antiscia

Any astrologer who concentrates on the relevance of the 360 degrees of the zodiac circle will find the use of antiscia illuminating. Antiscia! It sounds more like a sneeze than a word. But was it not once true that the soul was thought to separate from the body in the instant of a sneeze? (The origin of saying "Bless You"). In other words, a temporary division in half.

By folding the wheel of the zodiac across the solstice axis of zero Cancer and zero Capricorn and reflecting the two halves of 180 degrees to each other, some unexpected sets of twins are created. The images and readings available in the various systems of pictorial astrological degree symbols often prove particularly amenable to this, with the antiscion to each zodiac degree giving a further dimension for consideration.[94]

Antiscia between longitudinal degrees on the round zodiac (zodiacal parallels) are a way of approaching things obliquely. They are mirror images,[95] almost but not quite the same, and herein lies their difference to a conjunction. The conjunction focuses two planetary energies into one forceful and inseparable combination; the antiscia allow two energies to become part of each other through separate reflection.

---

94. See my series on 'Antiscion Pairings' in *The Sabian Symbol International Newsletter*, 6 issues from 2004 - 2005. After having studied longitudinal degree symbols for many years I am still not personally convinced that an equal amount of energy is contained in each zodiacal degree. It would appear, from a comparison of the many different sets of degree symbols, that there are irregular swathes of energy in the zodiac greater than just one degree and that the bordering cusps of a single degree are not always watertight. However in the majority of cases longitudinal degree symbols do operate as they should and can be surprisingly meaningful.

There is only partial evidence in my view, that precession might also alter these symbols. As a rule of thumb I prefer to use the *La Volasfera* set of degree symbols for historical charts with dates before the 17th/18th century. The degree symbols of *Charubel* are probably the best bet for nineteenth century dates. For twentieth century charts I use the *Sabian symbols*, undeniably the cream of the crop for general usage. For twenty-first century charts I also consult Alice Kashuba's *Fairchild Symbols*. Martin Goldsmith has also produced an excellent synthesis of degree symbols old and new in *The Zodiac by Degrees*, Weiser, 2004.

95. Antiscia as 'mirror points' appears in *Liber Secundus*, quoting Antiochus who said: "Libra did not see Aries because the Earth was in the middle, (and) as if through a mirror reached the theory of antiscia."

Because the antiscia in longitude are formed from degrees that always reflect the Sun's waxing path to its waning path (in terms of one degree approaching the solstice and the other receding from it), a subtle mirror side of the opposite is apparent. It is the mirror shield of Perseus in which a gorgon can be observed without petrification.

But there is nothing sinister about antiscia. It allows energy to flow between two places with potent force, and should one of those places be harbouring a difficult planetary energy it can be observed and assessed more dispassionately by the other, which is a useful consideration in transits.

As an illustration of how antiscia can be employed in interpretation in natal astrology let us examine the chart of a man who wrote the ultimate story of splitting things into two: Robert Louis Stevenson and *The Strange Case of Dr Jekyll and Mr Hyde*.

A TALE OF DARK SECRETS
Antiscia on the birth chart of Robert Louis Stevenson

R.L.Stevenson
13 November 1850. 1.30pm. Edinburgh, Scotland 55N57 03W13
Source: The Astrological Association

SUN	17S59
MOON	10S45
MERCURY	14S39
VENUS	27S49 (OOB)
MARS	19S22
JUPITER	04S14
SATURN	03N27
URANUS	10N02
NEPTUNE	10S42
PLUTO	05S09
NORTH NODE	17N58
SOUTH NODE	17S58
ASCENDANT	15S17
MIDHEAVEN	22S43

146 *Declination in Astrology*

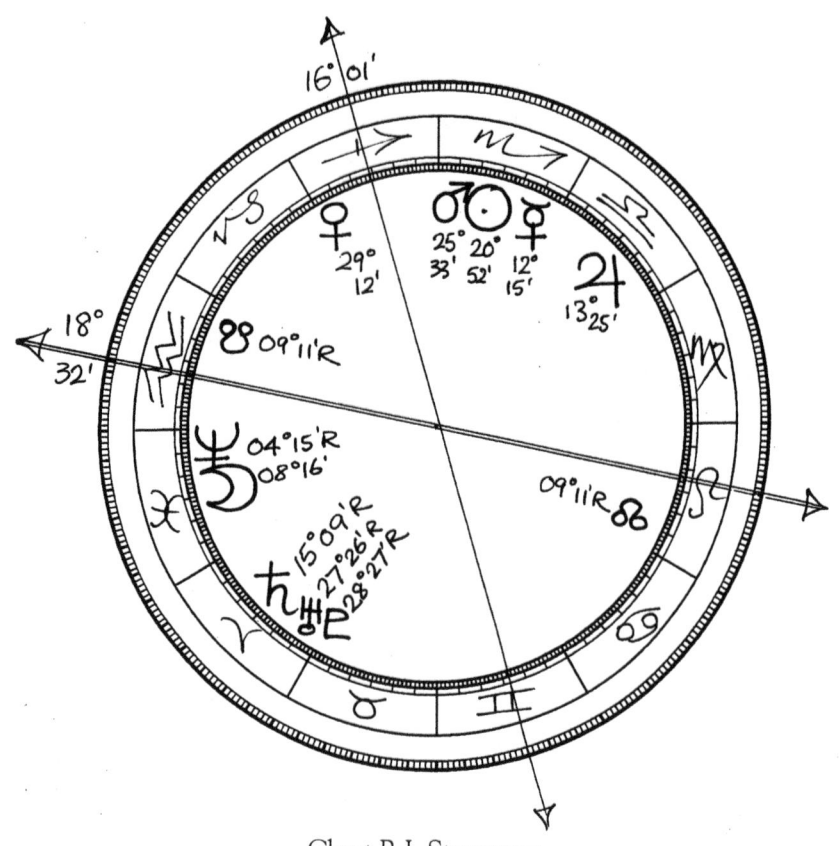

Chart R.L.Stevenson

NORTH NODE	17N58
URANUS	10N02
SATURN	03N27

JUPITER	04S14
PLUTO	05S09
NEPTUNE	10S42
MOON	10S45
MERCURY	14S39
ASCENDANT	15S17
SOUTH NODE	17S58
SUN	17S59
MARS	19S22
MIDHEAVEN	22S43
VENUS	27S49 (OOB)

"Both sides of me were in dead earnest..." wrote Robert Louis Stevenson, in his famous story of a personality splitting in two. As the author of *Treasure Island* and *The Strange Case of Dr Jekyll and Mr Hyde* he has a birth chart worthy of study at any level, but does it show a mind "commingled out of good and evil," to use his phrase. Was he both Jekyll and Hyde?

Stevenson was born with the majority of planets in south declination, a weaver of inward plots and pictures in the mind. His Sun in Scorpio also gave him a claim to the dark and secretive side of existence that is allowed this zodiac sign. The foggy city streets, through which the unpleasant Mr Hyde stalked, carry the same sense of uncertain menace as the lonely West Country roads in *Treasure Island*, where cold sea mists are pierced only by the sinister tapping of Blind Pew's stick. When Ralph Steadman, one in a long line of illustrators of the famous pirate story, added a preface in 1985 he described the content as "a dark tale". As he said in this illustrated edition "Everybody knows something, senses a dark secret, but nobody knows everything..."[96]

For a tale of dark secrets however, nothing beats Stevenson's enduring legacy, *Dr Jekyll and Mr Hyde*, a story whose title has entered the language on its own terms and now even outstrips his own name in recognition.

Jekyll and Hyde was written in three days in 1886, purportedly after a vivid dream and keeps its secret until the very end. Up until the last pages we are led to believe that Jekyll and Hyde are two separate people rather than one brilliant scientist who has discovered a potion that gives total character transformation. It is the morally upright Dr Jekyll who is the real Scorpio caricature, hiding away from the Sun in his locked laboratory, earnestly probing the deepest mysteries of the human soul, risking his very life with an unknown drug - and not being forthcoming about his secret discovery either. The agony and exhilaration of accepting his dark side, which eventually takes over completely, is the thought-provoking basis of the plot.

On Stevenson's chart there are two immediately noticeable antiscion contacts. Firstly the Sun at 20°52' Scorpio is at the exact zodiac antiscion of the Moon's South Node at 09°11' Aquarius. The residue of the past (South Node) has a direct line to the heart of the man (the Sun). Like Dr Jekyll's pious books that the crude Mr Hyde scribbled blasphemies over, Stevenson's philosophical ninth house Sun was subject to murky intrusions. Strange karmic memories (South Node Aquarius in twelfth house) affected him

---

96. Robert Louis Stevenson, *Treasure Island*, illustrated by Ralph Steadman, Harrap, London, 1985

constantly in the form of nightmares and ill-health delirium but he was able to use them to his advantage and transmute them into fantastic adventures that enthralled millions. The zodiacal parallel linked these two points on his chart in a potent yet beneficial way.

Dreams (twelfth house) were the acknowledged source of much of his inspiration. As a child he had thrilled to those bedtime stories of the supernatural that he coaxed from his beloved nurse. They were his access to a deeper and more mysterious world than his mother would admit existed, and the taboo made them enticingly sweet. In this powerful and ambivalent feminine influence we may also see early evidence of the workings of his out-of-bounds Venus, an energy almost as far south as it could go.[97] An exceptionally potent muse.

The extreme Venus granted Robert Louis Stevenson a talent in the arts along with a socially inclined personality. As a young man his fascination for the low-life of Edinburgh made him a regular patron of the lantern-lit pubs and clubs where he could laugh and drink openly with the underclasses. His acquaintances with prostitutes and others of society's colourful misfits in those cosy, whisky-reeking dens was a satisfying counterbalance to the proper world of his law studies and his father's stricter Presbyterian background.

The second of the exact antiscion contacts involves Mercury, the planet above all that should be strong in the chart of a writer. Mercury at 12°16' Scorpio is at the zodiac antiscion to the ascendant at 18°31' Aquarius, exact to within a degree. With Mercury and the ascendant in such mutual harmony Stevenson's literary gifts could flow unimpeded and streamed effortlessly from within him towards the outer world. They would become his signature, the lens through which he was seen, and the effective force in his personality. He had always wanted to be a writer from an early age. It was his sole ambition, and, appropriately, his first public essay was titled "Roads" (Mercury).

It may also have been his Scorpio Mercury sending antiscia to the Aquarian ascendant that urged him to write, under the guise of Dr Jekyll: "I hazard a guess that man will be ultimately known for a mere polity of multifarious, incongruous and independent denizens." Which in plain English means that the human may not just be one, but many strange and different people. In the rich imagination of this gifted writer who peopled his tales

---

97.   Venus peaked at 27S59 six days before his birth.

with an assortment of memorable characters from David Balfour to Long John Silver, this was undoubtedly true.

The special dynamic of both these sets of antiscia: Sun-South Node and Mercury-ascendant, is that they involve such strong parts of the horoscope. The Sun and the ascendant will always be of towering importance no matter what chart is under examination, but more than this the separate antiscion contacts work both ways. The Sun and the South Node, Mercury and the ascendant, are not only near exact antiscia in longitudinal degrees, but they are also near exact parallels by declination too.

The Sun is at 17S59 declination while the South Node is 17S58; the pair are parallel to hair's breadth accuracy. Mercury is 14S39 while the ascendant is 15S17; not quite such a close orb as the Sun and South Node but still only 38 minutes of a degree apart. The planetary pairs are both zodiacal parallels and declinational parallels. This is powerful antiscia.

6
Stars in Declination

First Magnitude Stars Close to the Celestial Equator

Zodiac positions of stars can be misleading as most of them are not 'in' the zodiac at all. How can they be? Only the stars that comprise the twelve zodiac constellations (plus a few others that have sneaked in sideways) can possibly be 'in the zodiac'. All others are a long way above or below the zodiac band and so have to be raised or lowered to meet it in order to give a zodiac (longitude) reading. However this symbolic method of raising and lowering a star to give it an equivalent zodiac degree has been successfully employed in astrology for centuries and has an undeniable validity.

Many astrologers who use the longitude positions of the fixed stars prefer to give more weight to those that are closer to the ecliptic, thus narrowing down the field, while others may prefer to use those of first degree magnitude only (the brightest stars) wherever they might appear in the sky.

Declination gives us similar options. It is possible to bring very high latitude stars normally way beyond the declination boundaries, like for example the Pole star Polaris, back into an inbound position through the process of "bouncing back" off the equator. The current declination of Polaris is approximately 89N16, only minutes short of the 90° ceiling which *is* the Pole, although its inbound declination would be - rather strangely - 4S34. While this symbolic calculation is correct it makes little appeal to our logic, that the most northerly star should end up in low declinations in the south. However its position in the 29th degree of Gemini by zodiacal longitude is equally unlikely if we adopt a literal view.

For the purpose of this present discussion we are looking at the actual stars of first magnitude that fall within or only just beyond the normal declination parameters, contained within a span of up to 29 degrees north and south. This means they could be in direct parallel or contra-parallel to natal or transiting planets and include the only first magnitude stars in the sky that have any possibility of being occulted or eclipsed by the Moon or other planets. There are only a dozen of these stars within the 29-degree limit and they are shown below. Because of their classical and traditional importance the Pleiades have also been included, under the name of their brightest light Alcyone, although none of the individual stars in that cluster are of first magnitude. Positions are given as at 1st January 2000:

North Declination		**South Declination**	
PROCYON (alpha Canis Minoris)	05 N 13 (25 Can 47)		
BELLATRIX (gamma Orionis)	06 N 21 (20 Gem 56)		
BETELGEUSE (alpha Orionis)	07 N 24 (28 Gem 45)		
ALTAIR (alpha Aquilae)	08 N 52 (01 Aqu 45)	**RIGEL** (beta Orionis)	08 S 12 (16 Gem 49)
REGULUS (alpha Leonis)	11 N 57 (29 Leo 49)	**SPICA** (alpha Virginis)	11 S 09 (23 Lib 50)
ALDEBARAN (alpha Tauri)	16 N 30 (09 Gem 47)	**SIRIUS** (alpha Canis Majorum)	16 S 43 (14 Can 05)
ARCTURUS (alpha Bootis)	19 N 11 (24 Lib 13)		
ALCYONE (& the Pleiades)	24 N 06 (29 Tau 59)		
		ANTARES (alpha Scorpii)	26 S 25 (09 Sag 45)
POLLUX (beta Geminorum)	28 N 01 (23 Can 13)		

One thing that becomes apparent on a closer study of the above is that some of these stars are in a different hemisphere to their zodiac positions. The great white Rigel for instance is at a declination of 8 degrees South yet its zodiacal position is in the northern sign of Gemini. How is this discrepancy possible?

Arcturus and Spica

To explain this better let's look at Arcturus and Spica, two stars that appear less than a degree of longitude apart in Libra on the tropical zodiac, yet by declination Arcturus is in the north and Spica in the south. A sky-map will

152   *Declination in Astrology*

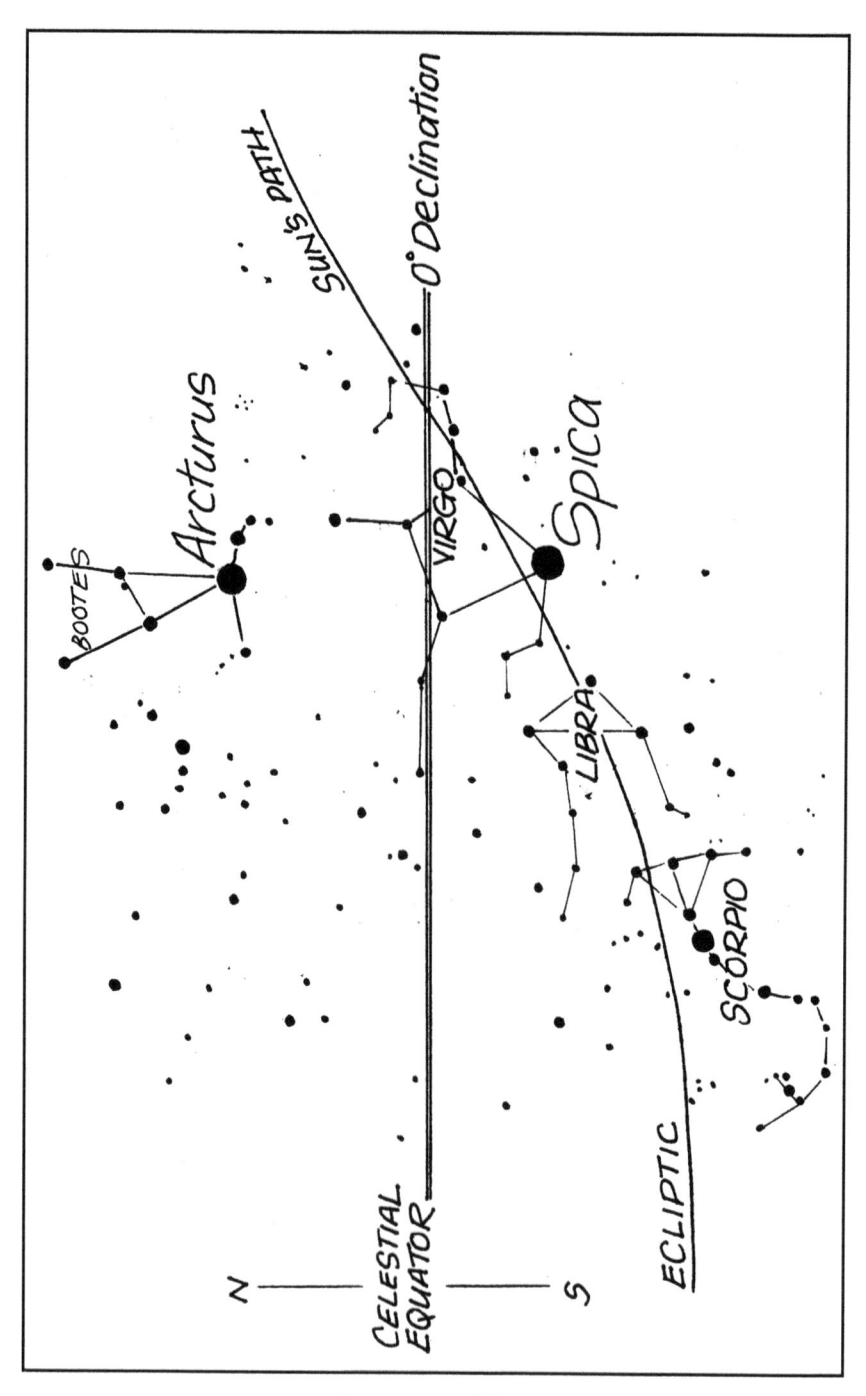

Arcturus and Spica

confirm that they are in a vertical line one above the ecliptic (the Sun's path) and one below, so that one star must be brought down and the other raised up to obtain their zodiacal measurement. The sky-map also shows that Arcturus is placed much farther above the ecliptic line than Spica is below it, which is correct as Arcturus is in the constellation of Bootes and not in the zodiac while Spica, the main star in Virgo, is. This ecliptic 'line' however is the Sun's path - not the celestial equator from which declinations are measured. Arcturus and Spica also stand one above and one below the celestial equator. Arcturus is 19N11, Spica 11S10. And here is the clue as to why a Libra star like Arcturus can be in the north: It is because the stars are fixed whereas the Sun and planets move around in the zodiac band. If a *planet* is 'in Libra' it has to be, in most cases, in that portion of the sky just south of the celestial equator, just after the ecliptic dives down below the equator after the autumn equinox. The *stars* however do not move along this band. They are fixed. They are where they are, north or south of the ecliptic and equator, a permanent backdrop to the moving planets.

Mighty Sirius

The mighty Sirius, to take another instance, is south of the equator and can not suddenly move off anywhere else. But at the time of year that the Sun arrives in that portion of the sky, just after northern midsummer when it is in Cancer, it (the Sun) happens to be north of the equator. Planets that move close to the Sun will also be following the Sun's path north of the equator (north declination) when they are in Cancer, but the stars could be above or below.

In fact there is no way of knowing from their zodiacal positions, whether any fixed stars are above or below the equator, nor how far they are away from the equator either. Sirius is usually low down near the horizon of the sky for those who live in the northern half of Planet Earth because it is a Southern Hemisphere star, but because it is in the region of the sky near tropical Cancer (the sidereal constellation of Gemini) it will appear in the northern sign of Cancer on a horoscope.

154   Declination in Astrology

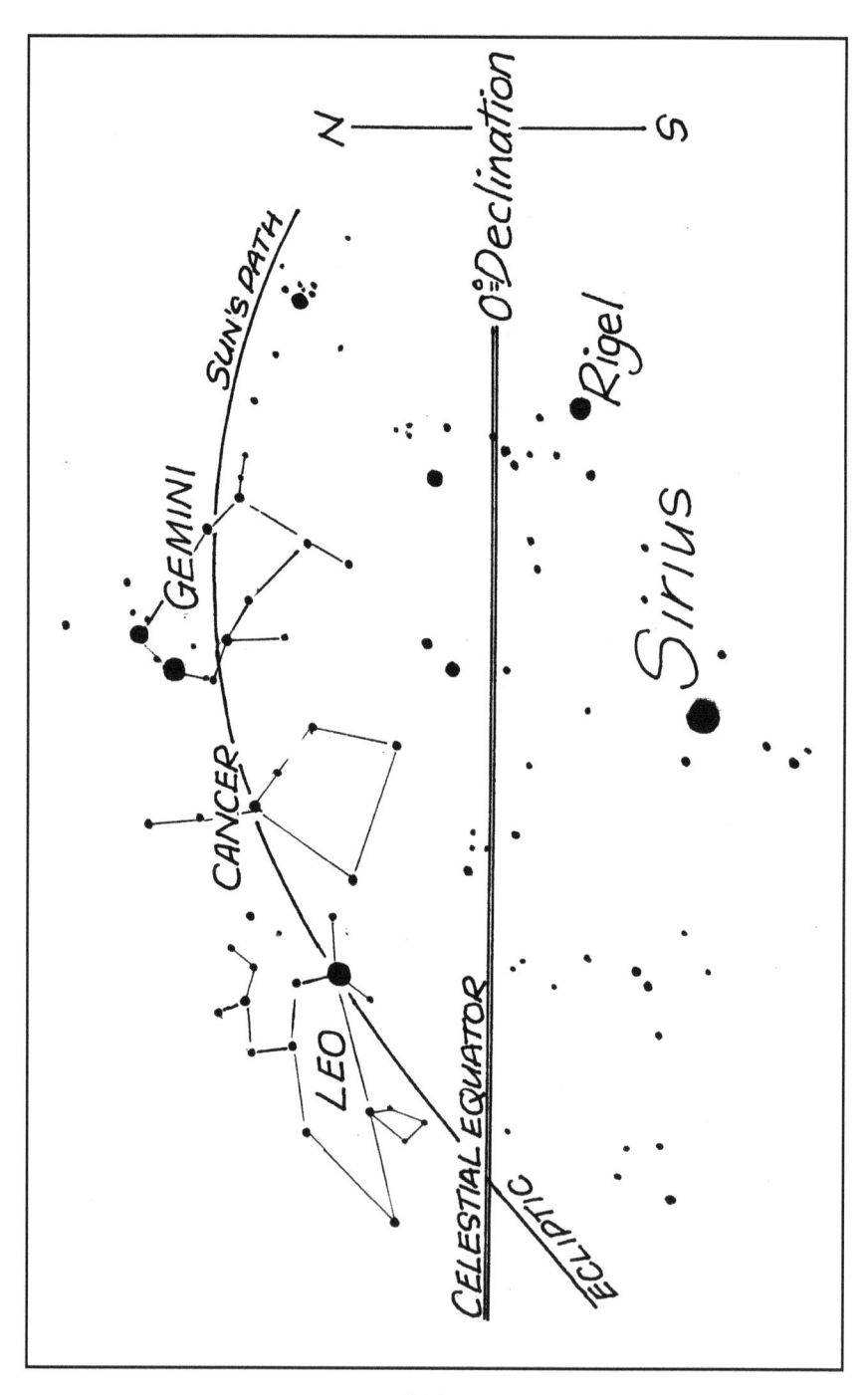

Sirius

Stars of Power

Only those stars that are situated close to the ecliptic, can ever be occulted by the Moon or other planets. The five first magnitude stars in this category are: Regulus, Spica, Aldebaran, Antares and Pollux.

Several of the stars on our list given above also make close contra-parallels to each other. Altair and Rigel, Regulus and Spica, Aldebaran and Sirius: these pairs all share the mathematical relationship of being equally spaced above and below zero. At equal distances from the celestial equator each pair of stars would be affected by any planet transiting their midpoint, including the Sun at both equinoxes. The start of all planetary ingress cycles when planets reach zero Aries and head north also have the added force of six mighty stars underlying. This is yet another subtle reason why the zero line of declination is such a powerful area.

Arguably the most eminent pair of stars in our list would be Aldebaran and Sirius at 16° North and South. Not only are high honour and renown traditionally associated with both of these in astrology but they are also the closest in orb of the three pairs of contra-parallels, focusing their energies together still further. Sirius, the brightest star in the sky, intimately bound to the highest powers in the mysticism of Ancient Egypt, links with another distinguished 'eye-star' Aldebaran the Eye of the Bull. Their positions at 16 degrees fall on the longitudinal midpoint of the cardinal directions, a recognised point of power in its own right.

Beneficial too are Regulus and Spica, the lion-heart and the wheat-sheaf, at 11 degrees North and South. With their complementary qualities of royal strength and skill in arts and sciences both were traditionally regarded as fortunate in their influence. 11 degrees is also the declinational midpoint, halfway between the extremes of zero and 23, another minor power point.

Altair and Rigel, our third pair of stars, are not quite so straightforward. The eagle star meets the foot of the hunter. Metaphorically one flies while the other connects to the ground. Both have shared contradictory traditional meanings in the past although neither has ever been classified as an 'evil' star. They also tenant the lesser power point of 8 degrees North and South.

It is remarkable that each of these pairs of stars falls on a declinational point of power. Charles and Lois Hannan, who have presented a great deal of research in this area, identifying and coining the term "power points", suggest there is a connection to the world at these points.[98] So with the traditional influences of renown attributed to these first magnitude stars

---

98.   Charles and Lois Hannan in NCGR Chicago Chapter's newsletter 1991, *Today's*

(especially Aldebaran-Sirius) one should look carefully at any natal planets sharing the same positions. At 8, 11 and 16 degrees North or South, worldly fame could be attached to that planetary influence.

Further meanings

The astrological influence or meaning of the larger stars was initially derived, at least in part, from their visual appearance, their spectral classes. A red star had a martial quality and in our list this would have included Betelgeuse and Antares. Golden yellow stars like our Sun were linked with material fortune and outer success and in our list this would have included Procyon, Aldebaran, Arcturus, Alcyone and Pollux. White stars were more placidly beneficial, stimulating personal creativity in body and mind, and Bellatrix, Altair, Rigel, Regulus, Spica, and Sirius were representative of these.

In our three pairs of 1st magnitude stars Altair and Rigel at 8° North and South are both White, as are Regulus and Spica at 11° North and South. Aldebaran and Sirius however at 16° North and South are a combination of Yellow and White, another indication that this pair comprises the most likely outwardly successful axis.

(See Appendix 2 for a complete list of all named stars and their declinations within 30 degrees North and South).

Astrologer 1991, and *The Other Dimension*, Summer 1999. Volume 4, Number 2. The exact points of power identified, beside 00NS00 (equinox) and 23NS26 (solstice), are:
    8NS45 (22.5 degrees of longitude either side of Aries/Libra axis),
    21NS34 (22.5 degrees of longitude either side of Cancer/Capricorn axis),
    16NS20 (15 degrees of longitude of the Fixed signs)
    11NS43 (midpoint between tropics and equator by declination).

"Death Shall Come on Swift Wings"

The Tomb and Stars of Tutankhamun

Following the line of thought that the Aldebaran-Sirius axis at 16 degrees North and South may bring world renown when appropriately triggered, let us return to a place and time that has all the ingredients: a fabulous treasure, a mummy's curse, global fascination and immortal fame. We are in Egypt in the Valley of the Kings at the ominous solar eclipse of 17 March 1923.

The official opening of the burial chamber of Tutankhamun had taken place just one month before. Through cinema newsreels the world had seen or was still hearing and reading of the incredible discovery of the age: a pharaoh's tomb unearthed intact. The archaeologist Howard Carter and his financial backer the Earl of Carnarvon were standing at the pinnacle of their worldly success, yet the friendship between this odd couple had suddenly disintegrated at the same time.

Tutankhamun

The opening of the antechamber of the tomb (as distinct from the inner burial chamber) had taken place almost four months previously in late November 1922. It was on this occasion it is often said that the 56-year-old Earl of Carnarvon received the mosquito bite that would trouble him throughout that winter. Howard Carter had also returned to his accommodation in Luxor to find his pet canary dead in its cage; a frightened servant said it had been attacked and killed by a cobra. These odd incidents together with many others, plus the various moments of archaeological breakthrough, form a whole string of dates and times that comprise the saga of the discovery of Tutankhamun. From an astrological point of view some of these are reliable while others are probably not, but they all come to a head in the winter of 1922/23. If there is an underlying pattern to examine, the solar eclipse of 17 March 1923, just days before the spring equinox, seems to act as the resolute focal point.

At the full moon stage of this new moon and solar eclipse, Carnarvon died in Cairo of pneumonia following blood poisoning. The story of all the lights going out over Cairo at the same instant sounds like media hype but was confirmed by his son who was at the bedside when the building was plunged into darkness. It was also documented that in Highclere Castle in England the Earl's beloved dog howled and dropped dead that night at the same hour. When the mummy was finally unwrapped it was said to have a blemish on its cheek identical to Carnarvon's facial mosquito bite. During his feverish last days Carnarvon kept repeating "a bird is scratching my face." The mythical clay tablet found at the tomb by Howard Carter with the inscription "Death shall come on swift wings to whoever toucheth the tomb of the Pharaoh", is probably a fabrication. (Carter denied its existence). Nevertheless events would now go into top gear. Carnarvon's sudden death, followed by the unexpected deaths of others associated with the dig, fuelled a media frenzy. If the discovery of the treasure in itself wasn't the story of the year, the suggestion of a mummy's curse made it a contender for the story of the century.

Solar Eclipse
17 Mar 1923. 2.51pm EET
Luxor, Egypt 25N41 32E24.

SUN	01S37
MOON	02S05
MERCURY	11S03
VENUS	16S26
MARS	15N03
JUPITER	16S10
SATURN	04S40
URANUS	06S53
NEPTUNE	16N17
PLUTO	20N24

NORTH NODE	03N44
SOUTH NODE	03S44
ASCENDANT	16N23
MIDHEAVEN	15N20
PLUTO	20N24
ASCENDANT	16N23
NEPTUNE	16N17
MIDHEAVEN	15N20
MARS	15N03
NORTH NODE	03N44

SUN	01S37
MOON	02S05
SOUTH NODE	03S44
SATURN	04S40
URANUS	06S53
MERCURY	11S03
JUPITER	16S10
VENUS	16S26

The Aldebaran-Sirius axis, the fame axis, is at the declination power point of 16 degrees. In 1923 the exact declinations of the two stars were 16N21 (Aldebaran) and 16S36 (Sirius).[99] Within the same degree on this solar eclipse chart were:

Venus 16S26
Jupiter 16S10
Neptune 16N17
and Ascendant at Luxor 16N23

The Sun and Moon were close together below the critical zero line waiting to break into an earthly manifestation at any moment: a change was imminent. The global cultural influence of the discovery of Tutankhamun and the accompanying story of the curse can hardly be understated. It affected fashion, architecture, literature, movie-films and awakened a popular interest

---

99. A few minutes different to their previously given positions in the year 2000. The movement and tilt of the Earth causes a slight change in the declinational measurement of the fixed stars over a period of time.

in Egyptology that has never since abated. The fact that this was a *solar* eclipse meant that the mighty Ra was symbolically darkened. Although not totally eclipsed in the sky over Egypt in this particular case,[100] astrologically it still gave the Moon command. The irrational and the past were close to consciousness. Seven of the ten planets including Sun and Moon were in south declination: inner, deeper, subjective vibes.

Looking at the Aldebaran-Sirius degrees in particular, the nature of the fame and its effect on the world should be connected to the meanings of the planets that were positioned there, namely Venus, Jupiter and Neptune. Venus and Jupiter obviously refers to the vast wealth, the beautiful artefacts of the pharaoh's treasure, while Neptune adds an otherworldly connection. The ascendant at the same degree (16N) re-emphasises the outer manifestation of the event plus perhaps the importance of place. 16 North is the horizon-line here so symbolically Sirius the "Dog Star" and Aldebaran "the Watcher of the East" are also involved as gods of the horizon. A powerful Egyptian concept.

The importance of Sirius or *Sothis* to Egyptian belief was of the highest divine status. Sirius was connected to Osiris (the name may be a derivative) the god of the Underworld. Sky-shafts in the Great Pyramid aligned a pharaoh's soul to this star so he could become at one with it at death. Its dog-star appellation is likely to refer in part to Anubis, the jackal-headed god who oversaw the process of mummification and weighed the soul of the departed against the Feather of Truth. Carter and Carnarvon were faced by an imposing statue of Anubis guarding the treasury when they first entered the burial chamber.

Sirius on our solar eclipse chart is most closely connected to Venus and Jupiter, the two benefic planets. The heavenly magnificence of Osiris incarnate comes to this world through the splendour and beauty of Tutankhamun's discovery. Fame for this previously minor Egyptian boy-king is assured, but what constitutes the dark side? Where is the signature of the curse?

At the other end of the 16-degree axis is Neptune, the planet of deception, conjunct Aldebaran. Howard Carter, the stubborn and meticulous archaeologist, remained immune to the death curse, living another 17 years. He achieved his fame yet was never observed to enjoy it. There were Neptunian factors: no one doubts he discovered the tomb and deserves the

---

100. This was an annular eclipse (the Moon too far from Earth to completely hide the Sun) with an eclipse path not centred over Egypt.

credit but there were rumours of deception, of behind-the-scenes dealing, of things being stage-managed and not quite as they seemed. He and Carnarvon (the two men were only eight years apart in age)[101] had secretly entered the burial chamber through a wall to view the tomb some while before they officially broke the sealed doorway in the presence of an invited audience and pretended it was their first glimpse. Worse, they were rumoured to have disposed of portions of the treasure hoard to private buyers before making their discovery public. These last 'rumours' were most likely invented by angry newsmen shut out from a story, but certain key items did disappear despite Carter's obsessive security checks. Neither did Howard Carter ever receive a knighthood, which seems an odd oversight by the British establishment. Aldebaran, a Master Star of ancient times, held the reputation of granting great energy and recognition through being ahead of others, though it also warned of making enemies.

Neptunian too were the rash of spirit messages warning Carnarvon specifically not to enter the sealed tomb, and as was his nature he did so with a jocular air that some feared might have offended ancient guardians of the hallowed space. Arthur Conan Doyle announced his belief that dark spirits had been aroused and separate mediums in England had given Carnarvon similar information before he set out to Egypt to join Carter for the last time. Many other psychic danger signals were received from around the world when the news of the first opening of the antechamber spread internationally. Carnarvon's death, recorded as 1.50am 2 April 1923 (according to most accounts [102]) only hours after the Full Moon at 15.10pm, has awesome astrology. The Sun and Moon are now contra-parallel (Sun: 04N27 Moon: 04S41) with Saturn both parallel the Moon by declination (Saturn: 04S13 Moon: 04S41) and conjunct by longitude (Moon: 17° 34' Libra, Saturn: 17° 13' Libra). This is pretty close to an exact occultation of Saturn by the Full Moon, not the jolliest of energies. Mercury was standing on the celestial equator (00N08). Was this the manifestation of the "swift wings"? Neptune was still with Aldebaran at 16N but Jupiter and Venus had moved away from their benefic parallels with Sirius of two weeks before. The intangibility of Neptune was now more out on its own.

---

101. Howard Carter: 9 May 1874. Swaffham, Norfolk, England. Died 2 March 1939 aged 64. George Stanhope Herbert, 5th Earl of Carnarvon, nickname "Porchy": 26 June 1866. Winchester, England. Died 2 April 1923 aged 56. Main sources: Alan MacDonald, *Tutankhamun's Tomb*, Scholastic, London, 2003 and Gerald O'Farrell, *The Tutankhamun Deception*, Sidgwick & Jackson, London, 2001.
102. Others give 5 April 1923.

sDeath of Carnarvon
2 April 1923. 1.50am EET
Cairo, Egypt 30N01 31E27.

SUN	04N27
MOON	04S41
MERCURY	00N08
VENUS	11S36
MARS	18N22
JUPITER	15S53
SATURN	04S13
URANUS	06S33
NEPTUNE	16N22
PLUTO	20N26
NORTH NODE	03N46
SOUTH NODE	03S46
ASCENDANT	21S26
MIDHEAVEN	15S02
PLUTO	20N26
MARS	18N22
NEPTUNE	16N22
SUN	04N27
NORTH NODE	03N46
MERCURY	00N08
SOUTH NODE	03S46
SATURN	04S13
MOON	04S41
URANUS	06S33
VENUS	11S36
MIDHEAVEN	15S02
JUPITER	15S53
ASCENDANT	21S26

The signature of the curse is therefore Neptune. Not specifically of the planet itself but simply because the nature of this side of the phenomenon is Neptunian. There is no solid evidence that there ever was a curse on the tomb of Tutankhamun, everything is rumour and hearsay. On the other hand one can not easily dismiss the long list of deaths, misfortunes and uncanny happenings from the time of the tomb's opening. Neptune has ensured that this otherwise well-documented piece of archaeological history is beset with confusion, muddled religious scholarship, otherworldliness and accusations of deception. Even trying to piece together the dates and facts for this account has been similarly confusing, most books and websites just copy previous erroneous reports or blatantly contradict each other. Along with the breathtaking glory of his death mask and possessions (Sirius-Jupiter-Venus), the reputation of Tutankhamun to the modern world remains steeped in Neptune.

7
Declination in Action: The Davison Composite

A declination-friendly chart

The standard mid-point composite chart in astrology, which takes the mid-point of each set of planets from two individual charts, is usually better suited to longitude calculation than declination. If we take the midway point of planetary declinations from two separate charts we tend to get everything pulled towards lower declination degrees. Out-of-bounds measurements disappear, unless both charts have the same planet out of bounds in the same hemisphere, and critical zero positions can get clogged up with a mass of North-South midpoints. Neither is it very reliable, in my opinion, to calculate the composite chart in longitude first, then convert it straightforwardly to a declinational equivalent. Apart from anything else, nothing will be out of bounds. Using the Davison Composite method however can give a more interesting declination chart because we are working with an actual moment in time rather than a symbolic average.

The Davison Composite chart (previously mentioned in the out-of-bounds section on Ronald Davison) is a chart derived from the midpoint in time and space between two nativities. As a simple example, if one person was born at 10am on 1 January 1966 and the other at 2pm on 1 January 1968, the midpoint in time between their births would be 12 noon on 1 January 1967. And if they were born in the same location it is a chart for this place that would be calculated and taken as the composite between them. (If born in different places the shortest path between the two locations produces a third point on which to base the calculation.) From a declination point of view the location is not necessarily so important, as angles and houses mean less than planetary positions.

We can see immediately that this Davison chart is a more reliable one to examine for declination purposes. Perhaps there will be planets out of bounds or in critical zero positions in the Davison chart that do not appear in either of the individual charts, and this can say a lot about the nature of the two people's relationship together. We might see how two seemingly quiet or unadventurous types can be dynamite together or how two wildly out-of-bounds individual charts may produce a calmer and altogether more peaceful composite. The possibilities are not only manifold but add a great deal more to the longitude interpretation.

Composites in Time
Composite charts are not limited only to the charts of people. A useful composite is to join one's own birth chart with the chart of a business, an institution, even a country. To interpret the result read the longitude indications in the usual way for a general overview then check for any out-of-bounds or zero-line planets to highlight the planetary energies that are unusually active.

Another useful exercise is to join your natal chart in a Davison Composite with the chart of a specific moment in time, like a powerful planetary conjunction, eclipse or lunation. Ingress charts are particularly useful as part of a composite, especially the annual Spring Equinox (the moment that the Sun reaches the celestial equator and enters zero degrees of Aries) as this combination can be read as a personal forecast for the year ahead. After you have looked at the standard longitudinal indications showing notable house areas etc., look at the declinations particularly for clues to extreme planetary energies. Any planets out of bounds or within two degrees of zero are your quick clues to the forces that could represent your magnified talents during that year.

Declination at Stonehenge

Stonehenge with its proven astronomical alignments is undeniably a solar temple, but we might more accurately call it a "standstill" temple. The main axis of the Neolithic monument on Salisbury Plain corresponds to the solstices, the Sun's annual standstills. As the Earth's tilt has not changed a great deal in the five thousand years or so since Stonehenge is reckoned to have been built, the midsummer Sun still rises over the Heel Stone on the day of the northern solstice and sets in midwinter at the opposite point on the southern solstice.

Yet the standstill of the Moon is also an important factor in its construction. The Years of the High Moon (as they are termed by Gerald Hawkins in one of his last books on Stonehenge)[103] are those years when the Moon is at its highest possible declination and come at intervals of 18-19

---
103. Gerald S. Hawkins and Hubert A. Allen Jr, *Stonehenge Earth and Sky*, Wessex Books, Salisbury, 2004.

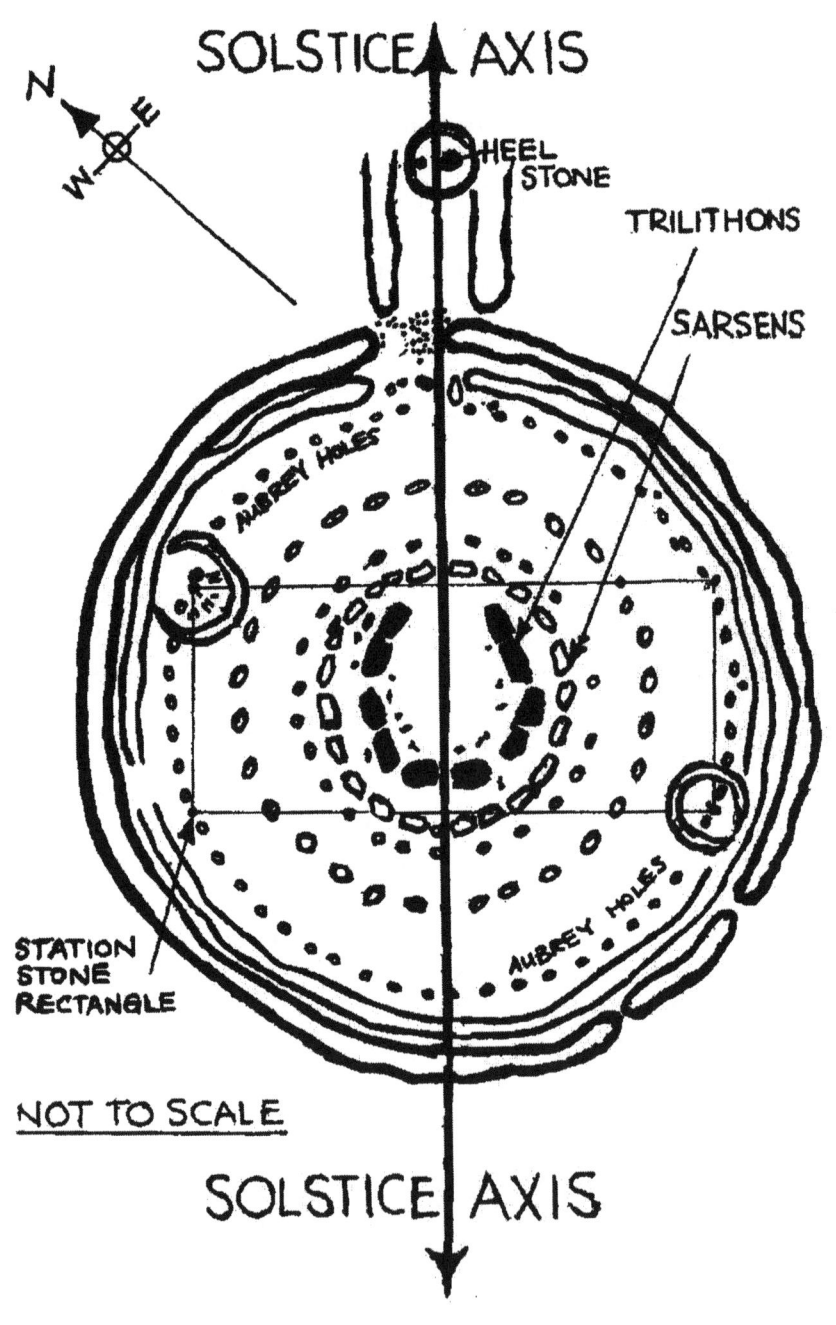

Stonehenge

years. As previously mentioned in the early part of this book, the Moon's out-of-bounds cycle lasts from 9-10 years followed by a similar inbound cycle, with the high point in the middle of the OOB cycle known as the major lunar standstill.

Three of these periods (from first to third major standstill) cover 56 years, a total corresponding to the number of Aubrey Holes, the outermost ring of cavities at Stonehenge which may originally have held wooden posts as markers. But it was the trilithons, the huge inner stone archways through which the Sun and the Moon are framed at their standstills, that prove that Stonehenge was visually oriented to the declination of both Sun and Moon in equal measure. These trilithons are special inner archways, as distinct from the outer ring of sarsen arches, and were a mystery for many years because the stones of their arches are positioned too close together for a human being to squeeze through. It has now been realised that their purpose was not for ceremonial processions to pass between but more likely for viewing a specific narrow band of the sky and horizon, especially as the openings are wider at the top.

At the equinoxes the Sun will rise and set due East and West, but at the solstices it rises and sets at its farthest extremes: points that are marked on the horizon from Stonehenge as a view through the windows of the deliberately placed stone archways. The important Heel Stone over which the midsummer Sun rises was only recently discovered (in 1979) to have been one of a pair through which the rising solstice Sun at its most north-easterly position would have been perfectly framed. Moonrise and moonset at the turning point of the major lunar standstill had similar stone arch windows to mark the occurrence.

Stonehenge also had four Station Stones placed at the corners of a rectangle within the Aubrey Hole circle whose diagonals crossed the centre of the monument and whose shorter sides lay parallel to the midsummer axis. These gave a viewing position for the standstill (solstice) sunrise along its shorter sides and a viewing position for the standstill moonset along its longer sides.

If Stonehenge is indeed a Standstill Temple, and whatever else it may have been it is certainly that, then it is a marker of Turning Points. If it marks the turning points of Sun and Moon as seen from the Earth, then it also marks the turning points of the Earth in its own orbit. But why it was necessary to haul some of these massive blocks of stone over land and sea all the way from West Wales to central Southern England in order to construct this cosmic computer remains an unanswered question.

Annual Energy Boosts

An exercise based on the Sun

The natal declination of your Sun, and its position on its annual path, relates to the time of year that you were born. Obviously - it is your birthday. But if you find the antiscion to this degree and relate it back to an actual date in the year, that date must also be tied to your birthday. The two dates are linked somehow. Perhaps it could be called a Second Birthday, and seen as a culmination of whatever began on the real birthday, the solar return.

In my experience, and before I studied declination, I found that there were even more annual dates that often acted regularly as new starts. These were certain times of the year that had nothing to do with my birthday or the position of other planets on my birth chart. Now I believe (in fact I know) that they are the **Contra-parallels of the Sun**. The two parallel points in the opposing hemisphere to those which contain the natal Sun and its antiscion, give two more calendar dates tied to the solar energy.

As an example someone born on December 1st with the Sun at 9°30' Sagittarius, would have the reflection to this, the antiscia, when the Sun reached 20°30' Capricorn on January 10th. The contra-parallels to these two points would be at 9°30' Gemini and 20°30' Cancer, whose calendar dates would be May 30th and July 12th. The declination of the Sun will be precisely the same at all four of these times: 21°53' from the equator. 21°53' *South* of the equator in December and January and 21°53' *North* of the equator in May and July.

So we have access to four annual energy boosts of possible new starts in any one year.

Three Types of Moon

It is interesting to symbolise the Moon's fluctuating path to the tides of the sea, which are, of course, ruled by the Moon.

It is a fact that the highest and lowest sea tides of the year reach their maxima around the time of the equinoxes. In the vocabulary of declination, the equinoxes resemble the area of 0° declination where the corresponding essences of longitudinal degrees are more stretched out. The first degree of declination North or South covers only five degrees of zodiacal longitude, whereas the 23rd degree North or South covers over 17 longitudinal degrees.

Equinox Moon energy applies to everyone whose natal Moon lies in Pisces, Aries, Virgo or Libra (the signs around the equinoxes). If we were to stand on a beach at the equinox on a New or Full Moon, we would observe the vast distance uncovered at low tide and the previously unseen treasures brought to light. This is analogous to examining the declination area of zero degrees whose crossing uncovers new views. Or put another way: while you may sail your boat from harbour on a high equinox tide, it could be totally grounded only a few hours later.

The sight of many sailing craft standing askew in the sand of a receding tide reminds us why the equinox period of zero declination gives the ability to be grounded and touch reality. It could also be seen as a period of rediscovering fundamentals from our past. Those with Pisces, Aries, Virgo or Libra Moons may poetically see beneath the ocean and explore the longest beaches in the world. Water has memory they say, and here our deepest memories lie freshly uncovered and blinking in the sunlight. The Equinox Moon (especially heightened for those with their Moon in the latter degrees of Virgo or Pisces, or the early degrees of Aries or Libra) could be called a **Beachcomber's Moon.**

With the solstice tides, the reverse holds true. The sea tides around the solstices are the very smallest in movement, so that those people with Solstice Moons (Moon in Gemini, Cancer, Sagittarius or Capricorn) may symbolise this energy. The water does not go up the harbour wall so far, but neither does it go down so far. Here we find that the compression of many zodiacal degrees of longitude into a smaller space equals a similar difference in tide lines.

Yet within that space, the considerable number of longitudinal degrees (many more than at the equinox) must relate to a sizeable volume of zodiacal experience. To stand on a beach at a solstice lunation is to see the sea currents flowing into and out of each other quickly, indicating perhaps the rapid mixing of many divergent ideas. The ebb and flow is fast and furious. The movement is rapid. High declination has an operation that is wilder and freer, offering glimpses more of the future than the past. While we may miss beachcombing our treasures from the past, we are in compensation buoyed up on the many new influences constantly sweeping in from the farthest global shores. The Solstice Moon (particularly strong for those whose Moon occupies the latter degrees of Gemini or Sagittarius or the early degrees of Cancer or Capricorn, and especially in those recurring periods when the Moon goes out of bounds) could be called a **Voyager's Moon.**

And what of the in-between Moons, those whose declination/zodiacal positions place them halfway between the above-mentioned extremes? These are the Moons in the four Fixed signs of Taurus, Leo, Scorpio and Aquarius, in our analogy representative of the times of the year between the solstices and equinoxes, the cross quarter festivals. The sea tides move in balance here, the lunar force steadies and is less inclined to swing in extremes. This is a **Constant Moon.**

Please bear in mind that these classifications are not taking into account the individual Moon phases that one may be born under, nor other irregular fluctuations like the void-of-course Moon etc.

8
The Path of Ra

A Shamanic Journey with the Sun

A few years ago I conducted an experiment with my colleague Lorraine Exley, an astrologer who is also a shaman - a person with the ability to enter into the inner spirit of outer forms. We hoped to uncover a pictorial degree symbol and divinatory meaning for each degree of declination north and south of the equator (including four out-of-bounds degrees).

Over a twelve-month period, from July 1998 to July 1999, the resultant images and experiences were recorded and collated. At first, we assumed that the images obtained might allow contemplation of possible meanings from natal planets in declination degrees. And while that may still be a valid use, we later concluded that the real purpose was to follow a shamanic journey with the Sun throughout the year.

Many of the images contained a likeness of the Sun, often depicted as a life force in the form of a globe or a golden circle. Unlike the more static pictures found in other sets of degree symbols, these declination symbols were more shamanic in nature; concerned with the flow of energy in the universe as it takes shape in various forms. They were moving pictures where energy bends through manifestations generated by the various parameters of the Sun's journey above and below the celestial equator. All the senses were captured in the symbols. Not only sight but touch, taste, smell, and hearing played as large a part in the description of the overall energy.

The entire set of these images can now be accessed on www.shamanicsun.com

A different time ratio
All previous sets of astrological degree symbols have been based on zodiacal longitude. 360 picture images. The declination degrees are quite different. Firstly, in declination, there are not as many solar degrees (48 as compared to 360); secondly and most importantly, they are irregular in time. As we have already seen, each of the first 15 degrees of declination, north or south, corresponds to three days of the Sun's movement on average (six days if you count the antiscia; the Sun returning to that same degree later in the year).

But in the area from 16° to the maximum declination of 23°26' North or South, the Sun stays longer and longer in each degree. At its highest point around the solstices the Sun can remain for an incredible 23 days in just one declination degree. Using the solar calendar this means that between June 11 and July 3 each year the Sun remains in the same declination symbol; a similar, slightly smaller number of days with a different symbol occurs around the southern solstice.

Another basic difference between zodiac degree symbols and declination degree symbols is the shape of their structure.

Dane Rudhyar often emphasised the circular nature of the Sabian symbols and that they formed a cycle of transformation in 360 phases. In his book *An Astrological Mandala* he pointed out that 1° Aries as a starting point in the process could begin anywhere, not necessarily in the first degree of Aries.[104] The important thing was the sequence, the position within the entire cyclic framework.

In the round zodiac, the Sun (or any planet) takes a step-by-step journey through 360 degrees and therefore 360 degree symbols. But in declination the Sun passes through the same degree twice in the course of a year, in an altered time ratio.

This presents a different kind of learning curve from that of the tropical zodiac, especially when degree symbols are employed. The implication with declination symbols is that we meet the same lesson twice in a six-month period from equinox to equinox. In fact, we return to the same degree symbol from which we began, before moving into the next half of the year and another set of paired declination symbols.

If we follow the Sun as our guide, we meet specific lessons in a proven sequence, but this sequence is not necessarily linear or straightforwardly cyclic. The declination journey is more like an initial rush at the equinoxes as we jump across degrees every two or three days, slowing down to longer and longer periods in each degree as we approach the solstices. This leads to a long unbroken period of more than three weeks in one degree around the solstice. But then we retrace our steps, encountering the same degree symbols in reverse order and for the same durations of time, until we rush again to the equinox to face ourselves and then step into the second half of the year.

As in climbing a mountain we start at the equinoxes with a steep incline, ascending quickly until the path gradually flattens and we spend

---

104. Dane Rudhyar, *An Astrological Mandala: The Cycle of Transformations and its 360 Symbolic Phases*, Vintage Books, New York, 1973.

longer traversing what is almost a plateau around the mountain's solstice peak. We then descend another side of the mountain but with a similar view of the levels we pass (similar degree symbols to ponder). Whatever the lessons contained in each degree, we are not expected to master them the first time we encounter them.

The Earth as a kingdom in liege to the Sun

By tropical zodiac movement we think of the Sun stepping through each day of the year in an even, forward, ever-onward motion. We count our age in solar years and understand that we grow a little older with each passing day. By declination the Sun does not follow this pattern. Although it still makes its birth/growth/decay/death cycle in the course of one year, its movement within the year is very different. Instead of the gradual step-by-step process through the days and zodiac degrees, the Sun by declination moves at various speeds through the degrees north and south and retraces its steps. The implication is that we live cyclically in tune with other solar rhythms.

> "I am far, far beyond that island of days where once, it seems, I watched a flower grow, and counted the steps of the sun..." [105]

This poetic lament, though written with no conscious bearing on the theory of declination, captures precisely the feeling of being shut out from some natural harmony. Old ceremonies like 'beating the bounds' survive into our times, where ancient parish boundaries were annually reactivated by a communal procession singing and chanting along its course. It ensured that important perimeters and farthest limits were clearly marked and kept in order, and harmony between spirit and land ensured.

The shamanic declination images can be seen as energy points between our own etheric bodies and the etheric body of the planet, and defining and honouring the Sun's path through an awareness of its journey through the declination degrees is to help maintain the delicate Earth/Sun balance. The solar harmony is discernible every day if we seek it as we connect with the vital yet subtle Steps of the Sun.

---

105.   Elizabeth Smart, *By Grand Central Station I Sat Down And Wept*, Nicholson & Watson, London, 1945.

Appendix 1
Ecliptic and Equator

The fundamental astronomy of it all

In my experience nothing has the potential to confuse students of astrology more than Spherical Astronomy's doctrine of the "Great Circles" and the complicated diagrams of celestial spheres with imaginary lines running all over them. Most of the problem lies in trying to get your head around two different viewpoints at the same time: a view of the sky from Earth drawn as a view of the sky towards the Earth. It is hoped that by separating these two views the basic concepts will become clearer.

On a planisphere, celestial globe or flat star chart of the sky, two lines will usually be found. One is labelled the Ecliptic the other the Celestial Equator. (See flat chart on the following page).

The **Celestial Equator** is the Earth's equator extended into space, with degrees of measurement shown above and below this line. These are the degrees of declination with which this book has been concerned.

The **Ecliptic** is the line or plane of the Sun's path, which always runs through the zodiac constellations. Measurements of celestial longitude (the 360 degrees of the zodiac) run along this line.

Although naturally these 'lines' are not visible in the sky, they represent a view from Earth. When we view the same phenomenon from outer space, as if we were looking at the solar system from the outside, we get something like the diagram of the zodiacal belt shown after the skymap on the following pages.

The diagram is not to scale but illustrates the fact that the solar system is almost flat like a disk. All the planets including the Earth move around the Sun in a similar plane. This plane is not completely flat however. The planets move up and down as they go round and round, and the width of the band, which is traditionally about 16 to 18 degrees wide, encompasses the zodiac constellations that lie outside it. That is why, from Earth, all the other planets are seen against the backdrop of the zodiac.

Appendix 1   175

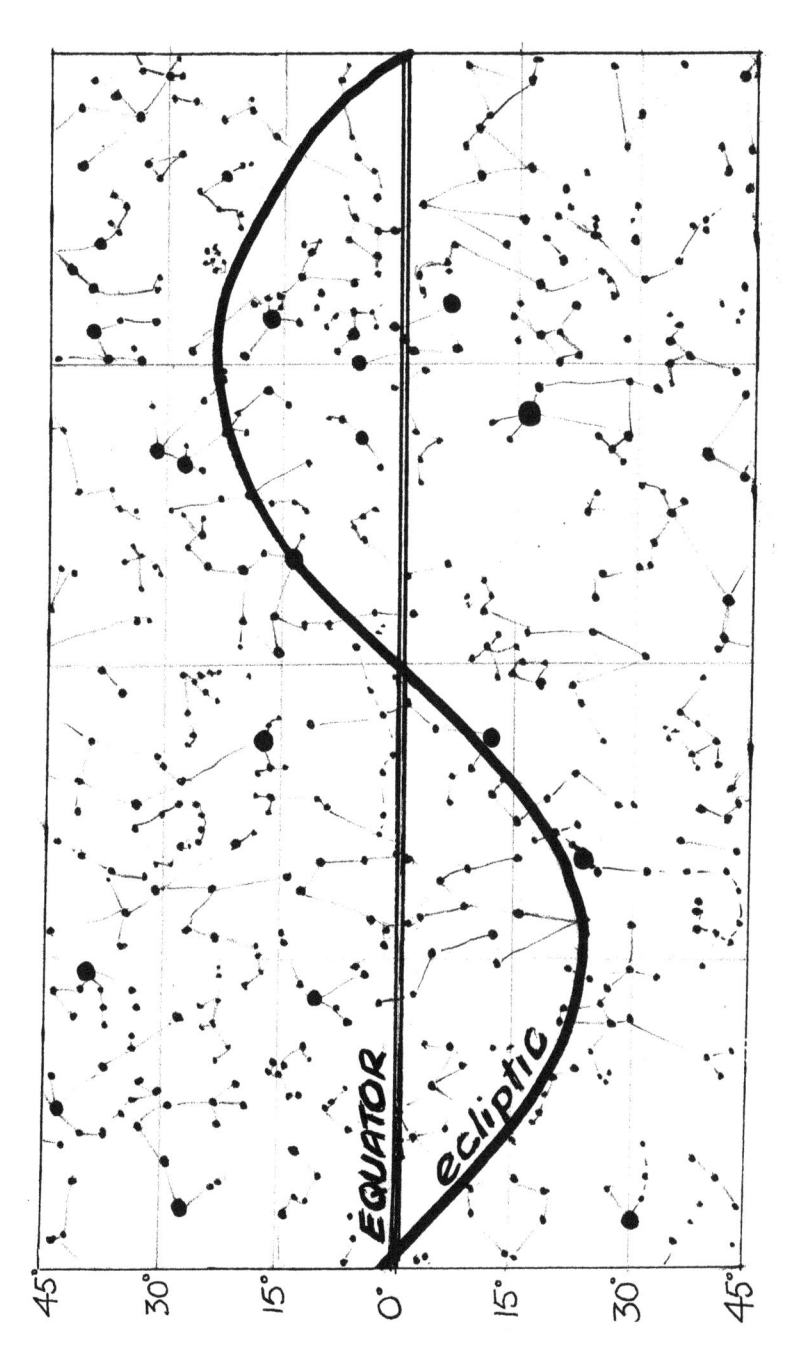

Sky-map showing ecliptic and equator

176   *Declination in Astrology*

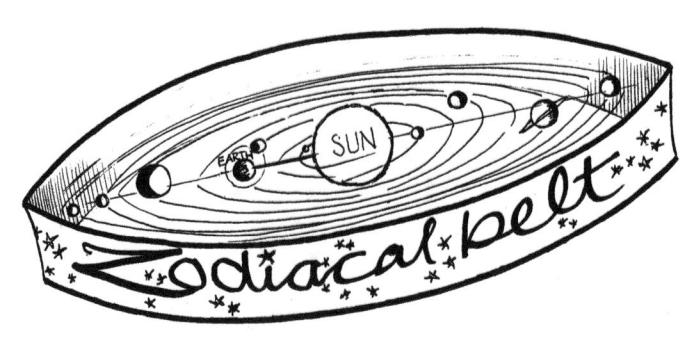

The Zodiacal Belt

The line in the diagram that connects the Earth to the Sun is the plane of the Earth's path around the Sun. This is the **Ecliptic.**

The word Ecliptic comes from 'eclipse', because this is the only place where the Sun, the Moon and the Earth can come into a direct alignment and therefore the only place where solar or lunar eclipses can occur. If the Moon, which is encircling the Earth in the diagram, has reached this line of the ecliptic it would be directly between the Earth and the Sun, causing an eclipse of the Sun to the Earth. If the Moon reached behind the Earth and crossed the ecliptic on the other side it would be blocked from receiving sunlight and would then be in total shadow, (an eclipse of the Moon).

In the following diagram the Earth and the Sun have been extracted from the larger picture:

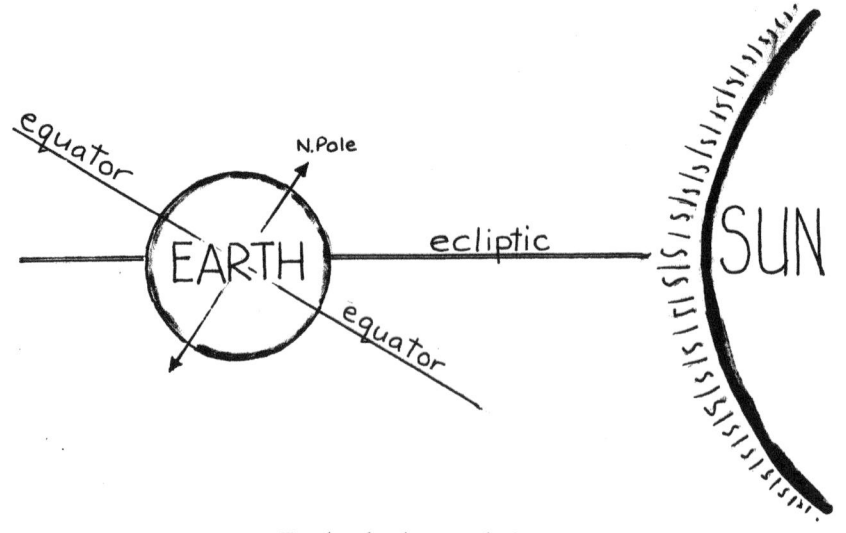

Earth tilted towards Sun

Here we can see that the Earth is tilted on its axis as it orbits the Sun. It inclines or *declines* at an angle of 23°26' to the ecliptic and it remains at this same tilted angle throughout its orbit. (The measurement of the angle is the obliquity of the ecliptic). In the picture the Sun's rays are directly hitting the northern hemisphere of the Earth so it is June or July, summer in the northern hemisphere. Six months later in December the Earth will have moved around the ecliptic to the other side of the Sun. As it remains tilted at the same angle the northern part of the Earth will now be pointing away from the Sun while the southern part will be closer. (See diagram below). Thus the Sun's rays now hit the southern hemisphere directly and it is summer in the south.

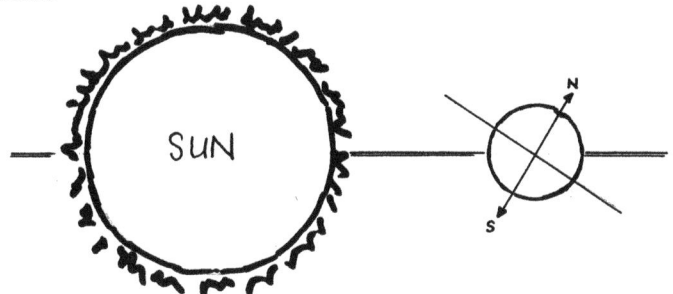

Sun-Earth

Midway between these two summer and winter extremes, in March and September, the Earth will be in a position for the Sun's rays to hit its equator directly. These are the only times and places that the equator and the ecliptic can cross or intersect each other. When the Sun is directly over the equator in this way it produces the equinoxes on Earth and day and night are equal. It is the point of zero degrees Aries (and zero degrees Libra) on the tropical zodiac.

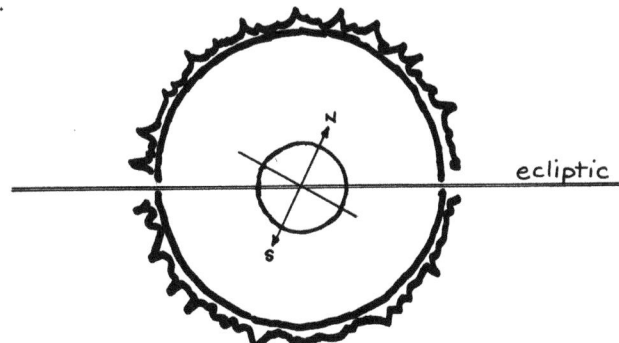

Earth on Sun at Equinox

We can see that if the Earth was not tilted and its equator was always in line with the ecliptic throughout the year, there would be no summer or winter, no longer or shorter days, no difference in the seasons at all. The birth/growth/death cycles of nature would not exist and we would find it difficult to count our age or our history in terms of years.

The precession of the Equinoxes

Over a vast period of time the Earth's axis completes a slight cyclical wobble which in turn causes the equator to vary its angle to the ecliptic. This means that the point the equator crosses the ecliptic (the equinox point) will also slowly move. Against the backdrop of the zodiac stars it moves retrogressively about 1 degree in 70 years, and this is what is known as the Precession of the Equinoxes. The Aries equinox or Spring Point currently points to the end of Pisces/beginning of Aquarius, hence we are said to be entering the Age of Aquarius. To travel through one-twelfth of the sky, or one zodiac Age, takes approximately 2,160 years. The whole cycle of precession encompasses 25,920 years.

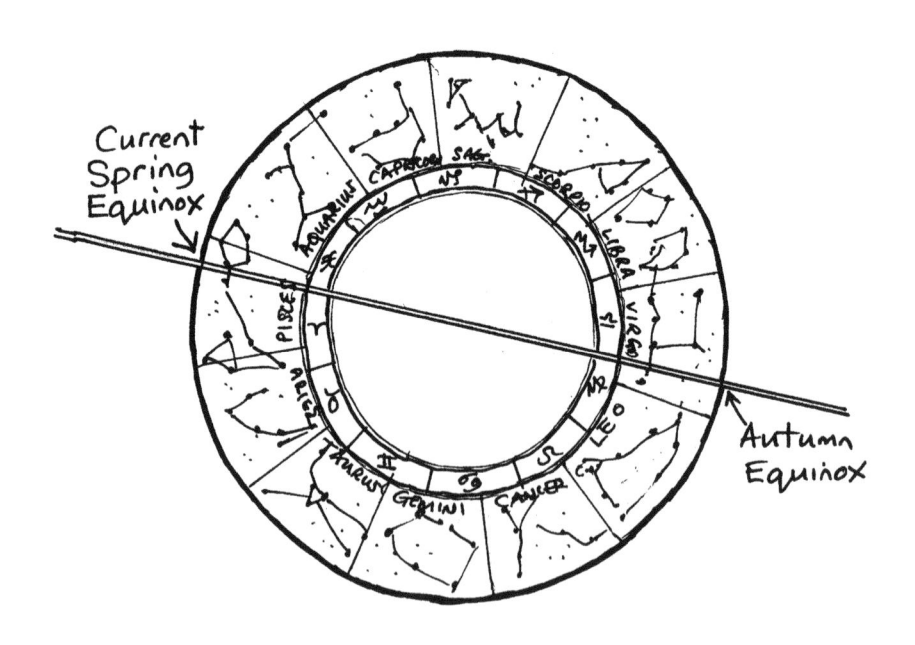

Constellations and Equinoxes

The tropical zodiac, which always begins at the equinox point, is therefore out of step with the zodiacal constellations or sidereal zodiac that lie behind it. The difference between the two zodiacs will continue to become even greater for at least 10,000 years, after which time they will slowly realign. Everything works in cycles.

The idea that astrology, as we practice it today, began when the sidereal and tropical zodiacs coincided - as if our ancestors were not aware of precession - is a cherished myth that is unlikely to be true.

Appendix 2
Named Stars and their Declinations

Our previous list of the brightest 12 stars in the solar declination area is now expanded to include a total of 177 named stars that also lie in the region up to and including 29 degrees North and South. The fact that most all of these have traditional names - which it has to be said sometimes differ according to source - proves that they were all visually important. To avoid any confusion over star names, Bayer's method of identification using constellation and letters of the Greek alphabet is also given in brackets in every case, plus the zodiac position of the stars as at the year 2000.

AD 2000 positions

Name of star	Declination	Longitude
North		
HEZE (zeta Virginis)	00N05	21 Libra 52
ZANIAH (eta Virginis)	00N07	04 Libra 31
MINTAKA (delta Orionis)	00N22	22 Gemini 24
SADALMELEK (alpha Aquarii)	00N48	03 Pisces 45
ZAVIJAVA (beta Virginis)	01N46	27 Virgo 09
MARFIK (lambda Ophiuchi)	01N59	05 Sag 36
AL RISCHA (alpha Piscium)	02N46	29 Aries 23
DENEB OKAB (delta Aquilae)	03N06	23 Cap 38
KAFFALJIDHMA (gamma Cetus)	03N13	09 Taurus 26
AUVA (delta Virginis)	03N24	11 Libra 28
MENKAR (alpha Ceti)	04N04	14 Taurus 19
ALYA (theta Serpens)	04N12	15 Cap 45
KELB ALRAI (beta Ophiuchi)	04N34	25 Sag 20
PROCYON (alpha Canis Minoris)	05N13	25 Cancer 47
KITALPHA (alpha Equuleus)	05N14	23 Aqu 07
BIHAM (theta Pegasi)	06N12	06 Pisces 50
BELLATRIX (gamma Orionis)	06N21	20 Gemini 56
ALSHAIN (beta Aquilae)	06N24	02 Aqu 25
UNUKHALAI (alpha Serpentis)	06N26	22 Scorpio 04

Appendix 2   181

TABIT (pi3 Orionis)	06N57	11 Gemini 55
BETELGEUSE (alpha Orionis)	07N24	28 Gemini 45
GOMEISA (beta Canis Minorum)	08N17	22 Cancer 12
ALTAIR (alpha Aquilae)	08N52	01 Aqu 45
AL TARF (beta Cancri)	09N11	04 Leo 15
ENIF (epsilon Pegasi)	09N52	01 Pisces 52
SUBRA (omicron Leonis)	09N54	24 Leo 14
MEISSA (lambda Orionis)	09N55	23 Gem 42
TARAZAD (gamma Aquilae)	10N36	00 Aqu 55
HOMAM (zeta Pegasi)	10N49	16 Pisces 09
VINDEMIATRIX (epsilon Virginis)	10N58	09 Libra 56
ACUBENS (alpha Cancri)	11N52	13 Leo 38
REGULUS (alpha Leonis)	11N57	29 Leo 49
RASALHAGUE (alpha Ophiuchi)	12N33	22 Sag 26
ALZIRR (xi Geminorum)	12N54	11 Cancer 13
DHENEB (zeta Aquilae)	13N51	19 Cap 47
KAJAM (omega Herculi)	14N02	01 Sag 33
RAS ALGETHI (alpha Herculis)	14N23	16 Sag 08
ROTANEV (beta delphinus)	14N35	16 Aqu 19
DENEBOLA (beta Leonis)	14N35	21 Virgo 36
ALGENIB (gamma Pegasi)	15N11	09 Aries 09
MARKAB (alpha Pegasi)	15N11	23 Pisces 28
ALPHERG (eta Piscium)	15N21	26 Aries 49
COXA (theta Leo Minor)	15N26	13 Virgo 25
PRIMA HYADUM (gamma Tauri)	15N37	05 Gem 48
SUALOCIN (alpha delphinus)	15N54	17 Aqu 22
ALHENA (gamma Geminorum)	16N24	09 Cancer 06
ALDEBARAN (alpha Tauri)	16N30	09 Gem 47
AL JABHAH (eta Leonis)	16N46	27 Leo 54
MARSIK (kappa Herculi)	17N03	25 Scorpio 42
HYADUM II (delta Tauri)	17N32	06 Gemini 52
DIADEM (alpha Coma Berenices)	17N32	08 Libra 56
SHAM (alpha Sagitta)	18N00	01 Aqu 03
SOUTH ASELLUS (delta Cancri)	18N09	08 Leo 43
MUFRID (eta Bootes)	18N24	19 Libra 19
AIN (epsilon Tauri)	19N11	08 Gem 28
ARCTURUS (alpha Bootes)	19N11	24 Libra 13
MESARTIM (gamma Arietis)	19N17	03 Taurus 11
PRAESEPE Cluster (M44 Cancri)	19N41	07 Leo 20

BOTEIN (delta Arietis)	19N44	20 Taurus 51
ALGIEBA (gamma Leonis)	19N51	29 Leo 36
ZOSMA (delta Leonis)	20N32	11 Virgo 18
MEKBUDA (zeta Geminorum)	20N34	14 Cancer 59
SHARATAN (beta Arietis)	20N47	03 Taurus 58
AL HECKA (zeta Tauri)	21N09	24 Gem 47
NORTH ASELLUS (gamma Cancri)	21N28	07 Leo 32
KORNEPHOROS (beta Herculi)	21N29	01 Sag 04
WASAT (delta Geminorum)	21N58	18 Cancer 31
TEJAT (eta Geminorum)	22N30	03 Cancer 26
DIRAH (mu Geminorum)	22N30	05 Cancer 18
ALTERF (lambda Leonis)	22N58	17 Leo 52
ADHAFERA (zeta Leonis)	23N25	27 Leo 33
HAMAL (alpha Arietis)	23N27	07 Taurus 40
KERB (tau Pegasi)	23N43	01 Aries 03
MEROPE (23 Tauri)	23N56	29 Taurus 42
ATLAS (27 Tauri)	24N03	00 Gemini 21
ALCYONE (eta Tauri)	24N06	29 Taurus 59
ELECTRA (17 Tauri)	24N06	29 Taurus 24
PLEIONE (28 Tauri)	24N07	00 Gemini 23
CELAENO (16 Tauri)	24N17	29 Taurus 26
MAIA (20 Tauri)	24N21	29 Taurus 42
TAYGETA (19 Tauri)	24N27	29 Taurus 34
SADALBARI (mu Pegasi)	24N35	24 Pisces 23
ALGENUBI (epsilon Leonis)	23N46	20 Leo 42
ASTEROPE (kappa Tauri)	24N33	29 Taurus 44
SARIN (delta Herculi)	24N50	14 Sag 45
MEBSUTA (epsilon Geminorum)	25N07	09 Cancer 56
RAS ELASED BORE (mu Leonis)	26N00	21 Leo 26
MAASYM (lambda Herculi)	26N06	19 Sag 53
ALPHECCA (alpha Coronae Borealis)	26N43	12 Scorpio 17
IZAR (epsilon Bootes)	27N05	28 Libra 06
ALBIREO (beta Cygni)	27N58	01 Aqu 14
POLLUX (beta Geminorum)	28N01	23 Cancer 13
SCHEAT (beta Pegasi)	28N04	29 Pisces 22
EL NATH (beta Tauri)	28N36	22 Gem 34
ALPHERATZ (alpha Andromedae)	29N05	14 Aries 18
NUSAKAN (beta Coronae Borealis)	29N06	09 Scorpio 07
METALLAH (alpha Triangulum)	29N34	06 Taurus 51

Appendix 2   183

South

ALNILAM (epsilon Orionis)	01S12	23 Gemini 27
SADALACHBIA (gamma Aquarii)	01S23	06 Pisces 42
PORRIMA (gamma Virginis)	01S27	10 Libra 08
ALNITAK (zeta Orionis)	01S57	24 Gemini 41
MIRA (omicrom Ceti)	02S59	01 Taurus 31
YAD PRIOR (delta Ophiuchi)	03S41	02 Sag 17
SITULA (kappa Aquarii)	04S14	09 Pisces 24
YED POSTERIOR (epsilon Ophiuchi)	04S41	03 Sag 30
CURSA (beta Eridani)	05S05	15 Gemini 16
SADALSUUD (beta Aquarii)	05S34	23 Aqu 23
HATSYA (iota Orionis)	05S54	23 Gemini 00
SYRMA (iota Virginis)	05S59	03 Scorpio 47
BEID (omicron 1 Eridani)	06S50	29 Taurus 26
KEID (omicron 2 Eridani)	07S39	00 Gemini 11
ANCHA (theta Aquarii)	07S47	03 Pisces 15
RIGEL (beta Orionis)	08S12	16 Gemini 49
ZUBEN ELAKRIBI (delta Librae)	08S30	15 Scorpio 16
ALPHARD (alpha Hydrae)	08S40	27 Leo 17
ZIBAL (zeta Eridani)	08S49	13 Taurus 49
AZHA eta Eridani)	08S54	08 Taurus 45
NORTH SCALE (beta Librae)	09S22	19 Scorpio 22
ALBALI (epsilon Aquarii)	09S30	11 Aqu 43
SAIPH (kappa Orionis)	09S40	26 Gemini 24
RANA (delta Eridani)	09S46	20 Taurus 52
SINISTRA (mu Ophiuchi)	09S46	29 Sag 44
BATEN KAITOS (zeta Ceti)	10S20	21 Aries 57
HAN (zeta Ophiuchi)	10S33	09 Sag 13
SPICA (alpha Virginis)	11S09	23 Libra 50
GIEDI (alpha Capriconi)	12S30	03 Aqu 45
GIEDI SECUNDA (alpha 2 Capriconi)	12S32	03 Aqu 51
ALSHAT (nu Capricorni)	12S46	04 Aqu 25
KHAMBALIA (lambda Virginis)	13S21	06 Scorpio 57
ZAURAK (gamma Eridani)	13S30	23 Taurus 52
SCEPTRUM (53 Eridani)	14S18	05 Gemini 15
LABRUM (delta Crateris)	14S46	26 Virgo 41
DABIH (beta Capricorni)	14S47	04 Aqu 02
ZUBEN ELAKRAB (gamma Librae)	14S47	25 Scorpio 07
MULIPHEIN (gamma Canis Majorum)	15S37	19 Cancer 37

SABIK (eta Ophiuchi)	15S43	17 Sag 57
SKAT (delta Aquarii)	15S49	08 Pisces 52
SOUTH SCALE (alpha Librae)	16S01	15 Scorpio 04
DENEB ALGEDI (delta Capricorni)	16S08	23 Aqu 32
ZUBEN HAKRABI (nu Librae)	16S14	18 Scorpio 46
ALGORAB (delta Corvi)	16S31	13 Libra 27
NASHIRA (gamma Capricorni)	16S40	21 Aqu 47
SIRIUS (alpha Canis Majorum)	16S43	14 Cancer 05
DORSUM (theta Capricorni)	17S14	13 Aqu 50
GIENAH (gamma Corvi)	17S31	10 Libra 43
BOS (rho Capricorni)	17N49	05 Aqu 09
ARNEB (alpha Lepus)	17S49	21 Gemini 32
MIRZAM (beta Canis Majorum)	17S57	07 Cancer 11
DIFDA (beta Ceti)	17S59	02 Aries 35
OCULUS (pi Capricorni)	18S13	04 Aqu 42
ALKES (alpha Crateris)	18S18	23 Virgo 41
JABBAH (nu Scorpii)	19S27	04 Sag 38
CASTRA (epsilon Capricorni)	19S28	20 Aqu 11
AKRAB (beta 1 Scorpii)	19S48	03 Sag 11
ARMUS (eta Capricorni)	19S51	12 Aqu 44
NIHAL (beta Lepus)	20S45	19 Gemini 40
ANGETENAR (tau 2 Eridani)	21S00	02 Taurus 38
AL BALDAH (pi Sagittarii)	21S01	16 Cap 14
POLIS (mu Sagittarii)	21S03	03 Cap 12
MANUBRIUM (omicron Sagittarii)	21S44	14 Cap 59
MINKAR (epsilon Corvi)	22S36	11 Libra 40
ISIDIS (delta Scorpii)	22S36	02 Sag 34
KRAZ (beta Corvi)	23S22	17 Libra 22
STAR CLUSTER 22M (M22 Sagittarii)	23S55	08 Cap 18
TRIFID & LAGOON (Nebula M8, M20, M21)	24S19	01 Cap 03
ALCHITA (alpha Corvi)	24S44	12 Libra 14
AZMIDISKE (xi Puppis)	24S52	06 Leo 03
KAUS BOREALIS (lambda Sagittarii)	25S25	06 Cap 18
NUNKI (sigma Sagittarii)	26S17	12 Cap 22
TEREBELLUM (omega Sagittarii)	26S18	25 Cap 50
WEZEN (delta Canis Majorum)	26S23	23 Cancer 24
ANTARES (alpha Scorpii)	26S25	09 Sag 45
ADARA (epsilon Canis Majorum)	28S58	20 Cancer 46
ALUDRA (eta Canis Majorum)	29S18	29 Cancer 32

FOMALHAUT (alpha Pisces Australis)   29S38   03 Pisces 51
KAUS MEDIUS (delta Sagittarii)   29S49   04 Cap 34
ASCELLA (zeta Sagittarii)   29S53   13 Cap 38

Appendix 3
Investigating Yods

My springboard for this feature was a study by Ed Dearborn on the 150-degree aspect ("The Ramifications of the Quincunx" [105]) in which the distinction between a quincunx and an inconjunct aspect was considered and the combinations of different house meanings in a Yod were examined.

Ed supported the findings of J.Lee Lehman [106] (who cites ancient sources) that the 150-degree aspect is more challenging, and consequently more driven and powerful, if one of the zodiac signs involved is a Fixed one. This is technically an inconjunct aspect. If neither of the signs involved in the 150-degree measurement is Fixed then the aspect is called a quincunx.

The triangular figure of the Yod, derived from two 150-degree aspects and one of 60 degrees, is host to many general interpretations including the popular "secret talents emerging" or "stress-related health problems". But both of these can be seen to have derived from drawing a Yod across the 1st-6th-8th houses of a horoscope with the focal planet in the 1st and taking that as a basis for all meanings. As Mr Dearborn's study points out other house combinations can tell different stories. For one of the best general interpretations of a natal Yod I endorse Robert Blaschke's suggestion that it can produce a life with "many fated changes in direction due to circumstances beyond (one's) direct control, thus leading to an evolving spiritual philosophy containing surrender to the Will of God".[107]

A Yod will always have one planet (or angle) in a Cardinal sign, one in a Fixed sign and one in a Mutable sign, hence both the oddness and the inherent wholeness of a Yod's energy. But the combinations will differ. It may be composed of 2 inconjuncts and a sextile, or 1 inconjunct 1 quincunx and a sextile. **It is the Yod with a Fixed sign planet at its apex that is the most powerful as it is composed of 2 inconjuncts.** 4 out of a possible 12

---

105. Later published as 'The Inconjunct, The Quincunx, and Yod' in *The Mountain Astrologer, Mercury Direct* (Cedar Ridge, California, USA), August/September 2006.
106. J.Lee Lehman, *Aspects* Volume 17, No.11, Summer 1992.
107. Robert P. Blaschke, *Earthwalk Astrology Newsletter*, February 2005. www.earthwalkastrology.com

different combinations of Yods (talking of signs not houses) are Fixed sign Yods or Inconjunct Yods.

The Fixed sign Yods may be challenging for an additional reason as they will contain the only combinations of three zodiac signs that have no zodiacal parallel or contra-parallel relationship to each other. They are not "beholding" to each other, to use Ptolemy's expression, so their lever for adjustment is more exaggerated. The fated life-script more hard won. For example, a Yod with Taurus at its apex connects through its two other corners with Sagittarius and Libra. None of these three signs relate to each other by antiscia. But a Yod with (say) Aries at its apex connects with Scorpio and Virgo. Aries and Virgo are signs in parallel. Similarly a Yod with Gemini at its apex connects with Scorpio and Capricorn. Gemini and Capricorn are signs with a contra-parallel or equinoctial point connection.

The 4 easiest Yods are therefore those containing two signs with a parallel, rather than a contra-parallel, relationship. These are the Yods with a focal planet in either Aries, Virgo, Libra or Pisces. It will be noted that these are the equinox signs, those that begin or end on the line of zero declination, and should therefore indicate that they have a more natural ability towards solvency, towards making their energies conscious.

The 4 contra-parallel Yods are those with focal planets in Gemini, Cancer, Sagittarius and Capricorn. These are the signs in the highest declinations north and south, the solstice signs. Their energy flow may therefore be more climactic, but nevertheless encompasses the symbolic pause of the Sun's standstill. The Finger of God (the focal planet) stops and reflects, ideally allowing an outer understanding of the Yod's internal tension.

The Fixed Yods, with focal planets in the signs of Taurus, Leo, Scorpio and Aquarius are, as seen by declination, firmly fixed in central positions either north or south of the celestial equator. They are not about to change direction or change hemispheres. They are Fixed, and are therefore forced harder to adjust to the lesson of the Yod. This all tends to back up the rule that the 4 Fixed sign Yods do not have the ease of flow that the others possess and are therefore more like squares in their mode of operation.

Similarly in the so-called release point of a Yod, (the zodiac degree in exact opposition to the Yod's focal point), the energy will be Fixed for the Fixed Yods. The release point may be through a natal planet or a transiting or progressed planet reaching this opposition point, but it is likely to mark out a slower yet more permanent manifestation in the Fixed Yod. Both the Equinox and the Solstice Yods would have Cardinal or Mutable signs at their respective release points, indicating once again an easier though perhaps less drastic release-flow of energy.

One last observation. It goes without saying that the nature and energy of a Yod of any type will differ according to the actual planetary energies involved.

Perfect Yods

An interesting Yod to consider would be one whose focal planet was positioned exactly at zero degrees of Aries or Libra, especially if this were the Sun as the declination would also be exactly zero. The two remaining points of the Yod triangle would then be situated in zodiacal terms at zero degrees of Virgo and zero degrees of Scorpio, or zero Taurus and zero Pisces, and in declination terms (assuming straightforward longitude equivalents) at 11N28 and 11S28 in both cases. Thus a perfect figure is formed comprising a contra-parallel of two bodies whose mid-point is the critical power point of zero declination, and whose focal point (of the Yod) is also this same point of zero. A balance between hemispheres has achieved a 'perfect' manifestation for the Yod's three separate energies.

If we now consider a Yod whose focal planet is positioned exactly at zero degrees of Cancer or Capricorn, with equivalent declination resting at the solstice power point, the remaining corners of the Yod triangle would fall at zero degrees Sagittarius/Aquarius and zero degrees Gemini/Leo respectively. The Yod with its focal point at zero Cancer would have its remaining two corners in an exact declination parallel at 20S10. The Yod with Capricorn at the apex would find the other two planets at exactly 20N10. This is an interesting pattern as the balance between hemispheres is a little more lop-sided (than the previous Equinox figure) although there is a perfectly harmonious base to this Yod with its two planets in parallel. The figure is either directing harmonious south declination energy to the power point of the northern solstice or directing harmonious north declination energy to the power point of the southern solstice.

A Fixed Yod whose focal planet is positioned exactly at zero degrees of any of the Fixed signs (in declination either 11N28 or 11S28) would have the remaining points of its Yod triangle as follows:

> With its apex at zero Taurus (11N28) the other two planets will be found at zero Libra and zero Sagittarius (00N/S00 and 20S10).
> With its apex at zero Scorpio (11S28) the other two planets will be found at zero Aries and zero Gemini (00N/S00 and 20N10).

With its apex at zero Leo (20N10) the other two planets will be found at zero Pisces and zero Capricorn (11S28 and 23S26).
With its apex at zero Aquarius (20S10) the other two planets will be found at zero Virgo and zero Cancer (11N28 and 23N26).

These are a much more oddly balanced set of positions declination-wise producing Yods that look skewed across the hemispheres, yet their apparent asymmetry belies the fact that in every case either the equinoctial or solstitial power point is involved in the individual triangle. Energies are inharmoniously forced into manifestation.

If we produce a Fixed Yod whose focal planet falls at the mid-degree of a Fixed sign (16N20 or 16S20), we find the remaining points of the triangle will always fall at 05S55 and 22S36, or 05N55 and 22N36 respectively. If the apex is in the north (Taurus, Leo) the base points of the triangle both fall south, and vice versa. Once more we have an ungainly-looking triangle declination-wise and one that appears to have less obvious force.

What this seems to suggest is that there is less dynamism in the Yods centred on the mid-degrees of the Fixed signs than in those centred on zero degrees of the Fixed signs. If we argue that the mid-degrees of Fixed signs are not such strong power points as the zero degrees of Cardinal signs generally, then mid-degree Fixed Yods affirm their lesser status, owning no other planets on solstice or equinox points. They do however have their *focal* planet on the lesser power point of the mid Fixed degrees, whereas the others had power points at the farther corners.

Fixed sign Yods may also not only regain their force but consequently become easier to handle when the focal or apex planet is situated near the end of a Fixed sign. This is because they are fast becoming Mutable sign Yods or as we have called them Equinox or Solstice Yods. (Virgo or Pisces at the apex being Equinox Yods and Gemini/Sagittarius being Solstice Yods). A perfect Yod with a zero degree Mutable sign apex will always encompass an exact solstice or equinox point at its base. It will also appear to be something of an asymmetrical figure declination-wise, similar to the zero degree Fixed sign Yod, but it will be easier because it is not an Inconjunct Yod, in other words only one of its sides is an inconjunct - the other is a quincunx.

Transiting Yods

Usually we look for close natal sextiles on a chart and see when a planet transits the farther point to form a Yod. Unexpected turns of fate are then postulated.

The results however may vary considerably in their effects, not only bearing in mind the relative strengths of the planets in question but also in their declination equivalents. When the natal and transiting planets are converted into declination and then put back into their longitudinal declination equivalents (see Table of Longitude Equivalents in the earlier section of this book) the results may not look so much like a Yod at all.

While an exact longitude Yod is perfectly valid in its own terms, as is any exact longitude aspect, it will obviously be even more powerful if the declinational equivalents form the same dynamic pattern.

Appendix 4
Why a Contra-Parallel is not an 'Opposition'

The 180-degree opposition aspect in longitude is generally regarded as a challenging, face-off confrontation between two energies. It tenants opposite signs of the zodiac whose qualities may be complementary but are nevertheless opposite. The opposition aspect's potential for full awareness (in terms of the planetary energies in question) is usually a lifetime's work of to-ing and fro-ing between their poles, for symbolically at least two planets in opposition cannot see each other because the Earth is in the middle.

The contra-parallel aspect in declination however is quite different. Using straightforward solar equivalents in the first part of this argument for the sake of clarity, we can see immediately that a zodiac (longitude) opposition placed at zero degrees Aries to zero degrees Libra would actually be a parallel in declination. It would be slap on the equator. In other words it is more a conjunction than an opposition.

Admittedly this is a special case. Zero Aries/Libra has a magic all its own. Life on Earth as we know it depends on these zero-line points where the great circles of ecliptic and equator join. It is no wonder that the equator has been given such a life and death quality. But all other exact oppositions in longitude will translate as contra-parallels in declination although we could argue that there is an appreciable difference between the varying types. For example a zodiac opposition between planets anywhere in the first decanate of Aries/Libra will correspond to declination positions less than 5 degrees above or below the celestial equator. This charges both planets with a reciprocal interpretative energy of budding awareness that makes them very different to a position - say - at 17 degrees North and South. Certainly Aries and Libra are both Cardinal signs and so correspond to the thrusting birthing energy of zero declination, but then the last decanate of Virgo/Pisces also shares this near-zero area too. Virgo and Pisces are Mutable signs, distributors rather than initiators, yet in this declination position they are impatient to be making manifest. So two planets in these zodiac oppositions have as much in common as they have opposite. (An opposition from 1° Aries to 1° Libra is equivalent to a contra-parallel of only about 24 *minutes*

North and South of the zero line. This means they are less than one degree apart by declination and are therefore also a parallel).

At the other extreme a zodiac opposition from zero degrees Cancer to zero degrees Capricorn would encompass in declination the entire works. Standing at the farthest solar peaks, two planets in this position see the whole world stretched between them. Their broad view as North and South boundary guardians attaches an importance to them far exceeding that of just being two planets 'in opposition'.

But let's move away from these abstract arguments and focus on what happens in reality. In reality two planets in an exact longitude opposition are unlikely to correspond to an exact declinational contra-parallel anyway. They may be close or they may be nowhere near it. Similarly two planets in an exact contra-parallel will rarely be an exact opposition by longitude. The Sun is the only 'planet' (along with the Nodes) whose position in both declination and longitude has a constant equivalent. All the others follow their own agendas.

In any case the symbolism is different. A contra-parallel in declination is most obviously a bridging across two hemispheres. It is allowing North energy into a Southern planet and South energy into a Northern planet. Perhaps it is because (in declination) we do not see a conjunction in the same way as a longitude observer - I mean a parallel is equivalent in strength to a normal zodiacal conjunction but it is seen as stretching along a line. The harmony of two bodies in exact parallel is easily apparent. Even though not in the same place in the sky they are, so to speak, on the same waveband. Accordingly two bodies that are equidistant on lines above and below the equator (a contra-parallel) appear to partake of a similar kind of harmony.

The symmetry of a contra-parallel unites two planets across the hemispheres in a way that is quite different to a longitude opposition which appears to divide a zodiac chart in half. And this I would suggest is the basic contrast in meaning. Some authors have propounded little interpretative difference between a parallel and a contra-parallel, the combination of the two planetary meanings being the over-riding factor. The same could not be said for a longitude conjunction and opposition - think of a New Moon and a Full Moon - same two planets, totally different energy.

Finally any contra-parallel has as its midpoint the celestial equator itself, tying both bodies to this powerful area and affecting them whenever the equator is activated (as at each equinox for instance). Few opposing degrees in longitude have their midpoints at zero Aries/Libra or other Cardinal points so they do not have claim to such a uniting energy.

Index

A
Abbey Road 86
Addey, John 72, 77, 78
Age of Aquarius 178
albatross 138
Alcyone 151
Aldebaran 151, 160
All Saints day 35
Altair 151
Angel Gabriel 39
Annual Energy Boosts 168
Annunciation 39
Antares 151
Antiscia 14, 144
antiscia-related zodiac degrees 18
antiscion 17, 144
Anubis 160
Arcturus 151, 152
Aries point 12
Arthur 57
Ascension day 57
Astrologers' Quarterly 72, 73
Astrological Association of Great Britain 77
Astrological Lodge of London 73
Astrological Mandala 172
Astrology 77
astro-meteorology 139
Aubrey holes 167
Auster, the South wind 102
autumn equinox (see equinox)

B
Barbie Doll 91
Bat Man 81
Baum, L. Frank 68
Beachcomber's Moon 169
Beast from 20,000 Fathoms 121
Beatles 86, 124
Beatles' Week 125
Beatles 'White' album 90
Bellatrix 151
Beltane 34

Betelgeuse 151
Beyond the Steps - Planets out of bounds
    (see 'out of bounds')
Bird 96
Blake, William 95
Blaschke, Robert P. 186
blessed green 49
Boehrer, Kt 13
Bootes 153
Borea, the North wind 102
Buffy the Vampire Slayer 111
Burroughs, Edgar Rice 62, 66
Burton, Richard 96

C
Cain and Abel 138
Camelot 47, 57
Candlemas 35, 42, 58
Captain Video 105, 107
Capulet, Juliet 52, 53
caravanserai 115
Cardinal signs 9
Carnarvon, Earl of 157, 162
Carter, Charles E.O. 72, 74, 124
Carter, Howard 157
Cat People 1167
cazimi 6, 7
celestial equator 1, 12, 103, 174, 175
Chanel, Coco 91
Cheam Road zodiac 79
Chiron. The Rainbow Bridge 120
Christmas 39, 58
Churchill, Winston 79
clef de voûte 51
Clow, Barbara Hand 120
Coleridge, Samuel Taylor 135, 137
co-longitudes 24
commanding signs 102
conjunction 6
Constant Moon 170
Contra-parallels and Orbs 8
contra-parallel 8, 168, 191
Cornelius, Geoffrey 33, 74
Cornell, Cynthia 8

Council of Tours 42
cross quarters 33
crossing the line 137

D

Davison composite chart 164
Davison, Ronald Carlyle 71
Dearborn, Edward 186
"Death Shall Come on Swift Wings" 157
Declination at Stonehenge 165
Declination Degrees, Parallels, Planetary Eclipses and Occultations 6
declination equivalents 24
degree symbols 144, 170, 172
Disney, Walt 100
Doctor Who 109
Dog star (see Sirius)
Donald Duck 98
doppelganger 89
Doyle, Arthur Conan 161
Durer 95

E

Earth goddess 36
Earth point 12
Easter 39, 56, 57
Eastwood, Clint 96, 97
eclipse 7, 158, 175
ecliptic 152 -154, 174-176
Ecliptic and Equator 174
ecliptic intercept 16
Egyptian Book of the Dead 33
Elephant Man 126
Emerson, Ralph Waldo 139
Encyclopaedia of Psychological Astrology 75
Epiphany 42
equator 1, 12, 103, 136, 141, 174
equinox - spring 4, 10, 34
equinox - autumn 5, 10, 35
etheric body 173
Eve of All Hallows 35
Excalibur 49, 58
Exley, Lorraine 171
Experience 139
Extreme Venus 91

F

Faerie 38
Faraway Hill 104, 106
Fawkes, Guy 35
Firebrace, Brigadier 74
First Magnitude Stars close to the Celestial Equator 150
First Men in the Moon 130
FitzGerald, Edward 112, 113
fixed stars - declinations 150, 180
Flying Dutchman 107
Full Moon 59

G

Galahad 57, 58
Garbo, Greta 91
Garland, Judy 67, 70
Garrett, Helen Adams 136
Gawain and the Green Knight 46
Gillman, Ken 77
Glastonbury zodiac 79
Graves, Robert 51
great circles 174
Green, H.S. 124
Green Man 49
Greenwood marriage 36
Grimm, Brothers 43
Groundhog day 35, 36
Guinevere 59
Gunpowder Plot 35

H

halcyon bird 44
Halloween 34, 35
Hamlet 44
Hannan, Charles and Lois 155
Harrison, George 88
Harvey, Charles 76
Hawkins, Gerald 165
heart chakra 50
hemispheres - North and South 4, 5, 11, 12, 102, 137
holly king 49
Holy Grail 57
Holy Spirit 57

Hone, Margaret 74
Hood, Thomas 42
Horicks and Michaux 102
Horoscope Interpretation Outlined 8
hottest day 2

I

Imbolc 35, 58
inconjunct 186
ingress 13, 165
intercalary days 42
Introduction to Political Astrology 124
Invaders 109
Invisible Man 129
Iram 111
Island Of Doctor Moreau 130, 131

J

Jamsh'yd 111
Jayne, Charles 8, 16
Jekyll and Hyde 145, 147
Jesus Christ 38, 57
Juliet at Lammas Eve 52
juniper 43
Jupiter at zero 111
Jupiter-Saturn conjunction 7

K

karma 13
Khayyám, Omar 111, 116
King Kong 121

L

Lady day 39
Lady of the Lake 58
Lammas 35, 52
latitude 1
The Latitude Cycle 102
Lehman, J. Lee 186
Lennon, John 88, 125
Leo, Bessie 74
Let It Be 90
Lewisohn, Mark 87
Lewton, Val 117
Liberace 91, 93

Lilly, William 15
lion heat 55
Liverpool: Scorpionic City of Dreams 122
lobscouse 124
Lone Ranger 81, 82
Longitude Equivalents 24
lunar nodes (see Moon's nodes)
Lunar Ranger 81

M

Macmillan, Iain 87
Magritte 95
Malory, Thomas 57
Mars - out of bounds
    62, 66, 71, 94, 95, 98
Martin, Dean 96
Martinmas 35
masques 56
May day 34
May pole 36
May Queen and Halloween Jester 33
McCartney, Paul 87, 125
Mercury - out of bounds 62, 71, 77, 119
Merrick, Joseph 126, 127
Michaelmas 39
Mickey Mouse 98
Midsummer Night's Dream 37, 56
Midsummer's day 4, 39, 40
Midwinter's day 40
Millennium 41
Minnie Mouse 99
Moment of Astrology 33
Moon - out of bounds 14, 61, 71, 81, 86, 96, 98, 104
Moon's major standstill 14, 40, 167
Moon's minor standstill 14, 40
Moon's nodes 87, 128, 133
Moore, Clayton 85
Morte D'Arthur 57
Most Unusual Mouse 98
mummers 44
Mushtari 112
Muslim calendar 40

N

Neptune at zero 117, 122
New Moon 40
New Year's day/eve 41, 58
New York 121
North declination 12, 102
northern signs 4, 102
Notable Horoscopes 112

O

oak king 36, 49
obedient signs 102
Obliquity of the Ecliptic 10
occultation 6, 7, 155, 161
Omar Khayyám and the Seven-Ringed Cup 111
OOB (see 'out of bounds')
opposition 8, 191
orbs 8, 9
Orithyia 102
out of bounds 13, 61
Outer Limits 108

P

parallels 6
parallel conjunction 6
Parallels: Their Hidden Meaning 8, 16
Parker, Charlie 96
parliament of birds 44
Path of Ra 171
Parton, Dolly 91
Passover 57
Pearson's Weekly 129
Pentecost 56, 57
Perseus 145
Photograph of The Beatles 86
Picasso 95
planisphere 174
planetary eclipse 6
planetary hours 15
Play Misty for Me 96
Pleiades 151
Pluto 16, 87
Pluto at zero 126, 129
Pluto (Disney character) 98
Polaris 150

Pollux 151
Popeye 98
power points 155
precession of the equinoxes 178
Princess of Mars 63
Prisoner 109
Procyon 151
progression 14, 143
proteus syndrome 126
psychiatry 119
psychological thrillers 108
Ptolemy 15, 187
Puck 37

Q

Quantock Hills
quincunx 185

R

Ra 33, 160, 171
Raman, B.V. 112
Regulus 151
Return of the Ancient Mariner 136
Rigel 151
Rime of the Ancient Mariner 136
Roberts, Julia 91
Rodin 95
Romeo and Juliet 36, 52
Rosetti 95
Royal Arch 50
Rubáiyát of Omar Khayyám 111
Ruby Slippers 66
Rudhyar, Dane 102, 172

S

Sabian symbols 172
Saint Bride 35
Saint Brigid 35
Saint Michael 39
Samhain 34, 35
Santa Claus 37
Scarlet Pimpernel 81
Science Fiction and Soap Opera 104
Scofield, Bruce 40
Sergeant Pepper's Lonely Hearts Club Band 86

seven stars 51
seven lords of the universe 51
Shakespeare, William 37, 44, 53
shamanic journeys 171
shamen 49
sidereal zodiac 179
Silverheels, Jay 85
Sirius 150, 152, 153, 160
Sol Invictus 43
solar eclipse (see eclipse)
Solar Festivals 9, 33
solar-lunar festivals 56
solar parallels 15
Solomon's temple 50
solstice - northern 4, 165
solstice - southern 5, 165
solstice - summer 4, 10, 34
solstice - winter 5, 10, 35
Solstice Pause 38
Song of Amergin 51
Sothis (see Sirius)
South declination 12, 102, 136
Southern Cross 137
southern signs 102
Spica 151, 152
splitting of the atom 117, 121
spring equinox (see equinox)
St John's day 38
St Stephen's day 44
St Walpurgis night 35
standstills - lunar 14, 40, 165
standstills - solar 38, 165
Stars in Declination 150, 180
stars: spectral classes 156
Star Trek 108
Starr, Ringo 88
Steadman, Ralph 147
Steamboat Willie 98
Stevenson, Robert Louis 145, 146
Stonehenge 165, 166
Strange Case of Dr Jekyll and Mr Hyde 145, 147
summer solstice (see solstice)
Sun's Annual Journey 4
Sword in the Stone 56
Synastry 72, 76, 77

T

Table of antiscia-related zodiac degrees 18
Tale of Dark Secrets 145
Tanner, Nelda 103, 137
Tarzan of the Apes 62
Technique of Prediction 77
temple of the stars 79
Texas 83, 84
Three Types of Moon 168
tilt 10, 177
Time Equivalents 29
Time Machine 130, 134
Toulouse-Lautrec 95
Treasure Island 147
Treeves, Sir Frederick 128
trilithons 167
tropic of Cancer 4
tropic of Capricorn 5
tropical zodiac 4, 179
Tutankhamun 157
Twelfth Night 43
Twelfth Night 56
Twelve Days of Christmas 42
Twilight Zone 108
Two Astrologers 71, 77
Two Hemispheres 102
Two hemispheres and the Ingress 11

U

Under the Moons of Mars 63
Uranian school 12
Uranus-Pluto conjunction 125

V

Valentino, Rudolph 91, 92
Vedic astrologers 41
Venus at zero 122
Venus - out of bounds 91, 98, 148
vernal equinox (see equinox - spring)
Verona 53
vertue 15
via negativa 137
Virgin Mary 39
Voyager's Moon 169

W

War of the Worlds 130
Wells, H.G. 129, 132
West, Mae 91
Weston-super-Mare 76
Whit Sunday 35, 57
White Goddess 51
Wigglesworth, Harold 76
Williamson, Joseph 124
Willner, John 8, 102
winter solstice (see solstice)
Wizard of Oz 66, 67
Wolf Man 117
Wordsworth, William 142
wren 44

X

X Files 110

Y

yang and yin 41
Yods 186
Yule log 42

Z

Zain, C.C. 103, 117
zero line (see equator)
zodiac and declination equivalents 11
    (see also longitude equivalents)
zodiacal belt 176
zodiacal parallel 6, 17
Zorro 81

Lightning Source UK Ltd.
Milton Keynes UK
UKHW021847300921
391375UK00007B/143